Praise for *Research-Based Strategies*

"This book offers a guide for closing the achievement gap between resourced and under-resourced students. Growth is achievable, especially when classroom strategies are driven by research."

—Genie DePolo, Chief Academic Officer and Principal,
Manhattan Charter School and Manhattan Charter School 2, NY

"Hearing Ruby Payne discuss meta-analysis and effect size really opened my eyes. The addition of effect-size measurements for each strategy doubles the value of Research-Based Strategies.*"*

—Stephanie Doyle, Ed.D., Teacher, Caughman Road Elementary, SC

"There are no shortcuts to equity in classroom instruction, but this book is a must-use resource for teachers of under-resourced students."

—Kim Vann, Executive Director, Bright Futures USA, MO

D1311559

REVISED EDITION

RESEARCH-BASED STRATEGIES

Narrowing the Achievement Gap for Under-Resourced Students

USE WITH
RTI

All strategies are
research-based
best practices

Ruby K. Payne and Bethanie H. Tucker
    Research-Based Strategies: Narrowing the Achievement Gap for
    Under-Resourced Students. Revised Edition.
    350 pages
    Bibliography: pages 301–334

    ISBN: 978-1-938248-90-0

aha! Process, Inc.
    P.O. Box 727
    Highlands, TX 77562-0727
    (800) 424-9484 ■ (281) 426-5300
    Fax: (281) 426-5600
    Website: www.ahaprocess.com

Library of Congress Control Number: 2009929502

Copy editing by Dan Shenk and Jesse Conrad
Book design by Paula Nicolella
Cover design by Amy Alick Perich

The authors gratefully acknowledge permission to reprint from the following:
    Nonviolent Communication: A Language of Life (3rd ed.)
    by Marshall B. Rosenberg, published by PuddleDancer Press.
    Visit www.nonviolentcommunication.com for more information.

Printed in the United States of America

REVISED EDITION

RESEARCH-BASED STRATEGIES

Narrowing the Achievement Gap for Under-Resourced Students

USE WITH RTI

All strategies are research-based best practices

Ruby K. Payne, Ph.D., and Bethanie H. Tucker, Ed.D.

Table of Contents

| | | | | Type of strategy | | |
Strategy number	Strategy name	Page number	Effect size	Academic	Behavioral	Academic and behavioral
1	Analyzing Student Resources to Determine Interventions	19	1.07 .54			●
2	Self-Assessment and Development of Resources	23	1.07 .54			●
3	Mental Models for Academic Content	26	.75 .64 .55	●		
4	Mental Models for Processes	34	1.28 .64 .55	●		
5	Building Relationships of Mutual Respect Among Students and Teachers	37	1.62 .72 .52			●
6	Relational Learning	41	.74 .55 .55			●
7	Structured Partners in Learning	45	.82 .55 .47			●
8	Peer Mediation	47	.63 .63		●	
9	Task Mediation	49	.87 .75 .53			●

Strategy number	Strategy name	Page number	Effect size	Type of strategy			
				Academic	Behavioral	Academic and behavioral	
10	Teaching Cognitive (Input) Skills	51	1.28	●			
11	Input Skill: Planning (for Task Completion) Step Sheets	57	1.28	●			
12	Input Skill: Planning Backwards	60	1.28	●			
13	Input Skill: Academic-Task Preparations to Control Impulsivity	62	1.28	●			
14	Input Skill: Focusing	64	1.28	●			
15	Input Skill: Bringing Order Out of Chaos	67	1.28	●			
16	Input Skill: Sorting More Important from Less Important Information	70	1.28	●			
17	Input Skill: Planning and Labeling in Academic Tasks	76	1.28	●			
18	Input Skill: Nonfiction Reading Strategy	80	1.28	●			
19	Input Skill: Fiction Reading Organizer/Sorter	85	1.28	●			
20	Input Skill: Procedural Self-Talk	90	1.28	●			
21	Input Skill: Teaching Input Skills Using Games	92	1.28	●			
22	Scaffolding Output: Dealing with Blocking	97	.87	●			
23	Predicting/Planning Your Grade	98	1.33	●			
24	Directionality	101	.87	●			
25	Content Comprehension: Teaching the Purpose, Patterns, Structures, and Processes of Disciplines	104	1.28 .87 .75 .64 .63	●			
26	Problem-Solving Process: Instructions in Mathematics	110	1.28 .87 .75 .64	●			
27	Process Selection	113	.87	●			
28	Managing Cognitive Load: External Task Aids	115	.87	●			
29	Automaticity	117	1.28	●			
30	Activating Prior Knowledge	118	.63	●			
31	Compensating for Missing Prior Knowledge	122	.63	●			

Strategy number	Strategy name	Page number	Effect size	Academic	Behavioral	Academic and behavioral
			Type of strategy			
32	Minimizing Activation of Irrelevant Prior Knowledge	124	.75	●		
33	Using Worked Examples: Replacing Some Practice with Worked Examples for Students to Analyze	125	.57 .37	●		
34	Increased Time on Task	126	.62	●		
35	Teaching Another Student	128	.55			●
36	Structured Academic Controversy	130	.53			●
37	Physical Activity	131	.22	●		
38	Bowtie Feedback	133	.73	●		
39	Student Self-Assessment	141	1.33	●		
40	Formative Assessment	145	.68	●		
41	Question Making	147	.64	●		
42	Possible Selves	157	.44			●
43	Role Identity	159	.53 .52 .49			●
44	Future Self/Future Story	161	.54 .44			●
45	Anticipating and Accepting Challenges and Changes	165	1.16			●
46	Reframing	167	1.16		●	
47	Mediating to Change Behavior	169	1.16		●	
48	Story Book to Improve Behavior	171	.63		●	
49	Classroom Management/Procedures Checklist	173	.75		●	
50	Planning Behavior	178	.75		●	
51	If You Choose	180	.63		●	
52	Metaphor Story	181	.64		●	
53	Building a Reward System Based on Implementing Your Own Plan	183	.73		●	
54	Registers of Language	184	1.16	●		
55	Chronological Story Structure	187	.53	●		

Strategy number	Strategy name	Page number	Effect size	Type of strategy Academic	Behavioral	Academic and behavioral
56	Formal Discourse	189	1.16	●		
57	Folder Activity (Mental Model for Part to Whole): Language Arts Example	191	1.28	●		
58	Writing Organizers	193	1.28	●		
59	Mental Model for Formal Written Expression	197	1.28	●		
60	Voices	199	.53	●		
61	Generative Vocabulary Instruction	202	.62	●		
62	Language: Vocabulary Development	206	.62	●		
63	Sketching Vocabulary	214	.62	●		
64	Sign Language for Comprehension	216	.60	●		
65	Teaching Students Their Lexile Measures	218	.60	●		
66	Tucker Signing Strategies for Reading	220	.52	●		
67	Teaching Adverbs and Prepositions	222	.62	●		
68	Teaching Words for Feelings	225	.62			●
69	Karpman Triangle	229	1.16		●	
70	Setting Appropriate Boundaries	231	.63		●	
71	Bracketing Distracting Thoughts	233	.63		●	
72	Self-Affirmations	235	.47			●
73	Gratitude Journals	237	.47		●	
74	Harsh Environments and Self-Expression: Language Skills	239	.47			●
75	Service Learning	241	.58			●
76	Six-Step Process	243	1.62	●		

Introduction

This book offers strategies that are effective for all students (kindergarten through college/university)—and for teachers to use particularly in order to narrow or eliminate the achievement gap for under-resourced students.

Since the founding of aha! Process in the mid-1990s, the company's focus has been to provide strategies that can be readily implemented and integrated into any curriculum or program that will raise student achievement. This was the case with the first edition of *Research-Based Strategies* (2009) and remains the primary emphasis of this updated version.

Based on multiple responses from practitioners, the basic features of this book remain the same. As before, readers will find a "menu" of strategies (see Table of Contents) that can be used to meet the needs of today's under-resourced learners. To better facilitate addressing students' needs, the strategies have been clustered according to academics and behavior.

If you are familiar with the first edition of *Research-Based Strategies,* you will note that we have retained most of the strategies that appeared in the original. We have done this because both our research and your feedback have indicated that they work. In this edition we also have added more than 20 new strategies.

The Impact of Effect-Size Research

A major addition to this edition of *Research-Based Strategies* is information about the *effect sizes* of 76 strategies. Effect-size research actually began a number of years ago as researchers sought to determine a more precise measure of the effectiveness of the various strategies that educators use, along with the many environmental influences that impact students' lives.

In 1984, for example, Herbert J. Walberg's publication of "Improving the Productivity of America's Schools" in *Educational Leadership* (Vol. 41, No. 8) highlighted the potential value of effect-size measurements of classroom events and posted effects of a number of strategies and approaches.

The best-known current analysis of effect sizes of strategies and influences in the field of education has been conducted by Dr. John Hattie, professor and director of the Melbourne Education Research Institute at the University of Melbourne, Australia, and honors professor at the University of Auckland, New Zealand.

Hattie initially analyzed the results of 800 research studies and ranked the effects of 138 influences in his groundbreaking book, *Visible Learning,* in 2009. In 2011 he ranked the effects of 150 influences, published in *Visible Learning for Teachers.* More recently Hattie analyzed nearly 1,200 studies, kindergarten through college, identified 195 influences, and measured their effects, which he published in *The Applicability of Visible Learning to Higher Education* (2015).

For this edition of *Research-Based Strategies* we quote the effect sizes reported in Hattie's most recent analysis in 2015. Although the title of this article prominently refers to higher education, the list of influences in the study is summative, including both higher education and K–12.

Before we look at the effect sizes of individual influences, it will be beneficial to define key vocabulary labels used in Hattie's reports.

Simply stated, *influences* are all the things—external and internal—that affect how students live, think, and learn. Influences include classroom events, teacher strategies and approaches, relationships, community personal characteristics, and environmental factors.

Not all influences, of course, are created equal; they vary in terms of the impact or effect they have on students' lives and academic performance. Measurements of these effects are reported as effect sizes. As Hattie stated in his inaugural lecture (1999) at Melbourne University, Australia, "We need estimates of magnitude to answer the question, 'Exactly how well does the strategy work?'" Or: How impactful is this influence on a student's life?

Hattie explains his effect-size scale as follows—in eight basic points (paraphrased):

1. A score of 0 (zero) means there is no effect on student achievement from an influence or from implementing a particular teaching innovation. A student exposed to strategies or influences with an effect size of 0, 24/7 for a year, would be no better or worse off than she was at the starting point— no progress, no regression.

2. An effect size of 0 also can mean that the influence does nothing to change everything else that is happening. For example, open versus traditional classrooms have an effect size of 0. The difference between the two simply doesn't matter.

3. A negative effect indicates that the innovation or influence has a *detrimental* effect on student achievement. A year of 24/7 exposure to influences with an effect size of less than 0 would result in actual regression of learning. Seven influences on Hattie's list (he calls them "The Disasters") that have a negative impact on student performance are:

   - Summer vacation: -.02
   - Welfare policies: -.12
   - Retention (repeating K–12): -.17
   - Television: -.18
   - Home corporal punishment: -.33
   - Mobility: -.34
   - Depression: -.42

   A closer look at these "disasters" reveals that students from low socioeconomic backgrounds typically fare worse than their more affluent peers when it comes to the likelihood of encountering these disastrous influences. More information on this dynamic can be found later in the Introduction.

4. A positive effect indicates that the innovation has as increased effect (greater than 0) on students' achievement. Keep in mind, however, that the range of influences greater than 0 is huge, and greater than 0 does not necessarily mean expected annual growth.

5. By averaging the effects across the meta-analyses, Hattie has determined the average effect of strategies and influences to be .40. Hattie reports this to be the benchmark figure and "standard" from which to judge effects.

6. Influences with an effect size higher than .40 have a greater-than-average effect on student growth.

7. 1.0 indicates an increase of one standard deviation above the norm. This means that by the end of the school year a typical student receiving this treatment would make progress equal to the .4 average of the expected one-year progress, *plus an additional one-year benefit derived from that treatment.* The magnitude of a strategy or influence with an effect size of 1, therefore, is huge—more than double the average effect.

8. The influence with the highest reported effect of 1.62 (more about its impact in Strategies 5 and 76) could affect student progress by as much as three years above and beyond the average effect.

To review: Strategies or influences with an effect size of 0 have no effect on student academic growth. Students subjected to influences and treatments with an effect size of less than 0 can actually regress. Those receiving treatment or influences with an effect size of .4 will likely make typical or average progress, and those subjected to influences and strategies with an effect size greater than .4 could possibly make as much as a year or more progress over and above students exposed to "average" (.4) strategies.

Hattie acknowledges that the studies in his analysis were statistically measured to determine an overall effect. Additional factors and moderators (such as age, gender, maturation, socioeconomic class, and teacher efficacy) were not further analyzed, as these did not constitute the overarching goal of the study.

Our observations and research findings about specific effects of socioeconomic class on each of the influences have been added in this edition of *Research-Based Strategies,* reflecting the work's goal of "narrowing the achievement gap for under-resourced students."

In the following chart is a listing of the major influences included in Hattie's analysis as reported in the journal article "The Applicability of Visible Learning to Higher Education" (2015).

Some of the items in the list of influences that Hattie studied are teaching strategies.

He did not attempt to analyze all known teaching strategies, as the magnitude of the resulting report would doubtless be overwhelming. He did analyze many strategies, however, and he includes the remainder in a category of influences labeled (logically) as "strategies."

In his article Hattie has determined the effect size of the category of strategies that teachers use but are not considered individually to be significant—.60. Obviously, some of the strategies in this category are more effective than others. The .60 ranking is an average.

Hattie's Ranking: 195 Influences and Effect Sizes Related to Student Achievement

	Hattie (2015) higher ed N = 195	Hattie (2011) analysis N = 150	Hattie (2009) analysis N = 138
Teacher estimates of achievement	1.62		
Collective teacher efficacy	1.57		
Self-reported grades	1.33	1.44	1.44
Piagetian programs	1.28	1.28	1.28
Conceptual-change programs	1.16		
Response to intervention (RTI)	1.07	1.07	
Teacher credibility	.90	.90	
Micro teaching	.88	.88	.88
Cognitive task analysis	.87		
Classroom discussion	.82	.82	
Interventions for learning disabled	.77	.77	.77
Interventions for disabled	.77		
Teacher clarity	.75	.75	.75
Reciprocal teaching	.74	.74	.74
Feedback	.73	.74	.73
Providing formative evaluation	.68	.90	.90
Acceleration	.68	.68	.88
Creativity programs	.65	.65	.65
Self-questioning	.64	.64	.64
Concept mapping	.64	.60	.57
Problem-solving teaching	.63	.61	.61
Classroom behavior	.63	.68	.80
Prior achievement/knowledge	.63	.65	.67
Vocabulary programs	.62	.67	.67
Time on task	.62	.38	.38
Not labeling students	.61	.61	.61
Spaced vs. mass practice	.60	.71	.71
Teaching strategies	.60	.62	.60
Direct instruction	.60	.59	.59
Repeated reading programs	.60	.67	.67
Study skills	.60	.63	.59
Pre-term birth weight	.59	.53	.54

(continued on next page)

(continued from previous page)

	Hattie (2015) higher ed N = 195	Hattie (2011) analysis N = 150	Hattie (2009) analysis N = 138
Spelling programs	.58		
Tactile-stimulation programs	.58	.58	.58
Service learning	.58		
CAI * with learning-needs students	.57		
Mastery learning	.57	.58	.58
Preschool with at-risk students	.56		
Visual-perception programs	.55	.55	.55
Peer tutoring	.55	.55	.55
CAI in other subjects	.55		
Cooperative vs. individualistic	.55	.59	.59
Interactive video methods	.54	.52	.52
Socioeconomic status	.54	.52	.57
Classroom cohesion	.53	.53	.53
Metacognitive strategies	.53	.69	.69
Comprehension programs	.53	.60	.58
Scaffolding	.53	.53	.53
Cooperative vs. competitive	.53	.54	.54
Peer influences	.53	.53	.53
Frequent/effects of testing	.52	.34	.34
Phonics instruction	.52	.54	.60
Classroom management	.52	.52	.52
Home environment	.52	.52	.57
Teacher/student relationships	.52	.72	.72
Play programs	.50	.50	.50
Second-/third-chance programs	.50	.50	.50
Parental involvement	.49	.49	.51
Mathematics	.49	.40	.45
Writing programs	.49	.44	.44
Questioning	.48	.48	.46
School effects	.48	.48	.48
Self-concept	.47	.47	.43
Integrated curricula programs	.47	.39	.39
Student rating of teaching	.47	.48	.44

* computer-assisted instruction

(continued on next page)

(continued from previous page)

	Hattie (2015) higher ed N = 195	Hattie (2011) analysis N = 150	Hattie (2009) analysis N = 138
Small-group learning	.47	.49	.49
Concentration/engagement	.45	.48	.48
Relative age within class	.45		
Professional development	.45	.51	.62
CAI	.45	.37	.37
Science	.44	.42	.40
Early intervention	.44	.47	.47
CAI with college students	.44		
Motivation	.44	.48	.48
CAI with elementary students	.44		
Outdoor/adventure programs	.43	.52	.52
Teacher expectations	.43	.43	.43
School size	.43	.43	.43
Philosophy in schools	.43		
Intelligent tutoring systems	.43		
Communication strategies	.43		
Exposure to reading	.42	.42	.36
Comprehensive instruction	.42		
CAI in writing	.42		
Behavioral organizers	.41	.41	.41
Goals	.40	.50	.56
Social-skills programs	.40	.39	.40
After-school programs	.40		
Cooperative learning	.40	.42	.41
Enrichment	.39	.39	.39
Career interventions	.38	.38	.38
Psychotherapy programs	.38	.38	
Gaming/simulations	.37	.33	.33
Music-based programs	.37		
Drama/arts programs	.37	.35	.35
Worked examples	.37	.57	.57
Reducing anxiety	.36	.40	.40
Student-centered teaching	.36	.54	

(continued on next page)

(continued from previous page)

	Hattie (2015) higher ed N = 195	Hattie (2011) analysis N = 150	Hattie (2009) analysis N = 138
Creativity	.35	.35	.35
Attitude to content domains	.35	.35	.36
Inquiry-based teaching	.35	.31	.31
Bilingual programs	.35	.37	.37
Decreasing disruptive behavior	.34	.34	.34
Various teaching on creativity	.34	.34	
Adjunct aids	.34	.37	.37
Preschool programs	.33	.45	.45
Head Start programs	.33		
Principals/school leaders	.33	.39	.36
Inductive teaching	.33	.33	.33
Ethnicity	.32	.32	.32
Online, digital tools	.32		
Teacher effects	.32	.32	.32
Drugs	.32	.32	.33
Systems accountability	.31	.31	
Ability grouping for gifted	.30	.30	.30
CAI in mathematics	.30		
CAI with high school students	.30		
Collaborative learning	.29		
Mobile phones	.29		
Homework	.29	.29	.29
Home visiting	.29	.29	.29
Desegregation	.28	.28	.28
Early intervention in home	.27		
Teaching test taking	.27	.27	.22
Use of calculators	.27	.27	.27
CAI in reading/literacy	.26		
Volunteer tutors	.26	.26	
Use of PowerPoint	.26		
Teaching reforms	.25	.22	.22
Early intervention	.25		
Divorce or remarriage	.25		

(continued on next page)

(continued from previous page)

	Hattie (2015) higher ed N = 195	Hattie (2011) analysis N = 150	Hattie (2009) analysis N = 138
Mainstreaming	.24	.24	.28
Bullying	.24		
Values/moral programs	.24	.24	.24
Illness	.24	.25	.23
Religious schools	.24	.23	.23
Competitive vs. individual	.24	.24	.24
Individual instruction	.23	.22	.23
CAI in science	.23		
Programmed instruction	.23	.23	.24
Summer school	.23	.23	.23
Finances	.23	.23	.23
Matching style of learning	.23	.17	.41
Exercise/relaxation	.22	.28	.28
Visual/audiovisual methods	.22	.22	.22
Teacher verbal ability	.22	.22	
Extracurricular programs	.21	.19	.17
Class size	.21	.21	.21
CAI in small groups	.21		
School cultural effects	.20		
Aptitude/treatments interactions	.19	.19	.19
Learning hierarchies	.19	.19	.19
School counseling effects	.19	.18	
Co-/team teaching	.19	.19	.19
Special college programs	.18	.18	.24
Within-class grouping	.18	.18	.16
Family structure	.18	.18	.17
Web-based learning	.18	.18	.18
Personality	.17	.18	.19
Teacher immediacy	.16	.16	.16
Adopted children	.16		
Home-school programs	.16	.16	.16
Out-of-school curricula	.15	.09	.09
Sentence-combining programs	.15	.15	.15

(continued on next page)

(continued from previous page)

	Hattie (2015) higher ed N = 195	Hattie (2011) analysis N = 150	Hattie (2009) analysis N = 138
Distance education	.13	.11	.09
Problem-based learning	.12	.15	.15
Ability grouping	.12	.12	.12
Diet	.12	.12	.12
Juvenile-delinquent programs	.12		
Teacher education	.12	.12	.11
Diversity of students	.11	.05	
Mentoring	.09	.15	.15
Subject matter knowledge	.09	.09	.09
School calendars/timetables	.09	.09	
Detracking	.09		
Perceptual-motor programs	.08	.09	.08
Single-sex schools	.08		
Gender on achievement	.08	.12	.12
Charter schools	.07	.20	.20
Sleep	.07		
Whole language	.06	.06	.06
Types of testing	.06		
College halls of residence	.05	.05	.05
Multi-grade/age classes	.04	.04	.04
Parental employment	.03		
CAI in distance education	.01		
Student control over learning	.01	.04	.04
Open vs. traditional	.01	.01	.01
Summer vacation	-.02	-.02	-.09
Welfare policies	-.12	-.12	-.12
Retention	-.17	-.13	-.16
Television	-.18	-.18	-.18
Home corporal punishment	-.33		
Mobility	-.34	-.34	-.34
Depression	-.42		

Source: Adapted from J. Hattie, 2015.

Enter Marzano

U.S. educational researcher Robert J. Marzano, along with colleagues, also has analyzed classroom teaching strategies—and identified the following 10 strategies to be the most effective classroom interventions:

1. **Identifying similarities and differences**
   Breaking concepts into similar and dissimilar characteristics

2. **Note taking and summarizing**
   Identifying essential components and restating them in one's own words

3. **Reinforcing effort**
   Attributing success and shortcomings to effort rather than intelligence or luck

4. **Spaced repetition**
   Multiple exposure over time to content with a specific goal

5. **Graphical methods**
   Visuals, mental models, and other non-linguistic representations of concepts

6. **Cooperative learning**
   Structured group work that requires all students to be accountable both to self and other students

7. **Goals and feedback**
   Clarification of where students were, where they are now, where they need to be, and how they get there

8. **Hypothesis testing**
   Predicting outcomes, testing predictions, and interpreting outcomes

9. **Activating prior knowledge**
   Connecting new content to students' prior experiences

10. **Advance organizers**
    Outlines, mind maps, or other organization of new content

Source: Adapted and paraphrased from R. Marzano, D. Pickering, & J. Pollock, 2001.

'The Disasters'—Squared by Poverty

As listed earlier in the Introduction, Hattie refers to influences with an effect size of less than 0 as "The Disasters." Most of the negative influences are more frequently observed in under-resourced households than in more stable environments.

The parallel and added complications of poverty as related to the disastrous impact of the seven previously listed influences are highlighted in such studies as the following:

- "Summer Vacation Hurts Poor Children. While middle- and upper-class children flock to sports camps and travel on family vacations, America's poor children—mostly for lack of other options—often head to the couch or the streets" (Hammond, 2011).

- Welfare policies can have negative effects on children: "… [F]amilies receiving assistance from TANF must comply with requirements ranging from drug testing and attending job development classes to accepting minimum wage jobs that require single mothers to be away from their families during evenings and weekends" (Hurst, 2011).

- There is often an association between socioeconomic status and grade-retention rates (Baydar, Brooks-Gunn, & Furstenberg, 1993; Brooks-Gunn, Guo, & Furstenberg, 1993; Liaw & Brooks-Gunn, 1994; Smith, Brooks-Gunn, & Klebanov, 1997).

- Poverty and high rates of TV viewing are frequently linked ("Nielsen: Income," 2015).

- Home corporal punishment is more prevalent in households of poverty (Straus, 2001).

- Mobility is usually more harmful for children from poverty. In an article for the *Cornell Chronicle,* Susan Kelley reports findings that frequent moves are particularly harmful to children if they're poor. Children who move three or more times before they turn 5 have more behavioral problems than their peers—but only if they are poor (Morris, Huston, Duncan, Crosby, & Bos, 2001).

- Americans in poverty are more likely than those who are not to struggle with a wide array of chronic health problems, and depression disproportionately affects those in poverty (Brown, 2012; Hurst, 2011).

The Winners (Positive Influences on Student Achievement)

John Hattie says the influence that has the strongest positive effect on campuses, kindergarten through college, is teacher estimates of teacher performance (including self-analysis) with a 1.62 effect size. Hattie notes that teacher performance has a direct impact on student achievement.

Second through 10th, according to Hattie, are:

2. Collective teacher efficacy: 1.57
3. Self-reported grades: 1.33
4. Piagetian programs: 1.28
5. Conceptual-change programs: 1.16
6. Response to Intervention: 1.07

7. Teacher credibility: .90
8. Micro teaching: .88
9. Cognitive task analysis: .87
10. Classroom discussion: .82

As previously noted, Hattie analyzed many influences on student learning, one of which is classroom strategies. Marzano further analyzed classroom strategies. In other words, Hattie assessed the entire tree, while Marzano focused on one branch of the tree.

At the intersection of Hattie's and Marzano's insights is where students from poverty stand to benefit the most. And this is where we begin with *Research-Based Strategies*.

The Purpose of *Research-Based Strategies*

As noted at the outset of the Introduction, the purpose of this book is to narrow or eliminate the achievement gap for under-resourced students.

Does *Research-Based Strategies* have all the answers? No. But it does provide a number of tools to improve the process of increasing achievement, especially among students from poverty.

As with previous editions, this iteration of *Research-Based Strategies* features approaches that can be readily implemented and integrated into any curriculum or program that will raise student achievement. The listing of strategies found in the previous edition has been retained in this update, as teachers often reported this to be an effective organizational structure of materials for selecting responses to intervention (RTI).

These strategies are not a prescription of services. Rather, they are designed for you to implement after you have completed an analysis of your students' resources and needs. Whether you base this analysis on state assessment results, formative assessments, daily observation, or classwork matters little. The important thing is that you are monitoring students' progress and promptly making interventions as needed. Interventions made after a student has failed typically result in a student falling farther behind, often not being able to recover—and sometimes even dropping out of school as a result.

As before, we have incorporated the book *Understanding Learning: the How, the Why, the What*. This is provided to ensure that you have a basic understanding of learning theory that supports these interventions. In keeping with the premise that all learning is about the *what,* the *why,* and the *how,* the interventions are then formatted the same way—providing you the *what* (the strategy), the *why* (the need for the particular strategy), and the *how* (explanation or process). The research base for each also is provided. *Understanding Learning* is a quick read regarding what students must do inside their head in order to learn.

Historically in the United States, we have taken resourced students and put them into a box called school, and they come out more resourced. When under-resourced students came into school, many times they dropped out or failed because the resources/supports were not there for them. Our task now is to have under-resourced students enter this box called school and also come out more resourced.

How to Use This Book

The book is organized this way:

1. The first section of charts is called Observed Behaviors and Strategy Numbers. When you observe a behavior, next to the behavior is a strategy number.

2. When you know the strategy number, go to that page, read the explanation and the directions—so that you can then use the strategies with students. All of these 76 strategies also can be used as a part of the RTI process.

3. In the Appendixes, in addition to *Understanding Learning,* are several research studies on learning, particularly with regard to under-resourced individuals. The first Appendix is a new article (not in previous editions of *Research-Based Strategies*) about calibration of student work, which means the assignments are leveled to the difficulty of the grade-level standard.

We wish you wonderful success. It is going to take everyone working together to eliminate the achievement gap, which must not be allowed to continue to exist simply because a student is under-resourced. We can do this.

–Ruby Payne and Bethanie Tucker, 2017

Observed Behaviors and Strategy Numbers

With other people

Observed behavior	Strategy number to use
Does not work well with others	1, 5, 6, 7, 8, 43, 44, 46, 47, 48, 49, 50, 51, 52, 53, 60, 68, 69, 70, 71, 74, 75
Bullies others	1, 5, 8, 43, 44, 46, 47, 48, 49, 50, 51, 53, 54, 56, 60, 68, 69, 70, 71, 73, 74, 75
Socializes excessively	2, 5, 7, 8, 15, 35, 40, 42, 49, 50, 51, 53, 60, 70, 76
Has almost no friends, is isolated	1, 2, 4, 5, 6, 7, 34, 40, 43, 45, 46, 47, 48, 50, 51, 54, 60, 69, 70, 71, 73, 74, 75, 76
Has few words to resolve conflicts	1, 5, 6, 8, 22, 34, 36, 44, 48, 52, 54, 57, 60, 61, 62, 63, 64, 65, 67, 68, 70, 74, 75, 76

With tasks/assignments

Observed behavior	Strategy number to use
Does assignment incorrectly	1, 2, 3, 4, 9, 10, 11, 17, 18, 19, 20, 26, 33, 38, 39, 40, 41, 57, 62, 76
Does not hand in work done in class	1, 23, 39, 40, 43, 50, 51, 52, 53, 57, 72, 76
Does not hand in work done outside of class	1, 2, 5, 6, 8, 11, 12, 16, 21, 38, 39, 40, 44, 46, 50, 51, 52, 53, 57, 70, 72, 76
Cannot transfer information from board to paper	10, 24
Does not follow directions	9, 10, 11, 12, 17, 20, 38, 39, 40, 41, 49, 51, 53, 57, 76
Will not attempt task	1, 2, 3, 4, 5, 6, 7, 9, 17, 18, 23, 25, 30, 33, 35, 38, 41, 50, 51, 52, 53, 72, 76
Misuses time	1, 10, 12, 17, 23, 25, 38, 39, 49, 50, 51, 53, 76
Skips steps/parts of assignment	4, 9, 10, 11, 13, 14, 16, 17, 18, 20, 33, 38, 39, 40, 41, 53, 57, 76

(continued on next page)

(continued from previous page)

With content

Observed behavior	Strategy number to use
Is overwhelmed by information presented	3, 10, 11, 16, 25, 28, 30, 31, 32, 33, 34, 38, 40, 41, 57, 61, 62, 72
Is not on grade level	1, 2, 3, 20, 38, 40, 76
Does not know purpose of content	3, 9, 25, 27, 30, 31, 32, 33, 61, 76
Does not remember information next day	3, 10, 14, 28, 29, 31, 34, 41, 61

With managing self/behavior

Observed behavior	Strategy number to use
Does not follow school rules	5, 6, 8, 42, 43, 44, 45, 46, 48, 49, 50, 51, 52, 60, 70
Interrupts teacher/class	5, 6, 44, 46, 47, 49, 50, 51, 52, 53, 55, 56, 60, 70
Entertains rather than does work	7, 23, 42, 45, 46, 47, 48, 50, 51, 53, 70
Sleeps in class	1, 2, 37, 42, 44, 49, 50, 53
Is disengaged, not motivated	1, 2, 5, 6, 7, 23, 25, 36, 37, 42, 43, 44, 45, 50, 53, 71, 72, 73, 74, 75
Has difficulty focusing	25, 28, 37, 41, 42, 45, 50, 53, 57, 64, 71, 72
Health issue or issues interfere with learning	1, 2, 37

With reading/writing/language

Observed behavior	Strategy number to use
Cannot determine what is more important and less important in text	3, 4, 18, 19, 25, 28, 30, 31, 32, 33, 35, 38, 40, 41, 55, 56, 57, 58
Writing samples are disorganized	3, 16, 20, 38, 39, 40, 41, 54, 55, 56, 57, 58, 59, 76
Writing samples are short, with limited vocabulary	22, 36, 38, 39, 41, 54, 55, 57, 58, 59, 61, 62, 67, 76
Writes below grade level	1, 22, 38, 39, 40, 41, 54, 55, 58, 59, 61, 62, 63, 67, 76
Does not complete constructed-response questions on tests	9, 14, 17, 20, 22, 38, 41, 54, 59, 61, 72, 76

(continued on next page)

(continued from previous page)

With reading/writing/language

Observed behavior	Strategy number to use
Uses inappropriate verb tenses in writing	39, 54, 61, 67
Cannot discriminate regarding main idea	16, 18, 31, 41, 55, 59
Is unwilling to read	1, 5, 6, 8, 25, 30, 31, 35, 41, 54, 65, 68, 72, 76
Cannot decode with fluency	61, 66, 76
Can read but does not understand what was read	19, 40, 41, 55, 61, 63, 64, 65, 67, 76
Has mostly casual-register vocabulary	38, 40, 42, 54, 61, 62, 63, 65, 67, 68

With math

Observed behavior	Strategy number to use
Has difficulty with problem solving	4, 11, 17, 20, 21, 26, 27, 28, 33, 34, 35, 38, 39, 40, 41, 57, 76
Cannot follow columns and rows	10, 15, 24
Cannot follow most math processes	4, 9, 10, 11, 17, 20, 21, 22, 26, 28, 33, 34, 41, 57
Does not know math facts in addition, subtraction, multiplication, and division	3, 24, 28, 29, 34, 35
Has difficulty with math vocabulary	17, 29, 34, 54, 61, 62, 63, 76
Has difficulty with math concepts	3, 4, 17, 28, 33, 34, 38, 40, 61, 76
Cannot rotate visual figures (geometry)	21, 24, 37
Has difficulty doing equations	4, 9, 10, 11, 17, 20, 27, 28, 29, 30, 33, 34, 35, 40, 41, 76

With external resource supports

Observed behavior	Strategy number to use
Has frequent unexcused absences	1, 2, 7, 17, 38, 42, 44, 45, 46, 47, 48, 49, 50, 51, 52, 53, 72, 75, 76
Has excessive tardies	1, 2, 12, 38, 42, 44, 46, 47, 48, 49, 50, 51, 52, 53, 72, 75, 76

Strategy 1

Analyzing Student Resources to Determine Interventions

Academic and
Behavioral
Strategy

Researchers

Awbrey, S. M. (2005).
DeVol, P. E. (2013).
DeWitz, S. J., Woolsey, M. L., & Walsh, W. B. (2009).
Hattie, J. (2015).
Strayhorn, T. L. (2011).
Vickerstaff, S., Heriot, S., Wong, M., Lopes, A., & Dossetor, D. (2007).

Effect Size

Response to intervention (RTI): 1.07
Socioeconomic status: .54

Added Effect of Poverty

Much of the success of under-resourced students is dependent on resource analysis to determine available resources and response to intervention (RTI). Interventions sometimes are identified that require resources unavailable to students with few resources.

Explanation

Interventions work only if they are based on resources to which a student has access *or* if the resource base is provided.

For the purposes of this book, the following resources are being examined:

Financial

Having the money to purchase goods and services.

Emotional

Being able to choose and control emotional responses, particularly to negative situations, without engaging in self-destructive behavior. This is an internal resource and shows itself through stamina, perseverance, and choices.

Mental

Having the mental abilities and acquired skills (reading, writing, computing) to deal effectively with daily life.

Spiritual

Believing in divine purpose and guidance; having hope or a future story.

Physical

Having physical health and mobility.

Support systems

Having friends, family, and backup resources available to access in times of need. These are external resources.

Relationships/role models

Having frequent access to individuals(s) who are appropriate, who are nurturing, and who do not engage in self-destructive behavior.

Knowledge of hidden rules

Knowing the unspoken cues and habits of different groups.

Language (formal register)

Having the vocabulary, language ability, and negotiation skills necessary to succeed in school and/or work settings.

NOTE: Motivation, as well as Integrity and Trust, also are included in the list of resources in *Bridges Out of Poverty*.

Directions

Questions to Determine Interventions

Whenever a student is struggling academically or behaviorally, the key guiding questions for determining interventions are:

1. What resources are available to the student?
2. What resources can the student develop or acquire with support?

The following grid provides guidelines for answering these two questions.

Resource	Questions to Determine Best Intervention
Financial	▪ Can the student afford the field trip, or is a scholarship needed? ▪ Can the student afford supplies for the project/science fair/other activity? ▪ Is the student hungry? Must a linkage to food be found?
Emotional	▪ Can the student verbalize choices? ▪ Does the student have the language to mediate situations without resorting to fists?
Mental	▪ Can the student read at the appropriate grade level? ▪ Can the student identify the final product or task? ▪ Does the student know what will be evaluated and how?
Spiritual	▪ Do students believe they have some control over the situation, or do they say there is nothing they can do? ▪ Does the student have a future story and a plan to go with it?
Physical	▪ Is the student clean? ▪ Are the student's clothes clean? ▪ Can students physically take care of themselves?
Support systems	▪ Is the student the primary support system for the student's household? ▪ Is there enough stability in the home that the student can have a place to keep and do work?
Relationships/ role models	▪ Does the student have at least one adult who is nurturing and caring? ▪ Does the student have three or more adults who care about the student's life? ▪ Are all of the student's significant relationships with peers?

(continued on next page)

(continued from previous page)

Resource	Questions to Determine Best Intervention
Knowledge of hidden rules	▪ Does the student use the "appropriate" school response to situations? ▪ Does the student try to be invisible?
Formal register	▪ Does the student have access to formal register at home? ▪ Does the student get right to the point when telling a story—or does the student begin at the end of the story and tell the story in no particular order?

Resource Analysis Grid

This student grid is for resource-development activities.

Rate each student's access to each resource on a scale of 1 to 10. Then build from the strength of the resources available. Coaches, for example, develop their game plans based on the skill sets of their athletes, and music and band teachers choose music that matches the skill sets of the student musicians they teach.

Name	Financial resources	Emotional resources	Mental resources	Spiritual resources	Physical resources	Support systems	Relationships/ role models	Knowledge of hidden rules	Formal register

Strategy 2

Self-Assessment and Development of Resources *

Academic and
Behavioral
Strategy

Researchers

DeVol, P. E. (2013).
DeVol, P. E., & Krodel, K. M. (2007).
DeVol, P. E., Payne, R. K., & Dreussi Smith, T. (2017).
DeWitz, S. J., Woolsey, M. L., & Walsh, W. B. (2009).
Hattie, J. (2015).
Payne, R. K., DeVol, P. E., & Dreussi Smith, T. (2009).
Souther, E. (2008b).
Strayhorn, T. L. (2011).
Vickerstaff, S., Heriot, S., Wong, M., Lopes, A., & Dossetor, D. (2007).

Effect Size

Response to intervention: 1.07

Socioeconomic status: .54

Added Effect of Poverty

Interventions (1.07 effect size) work only if resources are available.

Socioeconomic status plays a significant role in student achievement (.54). When students realize that their successes and struggles are often due to resources, they are better able to take control of their own destiny.

Explanation

Response to any environment includes the ability to name it. When one knows one's own resource base, resources can be leveraged because they can be named.

* For secondary and college/university students, adults, and communities

Directions

In carefully facilitated groups, as described in *The R Rules, Investigations,* and/or *Getting Ahead,* students analyze their personal resources and make plans for building on those that are stronger and developing those that are weaker.

Following is a sample grid for Student Resource Self-Analysis.

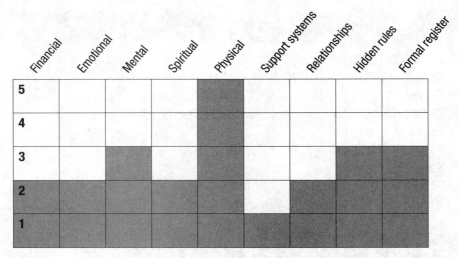

Source: Adapted from P. E. DeVol, R. K. Payne, & T. Dreussi Smith, 2017.

Approaches to Facilitating Student Resource Self-Analysis

A. R Rules

The R Rules is a curriculum (based on a workbook of the same name by Elizabeth Souther) for secondary students to identify, access, and build resources for school, work, and life. It is particularly well-suited for at-risk students or for alternative education (visit www.ahaprocess.com).

The R Rules program can be delivered as a one-semester, full-year, or multi-year course; workshop; advisory; dual-credit course; or an 18-session community model with children of families completing Getting Ahead classes.

The R Rules is a guide for teens to:

- Identify and access resources—individual, school, and community.
- Use tools and activities to create and use individual education, career, and transition plans.
- Explore economic realities and resources related to learning and earning.
- Work as members of a learning community to contribute, develop a voice, and make a positive difference.

B. Getting Ahead in a Just-Gettin'-By World

Getting Ahead is a workbook/program for adults and parents. It is used to develop capacity by increasing individual knowledge bases. Most individuals in poverty are problem solvers, but often they don't have the knowledge bases that others have. In a series of 16 sessions, people from poverty build knowledge bases out of which action frequently results.

Individuals in Getting Ahead make a future story for themselves and assess their own resources.

- Developed by Philip DeVol (*Bridges Out of Poverty* coauthor) to be used with individuals and small groups from poverty
- Teaches hidden rules of middle class and wealth
- Explains different resources and helps formulate a plan to build them

C. Investigations into Economic Class

This program is for college/university students and dual-enrollment high school students. It is a semester-long curriculum that guides students through an investigation of the history of class, causes of poverty, change theory, language development, and the process of assessing and building personal and community resources. This balance of intellectual development based on the study of economic class and personal self-discovery—enhanced by the relevance of the content—addresses a variety of needs of under-resourced students in postsecondary institutions.

The Investigations curriculum was developed by Philip DeVol and Karla Krodel; it mirrors the content and processes from Getting Ahead while also addressing specific college/university knowledge areas.

Strategy 3

Mental Models for Academic Content

Academic
Strategy

Researchers

Baghban, M. (2007).
Bailey, M., et al. (1995).
Donovan, M. S., & Bransford, J. D. (2005).
Groesser, S. N. (2012).
Guastello, E. F., Beasley, T. M., & Sinatra, R. C. (2000).
Gürses, A., Cetinkaya, S., Dogar, & Sahin, E. (2015)
Hattie, J. (2015).
Herman, T., Colton, S., & Franzen, M. (2008).
Idol, L., & Jones, B. F. (Eds.). (1991).
Jones, B. F., Pierce, J., & Hunter, B. (1988).
Kilpatrick, J., Swafford, J., & Findell, B. (Eds.). (2001).
Lin, H., & Chen, T. (2006).
Marzano, R. (2007).
Marzano, R., & Arredondo, D. (1986).
Mayer, R. E. (2005).
McCrudden, M. T., Schraw, G., & Lehman, S. (2009).
Payne, R. K. (2005).
Payne, R. K. (2013).
Resnick, L. B., & Klopfer, L. (1989).
Schnotz, W., & Kurschner, C. (2008).
Senge, P., Ross, R., Smith, B., Roberts, C., & Kleiner, A. (1994).
Shulman, L. S. (1987).

Effect Size

Teacher clarity: .75

Concept mapping: .64

Visual-perception programs: .55

Added Effect of Poverty

Brain scans reveal statistically significant disparities between resourced and under-resourced students in the areas of language and memory ability; visual and spatial cognition did not differ significantly in research tests. Mental images are effective for all students, but they are critical for those who are under-resourced.

Explanation

When a great discrepancy exists between the way the learner creates understanding and the way the expert communicates understanding, failure usually results. Mental models serve to fill this gap by building a bridge between abstract concepts and concrete understanding.

Mental models are drawings, stories, and analogies that translate ideas into sensory representations or experiences that help make sense of information and increase memory of information.

To translate the concrete to the abstract, the mind usually needs to hold the information in a mental model.

To understand any discipline or field of study, one must understand the mental models that the discipline uses. In effect, virtually all disciplines are based on mental models. For example, when an individual builds a house, many discussions and words (the abstract) are used to convey what the finished house (the concrete) will be. But between the words and the finished house are blueprints. Blueprints are the translators. Between the three-dimensional concrete house and the abstract words, a two-dimensional visual translates.

When mental models are directly taught, abstract information can be learned much more quickly and retained because the mind has a way to contain it or hold it.

Directions

One of the most important mental models for students to have is a mental model for time that includes past, present, and future. A mental model for time is vital to understanding cause, effect, consequence, and sequence. Without a model for time, an individual cannot plan. (Please note that there are cultural differences in mental models for time; however, all cultural mental models for time do have a way to address past, present, and future.)

To access a student's mental model in a particular instance, use sketching or ask for a story, analogy, or metaphor. Sketching is a particularly useful tool in better understanding what a student has stored in terms of mental models. To do sketching with students, have them draw a two-dimensional visual of how they think about a word, an idea, a person, etc.

Research by Richard Mayer (2005) found that adding visuals resulted in an 89% advantage in learning outcomes.

The following diagram shows that to translate the concrete to the abstract, the mind often finds it helpful to hold the information in a mental model. A mental model can be a two-dimensional visual representation, a story, a metaphor, or an analogy.

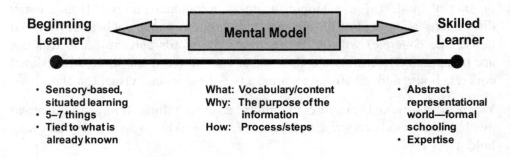

Beginning Learner	Mental Model	Skilled Learner
• Sensory-based, situated learning • 5–7 things • Tied to what is already known	What: Vocabulary/content Why: The purpose of the information How: Process/steps	• Abstract representational world—formal schooling • Expertise

When a great discrepancy exists between the way the learner creates understanding and the way the expert communicates understanding, failure results.

Explanation

Examples of mental models for academic content and processes follow.

Mental Model for Pythagorean Theorem

Pythagorean Theorem: $a^2 + b^2 = c^2$

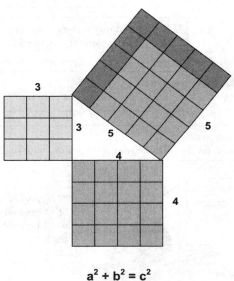

$$a^2 + b^2 = c^2$$

$$3^2 + 4^2 = 5^2$$

$$9 + 16 = 25$$

$$25 = 25$$

Square of one side + Square of other side = Square of hypotenuse

Pythagorean Theorem is a theory of relationship and proportion. In other words, if you know two sides of a right triangle you can know the third side.

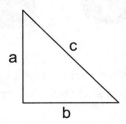

Mental Model for Persuasive Techniques

How can I get her to go out with me?
I have **10** ideas of **ways to persuade** her:

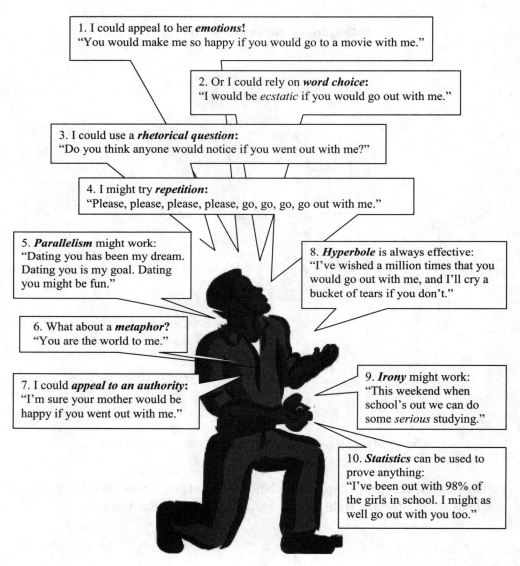

1. I could appeal to her *emotions*!
"You would make me so happy if you would go to a movie with me."

2. Or I could rely on *word choice*:
"I would be *ecstatic* if you would go out with me."

3. I could use a *rhetorical question*:
"Do you think anyone would notice if you went out with me?"

4. I might try *repetition*:
"Please, please, please, please, go, go, go, go out with me."

5. *Parallelism* might work:
"Dating you has been my dream. Dating you is my goal. Dating you might be fun."

6. What about a *metaphor*?
"You are the world to me."

7. I could *appeal to an authority*:
"I'm sure your mother would be happy if you went out with me."

8. *Hyperbole* is always effective:
"I've wished a million times that you would go out with me, and I'll cry a bucket of tears if you don't."

9. *Irony* might work:
"This weekend when school's out we can do some *serious* studying."

10. *Statistics* can be used to prove anything:
"I've been out with 98% of the girls in school. I might as well go out with you too."

Also see Strategy 58 for another mental model for persuasive techniques and reasoning—and Strategy 11 for a step sheet on persuasive writing.

Mental Model for Place Value

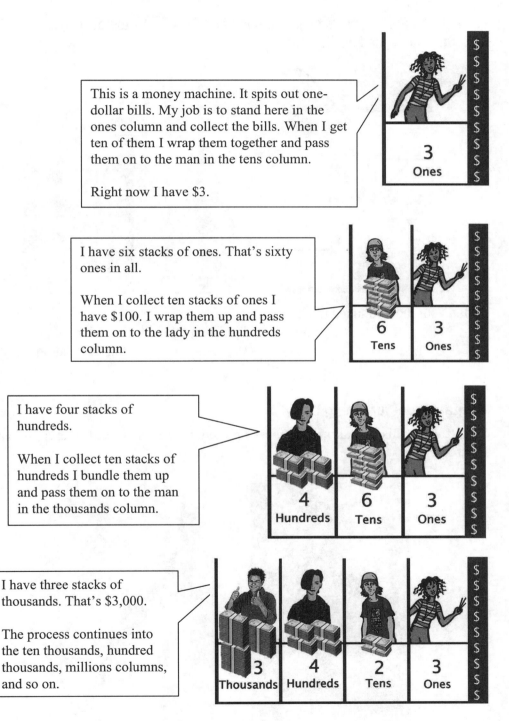

This is a money machine. It spits out one-dollar bills. My job is to stand here in the ones column and collect the bills. When I get ten of them I wrap them together and pass them on to the man in the tens column.

Right now I have $3.

I have six stacks of ones. That's sixty ones in all.

When I collect ten stacks of ones I have $100. I wrap them up and pass them on to the lady in the hundreds column.

I have four stacks of hundreds.

When I collect ten stacks of hundreds I bundle them up and pass them on to the man in the thousands column.

I have three stacks of thousands. That's $3,000.

The process continues into the ten thousands, hundred thousands, millions columns, and so on.

Mental Model for Inflation

There are two ways to get from the first floor to the top floor:
the stairs, and an elevator ...

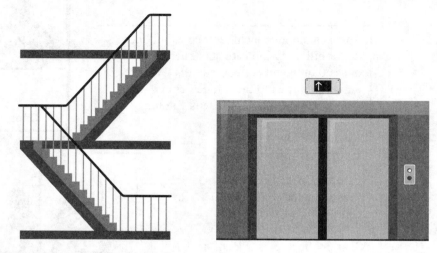

When your income takes the stairs ...
and the cost of living takes the elevator,
this is inflation!

Mental Model for Lining Up

To introduce this mental model, mess up the jelly beans and call it a crowd and
not a line.

Mental Model for Developing Characters

Leaves (appearance)

Twigs (details)

Branches (actions)

Bark (challenges/hardships)

Inner trunk (fears)

Soil (location)

Roots (family/background)

Strategy 4

Mental Models for Processes

Academic
Strategy

Researchers

Bransford, J. D., Brown, A. L., & Cocking, R. R. (Eds.). (2000).
Gürses, A., Cetinkaya, S., Dogar, C., & Sahin, E. (2015).
Hattie, J. (2015).
Idol, L., & Jones, B. F. (1991).
Jones, B. F., Pierce, J., & Hunter, B. (1988).
Marzano, R. (2007).
Marzano, R., & Arredondo, D. (1986).
Payne, R. K. (2005).
Payne, R. K. (2013).
Resnick, L. B., & Klopfer, L. (1989).
Senge, P., Ross, R., Smith, B., Roberts, C., & Kleiner, A. (1994).
Shulman, L. (1987).

Effect Size

Piagetian programs: 1.28

Teaching process skills (Piagetian programs) has an effect size with more than three times the impact of the average influence.

Concept mapping: .64

Visual-perception programs: .55

Added Effect of Poverty

Piagetian programs focus on thinking processes rather than outcomes. Process skills are those that are frequently underdeveloped among under-resourced students, but such skills can be taught.

Explanation

Jerome Bruner (1996) states that a theory of instruction should address four major aspects, one of which is the ways in which a body of knowledge can be structured so that it can be most readily grasped by the learner.

Directions

Mental models for processes posted on charts around the room can be referred to by students as often as needed, teaching the related skill of strategy selection. Sample mental models for processes follow.

Process Mental Model Example

Plan and Label—QTIPS

Math problem solving

Letter	Step	Teacher Directions	Symbol	Sentence Starter
Q	**Question**	Use sentence frame to underline question		I was asked to ...
T	**Think**	Thoughtfully, thoroughly, and totally read problem		
I	**Information**	Circle important information and labels; cross out unnecessary information		I knew ...
P	**Plan**	Choose plan, operation, or strategy: OPERATION STRATEGY STEPS		I used ...
S	**Solution**	Show your work; choose your answer; check your answer	X = 10	The answer is ... because ...

Source: Lodi Unified Schools, Marada Middle School, Stockton, CA, 2004–05.

Mental Model for Responding to Open-Response Questions: U R TOPS

U	UNDERLINE	UNDERLINE or highlight key words, ideas, power verbs, and important information.
R	READ	READ everything twice before you start to answer. Read charts, diagrams, and maps, then reread the question.
T	TOPIC	Create a TOPIC SENTENCE that clearly states your position, decision, or starts your answer.
O	ORGANIZE	ORGANIZE your thoughts to answer the question. Be clear, concise, and to the point.
P	PART	Look for specific PARTS to be answered. Label each part with a number.
S	SUPPORT	SUPPORT your answer with facts, figures, or statements from what is given.

Source: K. D. Ellis, 2004.

Strategy 5

Building Relationships of Mutual Respect Among Students and Teachers

Academic and
Behavioral
Strategy

Researchers

Brookover, W. B., Beady, C., Flood, P., Schweitzer, J., &
    Wisenbaker, J. (1979).
Comer, J. (1995).
Ferguson, R. (2008).
Gallagher, E. (2013).
Goleman, D. (2006).
Greenspan, S. I., & Benderly, B. L. (1997).
Hattie, J. (2015).
Payne, R. K. (2005).

Effect Size

"… [I]mpact on student learning is heightened when teachers believe their major role is to evaluate their impact" (Hattie, 2015, p. 81). This is what John Hattie labels "Teacher estimates of [teacher] achievement": 1.62

Teacher/student relationships: .72 for K–12 and .52 for college/university

Added Effect of Poverty

Teachers evaluating their own impact on student learning has the greatest effect of all the influences included in Hattie's research analysis—for all students. The unique characteristics of under-resourced students create a greater-than-average need for teacher reflection and ownership of student performance.

Explanation

In a research study of 910 first-graders, the at-risk students would not learn from the teacher, even with excellent instructional practices, if they perceived the teacher to be cold and controlling. A significant relationship—defined as one of mutual respect that includes high expectations, insistence, and support—is paramount between teacher and student.

> "All learning is double-coded, both cognitively *and* emotionally. How you feel about something is part of the learning and your openness to learning."
>
> —S. Greenspan & B. Benderly, 1997

> "No significant learning occurs without a significant relationship."
>
> —J. Comer, 1995

If a student and teacher do not have a relationship of mutual respect, the learning will be greatly reduced. For some students, learning won't occur at all. If a student and a teacher don't like each other—or even come to despise each other—forget about the learning. If, on the other hand, mutual respect is present, it can compensate for the dislike. Mutual respect is as much about nonverbals as it is about what one says.

Directions

Plan professional-development activities that address all the critical components of relationships of mutual respect:

- Support: the direct teaching of process and mental models
- Insistence: the motivation and persistence that comes from the relationship
- High expectations: the approach of "I know you can do it, and you will."

To assess teacher expectations, view self-videotaped lessons to assess personal reactions to "Factors that Influence Teacher Expectations."

Gender: sex-role stereotyping

Socioeconomic status

Race/ethnicity

Type of school: Students in inner-city schools or rural schools are sometimes presumed to be less capable.

Appearance: the expense or style of students' clothes and grooming habits

Oral-language patterns: The presence of any nonstandard-English speaking pattern can sometimes lead teachers to hold lower expectations.

Messiness/disorganization: Students whose work areas or assignments are messy are sometimes perceived as having lower ability.

Readiness: immaturity or lack of experience

Halo effect: Some teachers generalize from one characteristic a student may have.

Seating position: If students seat themselves at the sides or back of the classroom, some teachers perceive this as a sign of lower learning motivation and/or ability and treat those students accordingly.

Negative comments about students: negative comments that often come from other staff members

Outdated theories: Educational theories that emphasize the limitations of learners can lead to lowered expectations.

Tracking or long-term ability grouping: placement in "low" tracks or groups

Source: Adapted from W. Brookover, C. Beady, P. Flood, J. Schweitzer, & J. Wisenbaker, 1979.

View self-videotaped lessons to assess demonstration of teacher behaviors that demonstrate expectations.

1. Calls on everyone equitably.
2. Provides individual help.
3. Gives "wait" time.
4. Asks questions to give student clues about answer.
5. Asks questions that require more thought (not just yes/no questions).
6. Tells students whether their answers are right or wrong.
7. Gives specific praise.
8. Gives reasons for praise.

9. Listens.

10. Accepts feelings of student.

11. Gets within arm's reach of each student each day.

12. Is courteous to students.

13. Shows personal interest and gives compliments.

14. Touches students (appropriately).

15. Desists (does not call attention to every negative student behavior).

In Addition

Write each student's name on a Popsicle stick and put the sticks into a container. Pull a stick from the container and call on the student whose name is on the stick. This strategy contributes to efforts to call on all students equitably.

Show students videotaped lessons, then empower them by brainstorming with them what they can do to more positively influence their teachers' expectations of them. Research-based examples include:

1. Sit near the front of the class.

2. Smile occasionally.

3. Sit up straight.

4. Make eye contact. (If this is counter to a student's cultural practices, talk about choices and behavioral code switching.)

5. Tell your teachers when you think they do a particularly good job.

Respect often looks different through the eyes of teachers than it looks through students' eyes. It is possible, therefore, to mistakenly interpret students' behaviors as disrespectful when no disrespect is intended.

Brainstorm with students what respect and disrespect look and sound like to you and to them.

For the students disrespect looks like	For the students respect looks like
For the teacher disrespect looks like	For the teacher respect looks like

Strategy 6

Relational Learning

Academic and
Behavioral
Strategy

Researchers

Domagala-Zysk, E. (2006).
Faircloth, B. S., & Hamm, J. V. (2005).
Good, M., & Adams, G. R. (2008).
Green, G., Rhodes, J., Hirsch, A. H., Suarez-Orozco, C., &
    Camic, P. M. (2008).
Guay, F., Marsh, H. W., Senecal, C., & Dowson, M. (2008).
Hattie, J. (2015).
Halvorson, H. G. (2010).
Johnson, L. S. (2008).
Lazareve, O. F. (2012).
Payne, R. K. (2008).
Putnam, R. (2000).
Reis, S. M., Colbert, R. D., & Hebert, T. P. (2005).
Rimm-Kaufman, S. E., & Chiu, Y.-J. I. (2007).
Ross, D. D., Bondy, E., Gallingane, C., & Hambacher, E. (2008).
Sanchez, B., Reyes, O., & Singh, J. (2006).
Scales, P. C., Benson, P. L., Roehlkepartain, E. C., Sesma Jr., A., &
    van Dulmen, M. (2006).

Effect Size

Reciprocal teaching: .74

Peer tutoring: .55

Cooperative vs. individual learning: .55

Added Effect of Poverty

Under-resourced students generally possess fewer of the eight characteristics of relational learning (see list below) than their more affluent peers; therefore, they stand to benefit the most from this strategy.

Explanation

Researchers have identified eight characteristics of relational learning, as follows:

1. Relationships of mutual respect with teachers and administrators

2. A peer group to belong to that is positive and not destructive

3. Skills needed for maintaining positive relationships with peers

4. A coach or advocate who helps the student

5. If not a member of the dominant culture, the student has access to individuals (or histories of individuals) who have attained success and retained connections to their roots

6. Bridging social capital * (e-mail and social-media buddies, mentors et al.) to the larger society

7. At the secondary level, a very specific and clear plan for addressing one's own learning performance

8. A safe environment (emotionally, verbally, and physically)

* Social capital is terminology used by Robert Putnam in his book *Bowling Alone* (2000). It basically means who you know. He identifies two kinds—bonding and bridging. Bonding social capital involves people who are like you; bridging social capital involves people different from you.

Directions

A. A 'Corner Coach' for All Students

Explanation

This strategy is designed to enhance students' willingness to work with academic coaches.

Have students read about Muhammad Ali's corner coaches and the role they played in Ali's success as a boxer. Identify or allow students to select a "corner coach"—a teacher, a librarian, a cook, a custodian, or someone from home—for themselves.

Corner coaches assume three major responsibilities to the student:

1. Listen

2. Advocate when needed

3. Empower students to advocate for themselves by practicing the adult voice (see Strategy 60).

B. Preparations for Group Work

Teach Students How to Disagree

Explanation

Explain to students that disagreeing with others is acceptable in an academic setting, and when others disagree with them, such disagreement is not a personal attack. For example:

- Less helpful: "That's a dumb idea."
- More helpful: "I disagree because …"

C. Dedication Page

Explanation

"Psychologist James Shah discovered that when college students were subliminally exposed to their own father's name before completing a set of difficult problems, those students who associated Dad with the goal of high achievement worked harder and performed better" (cited in Halvorson, 2010).

Directions

Have student dedicate their projects to someone who supports their efforts. This name is likely to trigger motivation to put forth maximum effort.

Example: Dedicated to my 10th-grade English teacher _____.

D. Student Awareness of Supportive Relationships (for secondary and college students)

Directions

Students list major relationships in their lives, placing the name or title of each in one of several circles surrounding their own name in a center circle. They then draw solid lines from their own name to the names of those who support their efforts to achieve. They draw dotted lines from the circles of those who offer some but not steady support. Finally, they draw arrows away from the names of those who don't support or perhaps even try to sabotage their efforts.

Students' lists can remain private. The purpose is to identify ahead of time those to whom they can go in times of need.

Help students understand that they can maintain relationships with those who don't support their efforts or those who offer only partial support, but the solid-line relationships are the ones to go to for support.

Example:

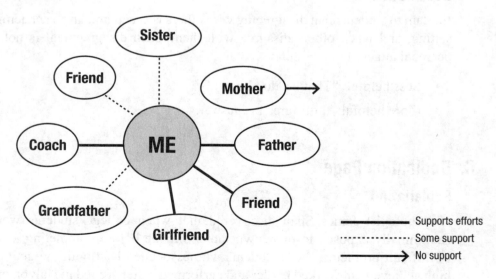

———————	Supports efforts
··················	Some support
———————→	No support

Strategy 7

Structured Partners in Learning

Academic and
Behavioral
Strategy

Researchers

Bransford, J. D., Brown, A. L., & Cocking, R. R. (Eds.). (1999).
Cheung, A., & Slavin, R. E. (2005).
Galton, M., Hargreaves, L., & Pell, T. (2009).
Gillies, R. M. (2004).
Gillies, R. M. (2008).
Lyman, F. (1981).
Mahalingam, M., Schaefer, F., & Morlino, E. (2008).
National Institute of Child Health and Human Development. (2000).

Effect Size

Classroom discussion: .82

Cooperative learning vs. individual learning: .55

Small-group learning: .47

Added Effect of Poverty

Since academic insecurity often correlates with poverty, under-resourced students sometimes benefit from intermediate pedagogical steps before being in the "limelight."

Explanation

Talking opens neural pathways, builds relationships, and enhances understandings. The think-pair-share (Lyman, 1981) strategy also serves as a reminder for instructors to give ample wait time, and pairing enables less confident students to field-test their opinions or ideas with a smaller grouping before sharing with the entire class.

By assigning all students to discussion groups, teachers give each student (on a daily basis) the opportunity to:

1. Communicate with a peer
2. Spend time with people who are "different from them"
3. Hear and give explanations at a level that is closer to the novice level of learning
4. Process new information

A sense of connectedness to teachers, subjects, and peers enhances motivation to achieve.

Directions

1. Students formulate an answer to a question individually.
2. Students share answers with peers.
3. Students are instructed to listen carefully to their partner's answer, noting similarities and differences in answers.
4. Pairs create a new answer that incorporates the best of both ideas and prepare to present the new answer if called upon.

Similar to the think-pair-share strategy, secondary teachers can instruct students to formulate, share, listen, and create.

Strategy 8

Peer Mediation

Behavioral
Strategy

Researchers

Farrell, A. D., Erwin, E. H., Allison, K. W., Meyer, A., Sullivan, T.,
    Camou, S., … Esposito, L. (2007).
Fisher, R., & Ury, W. (1983).
Hattie, J. (2015).
Huan, V. S. (2006).
Johnson, D. W., & Johnson, R. T. (1996).
Kunsch, C. A., Jitendra, A. K., & Sood, S. (2007).
Schellenberg, R. C., Parks-Savage, A., & Rehfuss, M. (2007).
Shamir, A., & Lazerovitz, T. (2007).
Shamir, A., Tzuriel, D., & Rozen, M. (2006).
Traore, R. (2008).
Tzuriel, D., & Shamir, A. (2007).

Effect Size

The list of John Hattie (2015) does not include peer mediation directly, but he
did analyze such related strategies as classroom behavior (.63) and problem-
solving teaching (.63).

Added Effect of Poverty

Involvement in peer mediation reinforces understanding of hidden rules of the
classroom among under-resourced students.

Explanation

Peer-mediation techniques teach questioning, choice identification, and the adult voice, all of which are critical for conflict resolution and positive peer/peer relationships.

Directions

Implementing peer-mediation programs involves planning and training. As peer mediators, students are taught the following procedures (Johnson & Johnson, 1996):

1. State what you want: "I want to use the book now."

2. State how you feel: "I'm frustrated."

3. State the reasons for your wants and feelings: "You have been using the book for the past hour. If I don't get to use the book soon, my report will not be done on time. It's frustrating to have to wait so long."

4. Summarize your understanding of what the other person wants, how the other person feels, and the reasons underlying both.

5. Brainstorm three optional plans to resolve the conflict.

6. Choose one plan and shake hands.

Strategy 9

Task Mediation

Academic and
Behavioral
Strategy

Researchers

Feuerstein, R. (1980).

Gürses, A., Cetinkaya, S., Dogar, C., & Sahin, E. (2015).

Hattie, J. (2015).

Kishiyama, M. M., Boyce, W. T., Jiménez, A. M., Perry, L. M., &
    Knight, R. T. (2009).

Sharron, H., & Coulter, M. (2004).

Sternberg, R., & Grigorenko, E. (2002).

Effect Size

Cognitive task analysis: .87

Teacher clarity: .75

Metacognitive strategies: .53

Added Effect of Poverty

There is a direct correlation in the research of Reuven Feuerstein (1980) between socioeconomic class and the amount of mediation provided, with students from lower socioeconomic class, on average, receiving less.

Explanation

Feuerstein discovered that children who receive inadequate mediation—explanation about the *what, why,* and *how* of events and phenomena—struggle to understand and assimilate new concepts and data.

Imagine two young children in separate houses, both sitting at a table drawing pictures. In both houses the door is open, and the wind is creating a draft. A gust of air blows papers off the table and across the room. In the first house an adult says, "Shut that door." The child follows orders and returns to her drawing. She completes the task but learned almost nothing from the episode.

In the second house an adult says, "The air is blowing through the door and creating a draft, which is blowing your papers across the room. Shut the door, and that would stop the draft." This child has learned not only *what* to do, but also *how* and *why.* She has been mediated. Mediation means that you identify the stimulus (the *what*), give it meaning (tell *why*), and then give it a *how* (Payne, 2005).

Directions

Mediate Almost Everything; Assume Nothing

Examples of opportunities to mediate students' learning are boundless. In fact, one rule of thumb in any classroom could be to assume almost nothing about what students already know—explain not only *what* they should be doing but also *why* and *how* they should carry through.

Examples of opportunities to mediate students' learning include:

Following safety precautions for
    lab work
Studying at regular intervals
Washing hands regularly
Looking both ways before
    crossing the street

Listening to opinions of others
Exercising daily
Developing rubrics

Strategy 10

Teaching Cognitive (Input) Skills

Academic
Strategy

Researchers

Awbrey, S. M. (2005).
Feuerstein, R. (1980).
Feuerstein, R. (2004).
Gürses, A., Cetinkaya, S., Dogar, C., & Sahin, E. (2015).
Hattie, J. (2015).
Jensen, K. (2015).
Kishiyama, M. M., Boyce, W. T., Jiménez, A. M., Perry, L. M., &
   Knight, R. T. (2009).
Perkinson, M. (2017).
Sharron, H., & Coulter, M. (2004).

Effect Size

Piagetian programs: 1.28

Teaching process skills (Piagetian programs) has an effect size with more than three times the impact of the average influence.

Added Effect of Poverty

Students whose past experiences are very different from those associated with performing academic tasks are typically less familiar with processes used to complete academic tasks.

Explanation

Input strategies are methods by which the brain prepares data for processing. Input skills are required for successful manipulation and intake of data. In EEG scans done at the University of California, Berkeley (2008), researchers found that most children from poverty have not developed the prefrontal cortex (executive function) of the brain in the way that most middle-class children have. The executive function of the brain is impulse control, working memory (holding one idea while you work with another), organization, and planning. The latter two are input skills—and these skills can be taught.

Cognitive Skills

INPUT: Data-gathering skills

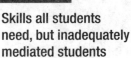

1. Use planning behaviors.
2. Focus perception on specific stimulus.
3. Control impulsivity.
4. Explore data systematically.
5. Use appropriate and accurate labels.
6. Organize space using stable systems of reference.
7. Orient data in time.
8. Identify constancies across variations.
9. Gather precise and accurate data.
10. Consider two sources of information at once
11. Organize data (parts of a whole).
12. Visually transport data.

Skills all students need, but inadequately mediated students have not acquired

ELABORATION: Efficient use of data

1. Identify and define the problem.
2. Select relevant cues.
3. Compare data.
4. Select appropriate categories of time.
5. Summarize data.
6. Project relationship of data.
7. Use logical data.
8. Test hypothesis.
9. Build inferences.
10. Make a plan using the data.
11. Use appropriate labels.
12. Use data systematically

Where we often start with instruction, assuming students already have input skills

OUTPUT: Communication of input and elaboration

1. Communicate clearly the labels and processes.
2. Visually transport data correctly.
3. Use precise and accurate language.
4. Control impulsive behavior

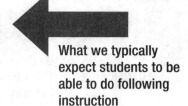

What we typically expect students to be able to do following instruction

Impact of Input Skills on Classroom Performance

Skill	Definition	How does lack of process impact classroom performance?
Use planning behaviors	Goal setting, identifying procedures in the task, identifying parts of the task, assigning time to the task, and identifying the quality of the work necessary for task	Does not turn homework in on time, unable to complete long term projects, cause/effect (if I do this, then this will happen), sequence, impulsive
Focus perception on specific stimulus	Strategy of seeing details and identifying everything noticed by the five senses	Cannot focus on assigned task, misses parts of the task, cannot find the information on the page
Control impulsivity	Strategy of stopping action until one has thought about the task	Cannot plan, gets in trouble, may be misdiagnosed as having ADHD, finishes assignments too quickly
Explore data systematically	Using a strategy to procedurally and systematically go through every piece of data	Cannot see patterns, relationships between data, does not have a method for checking work
Use appropriate and accurate labels	Precise use of words to identify and explain	Uses generic words instead of specific, cannot do "cloze" procedure tests
Organize space with stable systems of reference	An individual can identify with words the position of an item; can organize space	Disorganized, misplaces things, mixes up *b, d, p, q* (mimics dyslexia), cannot read a map, cannot line up numbers in math

(continued on next page)

(continued from previous page)

Skill	Definition	How does lack of process impact classroom performance?
Orient data in time	Strategy of assigning abstract values to time and the use of the measurements of time	Cannot sequence, loses track of time, does not turn things in on time
Identify constancies across variations	Strategy of knowing what always remains the same and what changes	Cannot see patterns, cannot make generalizations, cannot find main idea, or compare/contrast
Gather precise and accurate information	Use of specific vocabulary and word choice, identify precisely when something occurred in time and where it occurred in space	Cannot summarize because cannot distinguish between what's important and what's not, cannot tell where, when, how
Consider two pieces of information at once	The mind can hold two objects simultaneously and compare/contrast the two objects	Cannot compare/contrast, find patterns
Organize data (parts of a whole)	Go through data systematically, organizing space, identifying constancies and variations, and using vocabulary to label both the parts and the whole	Cannot explain why, does not recognize when someone is cheating
Visually transport data	The eye picks up data, then carries it accurately into the brain, examines it for constancies and variations, and labels the parts and the whole	Cannot copy from board or overhead

Sources: Developed by K. Jensen, 2015; adapted with permission.
Also adapted from work of R. Feuerstein, 2004.

Input: Quantity and Quality of Data Gathering—Music Applications

Music enhances skills that students use in other course content and many areas of life. Dr. Mary Perkinson, member of the Omaha Music Conservatory and assistant professor of Violin and String Education at the University of Nebraska, Omaha, stated (personal conversation, June 6, 2017) that music enhances students' math and language development in particular. Perkinson further identified …

How Music Can Help Develop Each of the 12 Input Skills

1. **Use planning behaviors.**

   Teachers rely on specific strategies to assist students with the theoretical study of the composition, the practice of the composition, and the performance of the composition—and they teach students how to plan each phase of the composition process.

2. **Focus perception on specific stimulus.**

   Students focus on the teacher's hand motions, following nonverbal cues and information that subsequently can be expressed with their instruments/voices.

3. **Control impulsivity.**

   Students prepare with a group to perform a piece from memory without stopping, regardless of what distractions occur.

4. **Explore data systematically.**

   Identify patterns in the composition, and label parts of the work using letters to identify larger patterns (i.e., a-b-a).

5. **Use appropriate and accurate labels.**

   Use appropriate labels to identify genre (baroque, classical, 20th century), and instrumentation (i.e., solo, duet, quartet, ensemble).

6. **Organize space using stable systems of reference.**

   Identify key signature, meter, tempo, articulations, and instrumentation, using music theory as the system of reference.

7. **Orient data in time.**

   Perform rhythms according to indicated note values, as well as interpret and perform compositions in light of the historical context.

8. **Identify constancies across variations.**

   Notice what rhythms, pitches, and articulations return frequently throughout the composition.

9. **Gather precise and accurate data.**

   Identify pertinent information, such as genre, historical context, and composer intent (through key signature, meter, and tempo) to produce an accurate representation of the composition.

10. Consider two sources of information at once.

Recognize the separate indications for the same note for note *pitch* and note *duration*.

11. Organize data (parts of a whole).

Recognize the broad compositional scheme and group similar notes, rhythms, and patterns together.

12. Visually transport data.

Read notes on the page and produce the appropriate physical responses.

Source: Adapted from M. Perkinson, 2017.

Strategy 11

Input Skill: Planning (for Task Completion) Step Sheets

Academic
Strategy

Researchers

Beatham, M. D. (2009).
Crook, S. R., & Evans, G. W. (2013).
Feuerstein, R. (1980).
Krueger, K. A., & Dayan, P. (2009).
Lodewyk, K. R., Winne, P. H., & Jamieson-Noel, D. L. (2009).
Marzano, R., & Arredondo, D. (1986).
Ngu, B. H., Mit, E., Shahbodin, F., & Tuovinen, J. (2009).
Spears D. (2011).

Effect Size

Piagetian programs: 1.28

Teaching process skills (Piagetian programs) has an effect size with more than three times the impact of the average influence.

Added Effect of Poverty

Stephen Crook and Gary Evans (2013) cite research documenting the lack of development of planning skills among many children living in poverty. They cite possible causes, including greater chaos in daily lives, more family moves and school changes, greater family turmoil and turnover, crowded and noisy households, higher levels of stress, and fewer structured routines and rituals.

Planning is number one on Feuerstein's list of process skills needed for data intake that is often underdeveloped among under-resourced students.

Explanation

This activity is called a step sheet, a tool that helps students who ask what they should do even before you finish the directions for an assignment. Step sheets provide procedural information for academic tasks. If students cannot plan, they often don't have procedural self-talk. They tend to do the first few steps, then quit. Step sheets help them successfully navigate tasks on a consistent basis.

Directions

Step sheets are best completed without assumptions about what students "should" know, beginning with a step that will help them think, "I can do that," and get started on the project. As students progress through additional similar tasks, they can assume more responsibility for developing step sheets for themselves.

Step Sheet

Steps	Amount of time
1.	
2.	
3.	
4.	
5.	
6.	
7.	
8.	
9.	
10.	
11.	
12.	

Sample Step Sheet: Persuasive Essay

This activity shows the steps for persuasive writing. It's another form of step sheet because it provides procedural information for an academic task.

Steps	Amount of time
1. Choose your topic or issue.	2 days
2. Make a list of pros and cons related to your topic.	2 days
3. Write your introduction, grabbing the reader's attention. In the introduction, write your thesis statement. (State your position in one statement. What position do you want to convince your audience is best?)	½ day
4. Write one to three paragraphs convincing the reader of your position, using facts, examples, statistics, and expert opinion.	1 day
5. Write one paragraph addressing cons of your topic and how they can be dealt with	1 day
6. Write your conclusion, restating your thesis.	1 day
7. Make an appeal for action.	1 day

Also see Strategies 3 and 58 for mental models on persuasive techniques and reasoning.

Strategy 12

Input Skill: Planning Backwards

Academic
Strategy

Researchers

Beatham, M. D. (2009).
Capezio, P. (2000).
Feuerstein, R. (1980).
Gürses, A., Cetinkaya, S., Dogar, C., & Sahin, E. (2015).
Hattie, J. (2015).
Krueger, K. A., & Dayan, P. (2009).
Lodewyk, K. R., Winne, P. H., & Jamieson-Noel, D. L. (2009).
Marzano, R., & Arredondo, D. (1986).
Ngu, B. H., Mit, E., Shahbodin, F., & Tuovinen, J. (2009).

Effect Size

Piagetian programs: 1.28

Teaching process skills (Piagetian programs) has an effect size with more than three times the impact of the average influence. Planning is high on the list of process skills identified by Reuven Feuerstein (1980) that often create a challenge for under-resourced students

Added Effect of Poverty

Research documents the lack of development of planning skills among many children living in poverty. Possible causes include greater chaos in daily lives including more family moves and school changes, greater family turmoil and turnover, crowded and noisy households, higher levels of stress, and fewer structured routines and rituals.

Explanation

To complete tasks requires planning, which often calls for procedural self-talk. The executive functions of the brains of many under-resourced children, which would support these tasks, tend to be inadequately developed. Planning and self-talk can be directly taught using games and procedural tools.

Directions

Walk students through planning experiences—starting with the end and moving toward the present.

Planning Backwards

Monday	Tuesday	Wednesday	Thursday	Friday

Strategy 13

Input Skill: Academic-Task Preparations to Control Impulsivity

Academic
Strategy

Researchers

Feuerstein, R. (2004).
Hattie, J. (2015).
Schraw, G., Brooks, D., & Crippen, K. J. (2005).
Shonkoff, J. P., & Phillips, D. A. (Eds.). (2000).

Effect Size

Piagetian programs: 1.28

Teaching process skills (Piagetian programs) has an effect size with more than three times the impact of the average influence. Planning is high on the list of process skills identified by Reuven Feuerstein (2004) that often create a challenge for under-resourced students.

Added Effect of Poverty

Students with limited resources must often exert self-control in areas of life not required of more affluent individuals, and their ability to control impulsivity becomes depleted.

Explanation

Feuerstein found that if you cannot plan, you cannot predict. If you cannot predict, you do not know cause and effect. If you do not know cause and effect, you do not know consequence. If you do not know consequence, you do not control impulsivity. If you do not control impulsivity, you have an inclination toward criminal behavior. As noted, a neurological study conducted at the University of California, Berkeley (2008), found that poor children's brains have not developed executive functions—one of which is the ability to plan (see Strategy 10). It can be learned.

Directions

Have students complete a "Preliminary Plans" or "Getting Ready" section on their step sheets or planning sheets, as follows, as a way of learning not to skip steps and not to start in the middle of a task.

Example: Elementary

Painting a picture		Time
Getting ready	1. Cover the floor with paper	2 minutes
	2. Fill a cup with water for washing the brush	1 minute
	3. Clip the paper to the easel	1 minute
	4. Put an apron on	1 minute 4 minutes to get ready!
Actions	5. Paint the picture	
	6. Put the painting on …	

Example: Middle School Through College

Writing a research paper		Time
Preliminary steps	1. Open a folder on a computer desktop labeled Research Project	2 hours
	2. Inside of the folder open …	
Action steps	3. Select your topic	
	4. List possible sources	

Strategy 14

Input Skill: Focusing

Academic
Strategy

Researchers

Baddeley, A., & Hitch, G. J. (2010).
Barrouillet, P., Bernardin, S., & Camos, V. (2004).
Bowman, H. (2011).
Engle, R. W., & Kane, M. J. (2004).
Feuerstein, R. (2004).
Gürses, A., Cetinkaya, S., Dogar, C., & Sahin, E. (2015).
Hattie, J. (2015).
Jones, S. M., Bailey, R., & Partee, A. (2016).
Killingsworth, M., & Gilbert, D. (2010).

Effect Size

Piagetian programs: 1.28

Teaching process skills (Piagetian programs) has an effect size with more than three times the impact of the average influence.

Added Effect of Poverty

The conditions associated with poverty often undermine the development of critical skills. Low-income children are more likely to have lower levels of executive functioning (Jones, Bailey, & Partee, 2016).

Explanation

The work of Reuven Feuerstein (2004) reveals that students who had very few opportunities as children to learn to focus closely on objects continue, in some instances, to struggle with seeing or perceiving details in their environments into adulthood. In fact, some studies indicate that many of these individuals miss as much as 50% of everything in their environments.

This phenomenon manifests itself in many ways in classrooms. Students will, for example, report to class, say, "I studied, and I'm ready for this test," and then they fail. We ask them why they didn't answer a question about a graph, and they say, "I didn't see it." The reality often is just that; they didn't see it. The graph was part of the 50% they missed because they don't have the skills needed to focus.

Directions

A. Provide students with checklists of the parts of textbook chapters and have them check each item off after they have found and read it in the chapter.

Print features

| bold print | headings | subheadings | labels | captions |
| italics | quotations | bullets | boxes | titles |

Graphic aids

| diagrams | figures | graphs | tables | charts |
| timelines | maps | | | |

Organizational aids

| index | glossary | preface | table of contents | headers |
| footers | appendix | | | |

Illustrations

| photographs | drawings | sketches | advertisements |

B. Students with the tendency to miss a large percentage (sometimes up to 50%) of the data around them are more likely to visually skip over potentially unfamiliar vocabulary, not focusing on new words enough to comprehend or even see them. The Knowledge Rating Scale strategy—also referred to in the vocabulary session of this book—is a useful tool for drawing students' attention to new vocabulary in the chapter.

After looking at a possibly unfamiliar word and thinking about how well they know the meaning of the word, they will be more likely to actually see the word in the context of the chapter.

Knowledge Rating Scale

Word	Know it well	Have seen or heard it	No clue
rhombus			x
triangle	x		
pentagon		x	
quadrilateral		x	
trapezoid			x
square	x		

Directions (for Primary Grades)

Include poems like the following in daily nursery-rhyme routines:

"Something I've Never Seen Before"
(sung to the tune of "Here We Go 'Round the Mulberry Bush")

> Every day on my way home, my way home, my way home,
> Every day on my way I am looking for
> Something I have never seen, never seen, never seen,
> Something I have never seen, never seen before.

Strategy 15

Input Skill: Bringing Order Out of Chaos

Academic
Strategy

Researchers

Curie, P., deBrueys, M., Exnicios, J., & Prejean, M. (1987).
Engle, R. W., & Kane, M. J. (2004).
Evans, G. W., Eckenrode J., & Marcynyszyn, L. A. (2010).
Feuerstein, R. (2004).
Gürses, A., Cetinkaya, S., Dogar, C., & Sahin, E. (2015).
Hattie, J. (2015).
Irvin, J., & Rose, E. (1995).
Teräs, M. (2007).
Zakin, A. (2007).

Effect Size

Piagetian programs: 1.28

Teaching process skills (Piagetian programs) has an effect size with more than three times the impact of the average influence.

Added Effect of Poverty

Reuven Feuerstein (2004) discovered that students from under-resourced backgrounds are less frequently taught organizational skills; therefore, they are less likely to feel the need to organize.

Explanation

Feuerstein defines organization as "Order out of Chaos" and explains that students must have organization before they will apply skills they learn. Teaching and requiring (assigning grades to the use of) designated organizational structures creates a sense of need for organization.

Directions

Point out potentially chaotic situations that have been organized, resulting in order out of chaos.

Examples include:

- School-bus schedules: Without organization, bus drivers would drive anywhere, picking up any children at any time of the day.

- Religious services: Without organization, people could arrive at any time and stand up and sing whenever they wanted to.

- Meals: Without organization, cooks could prepare one item early in the morning and the next late at night for the same meal.

- Books: Without organization, authors could arrange the contents of their books however they like.

In the discussion make a transition to bringing order out of chaos in students' lives and lessons, including organizing lockers, papers, notes, belongings, etc., as well as new subject matter in each of their heads.

Teach the use of such organizational processes as drilling down and generalizing their use to many situations.

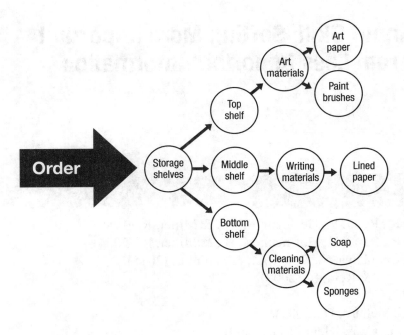

Explain that advance organizers, such as KWL (know, want to know, learned), are for the purpose of assisting students in organizing their thoughts (see Strategy 30 for diagram for KWL).

Illustrate the benefits of the activity by writing course concepts randomly and require students to arrange the items into a meaningful order. Include this activity in both class discussions and test questions. Point out that the result is an outline of the content. A simplified example follows:

Air Force	Normandy	European Theater	World War II
Army	Hitler	Germany	D-Day
Foxholes	Trenches	Eisenhower	

Strategy 16

Input Skill: Sorting More Important from Less Important Information

Academic
Strategy

Researchers

Feuerstein, R., Rand, Y., Hoffman, M. B., & Miller, R. (1980).
Feuerstein, R., Rand, Y., Hoffman, M. B., & Miller, R. (2004).
Gürses, A., Cetinkaya, S., Dogar, C., & Sahin, E. (2015).
Hagaman, J. L., & Reid, R. (2008).
Hattie, J. (2015).
Hock, M., & Mellard, D. (2005).
Kirkpatrick, L. C., & Klein, P. D. (2009).
Langford, P. A., Rizzo, S K., & Roth, J. M. (2003).
Marzano, R. (2007).
Reiner, M. (2009).
Richards, J. C., & Anderson, N. A. (2003).
Tanenhaus, M. K., Spivey-Knowlton, M. J., Eberhard, K. M., & Sedivy, J.
    C. (1995).
van der Schoot, M., Vasbinder, A. L., Horsley, T. M., & van Lieshout,
    E. C. D. M. (2008).
Weekes, H. (2005).

Effect Size

Piagetian programs: 1.28

Teaching process skills (Piagetian programs) has an effect size with more than three times the impact of the average influence.

Added Effect of Poverty

Under-resourced students often have learned to sort by criteria that are typically different from academic criteria.

Explanation

Memory is based on summarization and/or attachment to prior knowledge. Summarization is based on sorting the more important from the less important. To sort what is and is not important, one must identify similarities and differences (compare and contrast).

Sorting Information Using Patterns and Criteria

To store and retrieve information, one must be able to sort using criteria. If the patterns are known, however, one can sort faster. Because children from poverty often come into school behind, ways are needed to teach information much faster. Teaching patterns as a way to sort is one way to shorten the time needed to teach something.

The mind sorts data against patterns, mental mindsets, and paradigms to determine what is more important versus less important.

Items with the same attributes are assigned to a group.

Patterns can be identified using groups.

Abstract constructs are essential for grouping and patterning; these are necessary for success in school.

Developing Sorting Strategies

Attributes become a sort of screen that allows "important" data to continue and stops "unimportant" data.

By teaching patterns within data, students can find what is important more quickly and accurately.

Sorting and Comparing/Contrasting Aids Memory

To sort, the mind uses patterns and criteria (attributes).

Criteria may be:

- structure
- purpose
- number
- size
- direction
- design
- color
- shape
- detail
- type
- pattern
- function

Directions

Point out potentially chaotic situations that have been organized, resulting in order out of chaos.

A. Cartoons

Cartooning a chapter (with a limited number of frames) requires a student to identify and sort the most important points in a chapter.

Students identify the six major points or events in a chapter and make a cartoon showing these major points. Then they write a caption underneath each picture, creating a summary. Pictures can be drawn, or cut-out cartoon characters from the newspaper can be used to create the cartoons.

Cartoon Chapter		

B. Identifying Characteristics: Shapes—Alike and Different

The ability to differentiate shapes and attributes promotes an understanding of properties and variables in mathematics.

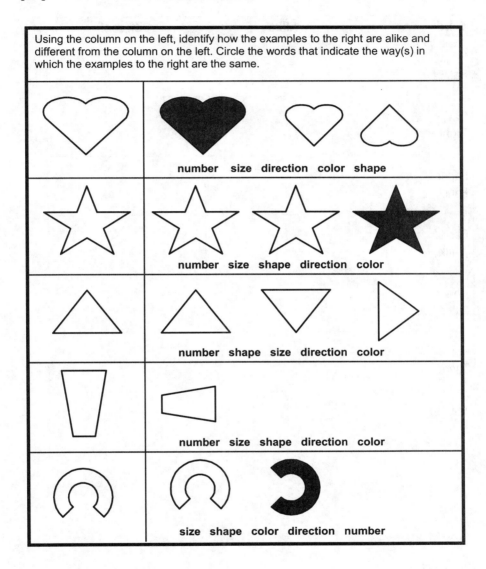

Using the column on the left, identify how the examples to the right are alike and different from the column on the left. Circle the words that indicate the way(s) in which the examples to the right are the same.

number   size   direction   color   shape

number   size   shape   direction   color

number   shape   size   direction   color

number   size   shape   direction   color

size   shape   color   direction   number

C. Identifying Characteristics: Words—Alike and Different

In the first column, write what the words have in common.

In the second column, write how the words are different.

Words	Alike	Different
Sugar Salt		
Day Night		
Paper Pencil		
Car Truck		
Now Later		
Here There		
Tall Short		

D. Comparing and Contrasting

In Robert Marzano's analysis (2007) of classroom instructional strategies (as opposed to influences analyzed by John Hattie, 2015), he identifies comparing and contrasting as the most effective classroom intervention.

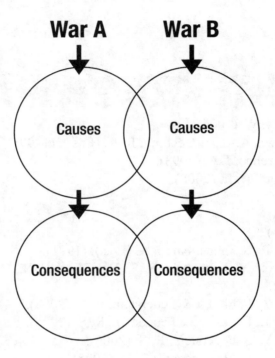

Use:

- Response signals (written response on white boards)
- Ready response (stand when you have an answer or put pen on desk when ready)
- Thumbs up/thumbs down
- Green card for true, red card for false
- System of ranking your agreement with number of fingers or height of raised arm

Strategy 17

Input Skill: Planning and Labeling in Academic Tasks

Academic
Strategy

Researchers

Bakunas, B., & Holley, W. (2004).

Bransford, J. D., Brown, A. L., & Cocking, R. R. (Eds.). (1999).

Chalmers, D., & Lawrence, J. A. (1993).

Collier, P. J., & Morgan, D. L. (2008).

Feuerstein, R. (1980).

Feuerstein, R. (1998a).

Feuerstein, R. (1998b).

Feuerstein, R., Klein, P., & Tannenbaum, A. (Eds.). (1991).

Feuerstein, R., Mintzker, Y., Feuerstein, R. S., Ben Shachar, N., Cohen, M., & Rathner, A. (2001).

Feuerstein, R., Rand, Y., Falik, L., & Feuerstein, R. S. (2003).

Feuerstein, R., Rand, Y., Falik, L., & Feuerstein, R. S. (2006).

Feuerstein, R., Rand, Y., & Feuerstein, R. S. (2006).

Gambill, J. M., Moss, L. A., & Vescogni, C. D. (2008).

Garcia-Ros, R., Perez-Gonzalez, F., & Hinojosa, E. (2004).

Gürses, A., Cetinkaya, S., Dogar, C., & Sahin, E. (2015).

Hattie, J. (2015).

Howie, D. R. (2003).

Kozulin, A. (2001).

Mohan, B., & Slater, T. (2006).

Payne, R. K. (2013).

Stoeger, H., & Ziegler, A. (2008).

Watson, S., & Miller, T. (2009).

Woodward-Kron, R. (2008).

Yumusak, N., Sungur, S., & Cakiroglu, J. (2007).

Effect Size

Piagetian programs: 1.28

Teaching process skills (Piagetian programs) has an effect size with more than three times the impact of the average influence.

Added Effect of Poverty

Plan-and-label activities reinforce skills that Reuven Feuerstein (1980) identifies as inadequately developed among under-resourced students: planning, procedural self-talk, and vocabulary.

Explanation

To complete tasks involves prefrontal brain activity—namely, planning—which usually requires procedural self-talk. Because the executive functions of the brains of children in poverty tend to be less developed, planning and self-talk can be directly taught.

There are at least four ways to systematically label tasks: numbering, lettering, assigning symbols, and color coding. It's important to note that a systematic approach to the labeling means that fewer pieces of the task are skipped or missed.

Directions

Planning and Labeling for Academic Tasks

For a task to be done correctly, a student must have:

- A plan
- A procedure
- Labels (vocabulary); labels are the tools the mind uses to address the task

There are several ways to teach this. It's easier to begin by using visual activities that have no words. This teaches students that all tasks must have a plan and labels.

Planning and Labeling in Math

This is an example of plan and label as it pertains to division. Each of the six steps is an example of the plan and labels the student must be able to identify and follow to work through the steps of division.

One, two, and three (1–3) are the parts of the equation that the student should be able to identify and label. Four, five, and six (4–6) are the steps or the plan that the students need to follow to be able to work the division problem. These steps identify the questions/plan that the students must be able to answer/follow to solve the division problem.

1. 6	Divisor: number of parts in a group
2. $\overline{240}$	Dividend: total number of parts
3.	Quotient: number of groups
4. $6\overline{\smash{)}240}$	Are there enough parts for a group?
5. $6\overline{\smash{)}240}$	Are there enough parts for a group? If so, how many groups?
6. $\begin{array}{r} \times\ 4 \\ 6\overline{\smash{)}24} \\ 24 \end{array}$	See if there are extra parts.

Planning and Labeling in Science

Below is a process/concept chart. The student tells what is done and explains how.

Step 1: The vinegar is poured into a dish. Why? … *Because it provides electrons and ions.*

Step 2: Pieces of cloth are dipped into vinegar. Why? … *Because it provides a conductor and insulator.*

Step 3: The cloth is placed between pieces of copper and zinc. Why? … *Because they give and take electrons.*

Step 4: There are four stacks of cloth, zinc, and copper. Why do we need to stack four? … *Because it makes a current.*

Step 5: Aluminum foil connects the top and bottom of the stack. Why? … *To create a circuit.*

Step 6: A light is placed at the top. Why? … *To close the circuit.*

How (process)	Why (concept)
1.	Electrons, ions
2.	Insulator
3. Copper, cloth, zinc	+ −
4.	Current + +
5.	Circuit
6.	Closes circuit

To do any task, a person must have both a process and internal language. Planning provides the process; labeling provides the language.

Strategy 18

Input Skill: Nonfiction Reading Strategy

Academic
Strategy

Researchers

Feuerstein, R. (1980).

Gaddy, S. A., Bakken, J. P., & Fulk, B. M. (2008).

Gajria, M., Jitendra, A. K., Sood, S., & Sacks, G. (2007).

Hall, K. M., Sabey, B. L., & McClellan, M. (2005).

Harris, K. R., et al., (2013).

Hattie, J. (2015).

McCrudden, M. T., Schraw, G., & Lehman, S. (2009).

Montelongo, J., Berber-Jiménez, L., Hernandez, A. C., & Hosking, D. (2006).

National Institute of Child Health and Human Development. (2000).

Rogevich, M. E., & Perin, D. (2008).

van den Bos, K.P., Nakken, H., Nicolay, P.G., & van Houten, E. J. (2007).

Williams, J. P., Hall, K. M., Lauger, K. D., Stafford, K. B., DeSisto, L. A., & deCani, J. S. (2005).

Williams, J. P., Stafford, K. B., Lauer, K. D., Hall, K. M., & Pollini, S. (2009).

Effect Size

Piagetian programs: 1.28

Teaching process skills (Piagetian programs) has an effect size with more than three times the impact of the average influence.

Added Effect of Poverty

Reuven Feuerstein (1980) identifies planning as a skill that is often inadequately mediated among under-resourced students. This strategy gives students a plan for getting started with tasks and organizing new information.

Explanation

To complete a task requires a systematic approach. Most state assessments include a high percentage of nonfiction text. Nonfiction is sorted differently from fiction.

Directions

Reading Strategies

Use these reading strategies with the article "The Wonder of Mughal Agra" and with the questions that follow the article.

"Plan and label" means you have a way to go through something systematically, and you have a way to label it or assign words to it so you can repeat it.

Feuerstein found in his research that when individuals do not have a systematic way to do anything (or a task), they miss as much as 50% of the original data.

1. Box in and read the title.
2. Trace and number the paragraphs.
3. Stop and think at the end of each paragraph to identify a key point.
4. Circle the key word or write the key point in the margin.
5. Read and label the key words in the questions.
6. Prove your answer. Locate the paragraph where the answer is found.
7. Mark or write your answer.

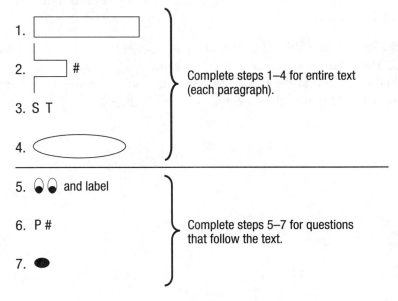

1.

2. #

Complete steps 1–4 for entire text (each paragraph).

3. S T

4.

5. 👀 and label

6. P #

Complete steps 5–7 for questions that follow the text.

7. ●

The Wonder of Mughal Agra

The Taj Mahal, one of the world's wonders, represents the architectural achievement of India during centuries of Muslim rule. The Mughal emperor, Shah Jahan, achieved the height of creation with the construction of a mausoleum, or tomb, for his wife, the empress Mumtaz Mahal.

They were married in 1612, and Shah Jahan became emperor in 1628. Devoted to each other, Mumtaz and the emperor traveled everywhere together, including the battlefield. On June 28, 1631, Mumtaz died while giving birth to their 14th child. Every Friday for six months Shah Jahan visited her temporary grave until construction began for her tomb in nearby Agra, a city located along a river.

Shah Jahan gathered the finest talent in his empire for the construction of the tomb. Individual artists and craftsmen worked with white and yellow marble, sandstone, diamonds, and other precious and semi-precious stones from as far away as China. An immense amount of labor was necessary; the workers were housed near the building site. The Taj Mahal took 22 years to build and was completed in 1648. The word "taj" means a high, conical hat worn in Islamic countries.

The Taj Mahal was more than just a tomb. It was also a setting for people to come and pay their respects to Mumtaz Mahal. The design of the site had to accommodate thousands of people and handle ceremonies connected with the anniversaries of the empress's death. A large rectangle was measured along the river and divided into two unequal parts. The mosque and tomb were placed in the larger portion on a raised terrace overlooking the river. The mausoleum was placed on the terrace, according to the emperor's instructions. A large gateway at the southern end was the only public entrance.

Shah Jahan, who created the Taj Mahal in memory of his beloved wife, died February 3, 1666. He was laid to rest in the vault on Mumtaz Mahal's right. He of course had no idea that the tribute to his wife would become a site visited by people from around the world for centuries after his own death.

1. What best describes the length of Muslim rule in India?

    A   More than 200 years
    B   Less than 100 years
    C   22 years
    D   From 1612 to 1666

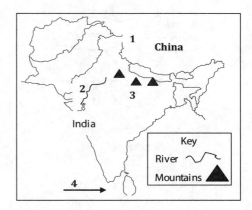

2. Based on the reading, what is the meaning of the word mausoleum?

    F   Architecture
    G   Rectangle
    H   Tomb
    J   Wonder

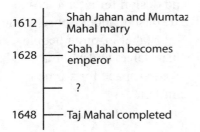

3. What event best completes the timeline above?

    A   Shah Jahan dies
    B   Shah Jahan visits the temporary gravesite
    C   Agra is built
    D   Muslims ruled India

4. Based on the map above, what is the most likely location for the Taj Mahal?

    F   1
    G   2
    H   3
    J   4

5. The term Mughal emperor is best connected with:

    A   Rule of China by Mumtaz Mahal
    B   Shah Jahan's rule of the Taj Mahal
    C   The design and purpose of the Taj Mahal
    D   Muslim rule of India

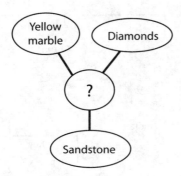

6. What is the correct title for the web shown above?

    F Agra buildings
    G Muslim rule
    H Construction materials
    J Artists and craftsmen

7. In addition to acting as a tomb, what else did the design have to accommodate?

    A Large numbers of people
    B Chinese architecture
    C Mausoleum law
    D Muslim rule of India

8. The Taj Mahal did not act as a:

    F   Mausoleum
    G Ceremonial site
    H School
    J Mosque

9. Which statement is not true about the Taj Mahal?

    A There is only one public entrance
    B Mumtaz Mahal is buried to the right of her husband
    C The mausoleum is on a raised terrace overlooking the river
    D Shah Jahan is buried there

10. What best summarizes the article?

    F Mughal emperors controlled China for a very long time
    G It provides details for measurements, construction, and design for a famous site
    H The design and purpose of the Taj Mahal inspired people
    J Shah Jahan and Mumtaz Mahal needed space for all their children

Strategy 19

Input Skill: Fiction Reading Organizer/Sorter

Academic
Strategy

Researchers

Feuerstein, R. (1980).
Conlon, T. (2009).
Hattie, J. (2015).
Idol, L., & Jones, B. F. (1991).
Jones, B. F., Pierce, J., & Hunter, B. (1988).
National Institute of Child Health and Human Development. (2000).
Stone, R. H., Boon, R. T., Fore, C. III, Bender, W. N., &
    Spencer, V. G. (2008).

Effect Size

Piagetian programs: 1.28

Teaching process skills (Piagetian programs) has an effect size with more than three times the impact of the average influence.

Added Effect of Poverty

Summarizing and sorting are two of the skills that Reuven Feuerstein (1980) identifies as inadequately developed among many under-resourced students.

Explanation

To summarize fiction, one has to remember the characters; the beginning, middle, and end (plot development); the setting; and the problem and/or goal. Any organizer that helps a student identify these things facilitates summarization and sorting.

Directions

Story Structure

Students complete each box with the information from the story.

Setting: Time Place	Three main characters:	Conflict or problem:
Events: Beginning	Middle	End

Source: K. D. Ellis, 2004.

Story Content Organizer

A graphic organizer guides students' thinking as they fill in and analyze text content to complete a visual map or diagram.

Following is an organizer for sorting what is important to remember in a story.

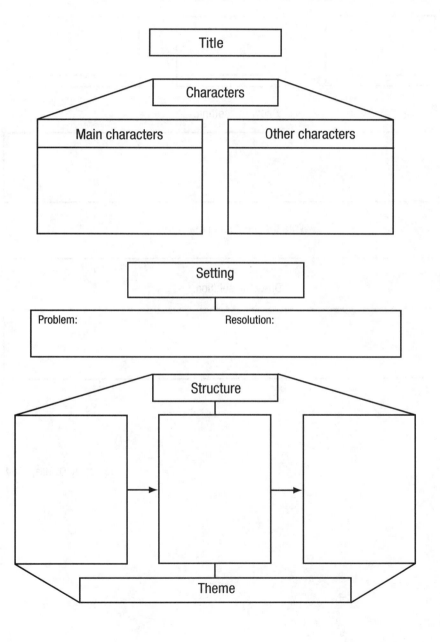

Story Map

Here's another organizer to sort what is important to remember in a story.

Draw and label three characters in the book:

_____	_____	_____

Show the setting:

Write the problem in the story:

_____

Draw the solution:

Source: K. D. Ellis, 2004.

Story Plot Chart

Another organizer to sort what is important to remember in a story.

Title:

Author:

Setting:

        Time:

        Place:

        General:

        Specific:

Problem or goal:

Circle one:

Humanity against humanity   Humanity against nature   Humanity against self

Events:

        1.

        2.

        3.

        4.

        5.

Event that solved the problem:

Message of theme:

Strategy 20

Input Skill: Procedural Self-Talk

Academic
Strategy

Researchers

Begley, S. (2007).

Callicott, K. J., & Park, H. (2003).

Fernyhough, C., & Fradley, E. (2005).

Feuerstein, R. (1980).

Gürses, A., Cetinkaya, S., Dogar, C., & Sahin, E. (2015).

Hattie, J. (2015).

Killingsworth, M., Gilbert, D. (2010).

Kishiyama, M. M., Boyce, W. T., Jiménez, A. M., Perry, L. M., & Knight, R. T. (2009).

Manfra, L., & Winsler, A. (2006).

Ostad, S. A., & Askeland, M. (2008).

Stamou, E., Theodorakis, Y., Kokaridas, D., Perkos, S., & Kessanopoulou, M. (2007).

Effect Size

Piagetian programs: 1.28

Teaching process skills (Piagetian programs) has an effect size with more than three times the impact of the average influence.

Added Effect of Poverty

Piagetian programs focus more on the thinking processes than the outcomes. Process skills are the skills that are frequently underdeveloped among under-resourced students, but the skills can be taught.

Explanation

To complete tasks involves prefrontal brain activity—namely, planning—which usually requires procedural self-talk. Because the executive functions of the brains of children in poverty tend to be less developed, planning and self-talk can be directly taught.

Directions

Student-Designed Step Sheets

Have students write procedural steps on step sheets (two examples appear below), then as a whole-group discussion, fill in any missing steps.

Steps: Statistics problem	Amount of time
1. Choose a statistical problem	1 day
2.	
3.	
4.	
5.	

Steps: Research paper	Amount of time
1. Choose your favorite author	1 day
2.	
3.	
4.	
5.	

Strategy 21

Input Skill: Teaching Input Skills Using Games

Academic
Strategy

Researchers

Feuerstein, R. (1980).
Feuerstein, R. (2004).
Gredler, M. E. (2004).
Jensen, K. (2015).
Kishiyama, M. M., Boyce, W. T., Jiménez, A. M., Perry, L. M., & Knight, R. T. (2009).
Leemkuil, H., Jong, T. D., & Ootes, S. (2000).
Rieber, L. P. (2005).
Shenk, D. W. (2012).
Shenk, D. W. (2017).

Effect Size

Piagetian programs: 1.28

Teaching process skills (Piagetian programs) has an effect size with more than three times the impact of the average influence.

Added Effect of Poverty

Piagetian programs focus more on the thinking processes than the outcomes. Process skills are the skills that are frequently underdeveloped among under-resourced students, but the skills can be taught.

Explanation

Input strategies help one gather data. Games are relational and competitive, and they build many of these skills.

Directions

Impact of Input Skills on Student Performance—and Games That Can Teach the Skills

Skill	Definition	How does lack of process impact classroom performance?	Games/activities that will strengthen this process
Use planning behaviors	Goal setting, identifying procedures in the task, identifying parts of the task, assigning time to the task, and identifying the quality of the work necessary for	Does not turn homework in on time, unable to complete long term projects, cause/effect (if I do this, then this will happen), sequence,	Logic puzzles, Set, chess, Blokus, http://fdlrs. brevard.k12.fl.us/ ThinkingMaps/flow. htm http://tao-game. dimension17.com/ http://www.logic-puzzles.org/index. php
Focus perception on specific stimulus	Strategy of seeing details and identifying everything noticed by the five senses	Cannot focus on assigned task, misses parts of the task, cannot find the information on the page	Any board game, knitting, crochet, sequential strategies (checklists)
Control impulsivity	Strategy of stopping action until one has thought about the task	Cannot plan, gets in trouble, may be misdiagnosed as having ADHD, finishes assignments too quickly	Any board game, http://fdlrs. brevard.k12.fl.us/ ThinkingMaps/flow. htm
Explore data systematically	Using a strategy to procedurally and systematically go through every piece of data	Cannot see patterns, relationships between data, does not have a method for checking work	Jigsaw puzzles, Set, using highlighter to find important pieces of information, http://tao-game. dimension17.com/

(continued on next page)

(continued from previous page)

Skill	Definition	How does lack of process impact classroom performance?	Games/activities that will strengthen this process
Use appropriate and accurate labels	Precise use of words to identify and explain	Uses generic words instead of specific, cannot do "cloze" procedure tests	Create mental models of new vocabulary, including questioning strategies
Organize space with stable systems of reference	An individual can identify with words the position of an item, can organize space	Disorganized, misplaces things, mixes up *b, d, p, q* (mimics dyslexia), cannot read a map, cannot line up numbers in math	Jigsaw puzzles, 9-square puzzles, counted cross stitch, Blokus, Rumis, http://www.learn4good.com/games/arcade/play_phit_blokus_version_of_tetris_for_kids_online.htm
Orient data in time	Strategy of assigning abstract values to time and the use of the measurements of time	Cannot sequence, loses track of time, does not turn things in on time	Comic-strip activity, sequence cards, using a timer
Identify constancies across variations	Strategy of knowing what always remains the same and what changes	Cannot see patterns, cannot make generalizations, cannot find main idea, or compare/contrast	Set, jigsaw puzzles, attribute trains, http://tao-game.dimension17.com/ www.creativepuzzels.com
Gather precise and accurate information	Use of specific vocabulary and word choice, identify precisely when something occurred in time and where it occurred in space	Cannot summarize because cannot distinguish between what's important and what's not, cannot tell where, when, how	Highlighters or highlighting tape, I Spy books, http://www.logic-puzzles.org/index.php App: Little Things
Consider two pieces of information at once	The mind can hold two objects simultaneously and compare/contrast the two objects	Cannot compare/contrast, find patterns	1-2-3 Oy, counted cross stitch, plastic canvas

(continued on next page)

(continued from previous page)

Skill	Definition	How does lack of process impact classroom performance?	Games/activities that will strengthen this process
Organize data (parts of a whole)	Go through data systematically, organizing space, identifying constancies and variations, and using vocabulary to label both the parts and the whole	Cannot explain why, does not recognize when someone is cheating	Jigsaw puzzles
Visually transport data	The eye picks up data, then carries it accurately into the brain, examines it for constancies and variations, and labels the parts and the whole	Cannot copy from blackboard or overheads	Feuerstein's dot puzzles, any activity where students must follow a pattern

Sources: Developed by K. Jensen, 2015; adapted with permission.
Also adapted from work of R. Feuerstein, 2004.

Teaching Input Skills with Chess

Longtime chess player, teacher, and coach (and coeditor of this book) Dan Shenk wrote a letter to the editor, which appeared in *The Goshen* (Indiana) *News* in 2012, about the Goshen Community Schools chess program he cofounded with Emory Tate Jr. in 1993. In the letter Shenk writes:

> … [W]e named the program Chess for Scholastic Success because the game has an amazing way of developing higher-order thinking skills in those who play regularly. Doctoral studies have shown that chess enhances concentration, problem solving, patience, deferred gratification, creativity, planning, cause/effect awareness, impulse control, sportsmanship, self-esteem, and resiliency in the face of adversity. Chess is not a panacea, of course, but it can be an important piece of the success puzzle.

By its very nature, chess addresses the following dozen input skills:

1. **Use planning behaviors.**
   Experienced chess players often plan several moves ahead before moving a chess piece.

2. **Focus perception on specific stimulus.**

   Players study positions on the chess board in detail.

3. **Control impulsivity.**

   Players resist the temptation to advance pieces prematurely, often favoring instead deferred gratification due to a long-range plan.

4. **Explore data systematically.**

   Players identify patterns in chess positions.

5. **Use appropriate and accurate labels.**

   Chess pieces, tactical and positional strategies, and (in particular) opening moves often are specifically named.

6. **Organize space using stable systems of reference.**

   The potential of each piece is analyzed in relation to other pieces—one's own and the opponent's.

7. **Orient data in time.**

   Moves are planned and generally executed in different phases of the game according to different principles that govern the opening, middle game, and endgame.

8. **Identify constancies across variations.**

   Players make mental notes both about recurring patterns on the board and how particular positions call for creative solutions that transcend chess principles.

9. **Gather precise and accurate data.**

   Players retain positions and patterns in their minds, then extrapolate accordingly.

10. **Consider two sources of information at once.**

    Multiple permutations of possible moves are often analyzed simultaneously.

11. **Organize data (parts of a whole).**

    Pieces are positioned in relation to their surroundings, frequently resulting in both logical and intuitive moves.

12. **Visually transport data.**

    Positions are viewed, then transported into the player's memory for eventual future reference.

Source: Developed by D. W. Shenk, 2017.

Strategy 22

Scaffolding Output: Dealing with Blocking

Academic
Strategy

Researchers

Feuerstein, R. (1980).
Gürses, A., Cetinkaya, S., Dogar, C., & Sahin, E. (2015).
Hattie, J. (2015).

Effect Size

Cognitive task analysis: .87

Added Effect of Poverty

Reuven Feuerstein (1980) determined that under-resourced students are more likely to block (freeze and say almost nothing when asked for an answer) than their more affluent peers.

Explanation

Inadequately mediated students, for whom instruction was less effective because their prerequisite input skills were underdeveloped, are often unable to communicate (output) data and will frequently block, saying little or nothing when asked a question.

Directions

When a student, who often blocks, answers a question inadequately, respond by saying,

- "Tell me more about that …"

- "What would you say to someone who thought …"

Then connect the additional information generated by the student with responses from other students.

Strategy 23

Predicting/Planning Your Grade

Academic
Strategy

Researchers

Covey, S. (1989).
Feuerstein, R. (1980).
Hattie, J. (2015).
Seligman, M. E. P., et al. (2005).

Effect Size

Self-reported grades: 1.33

Added Effect of Poverty

When students predict their grades, they have a future story for that course. In addition, surpassing their estimate tends to motivate them to work even harder.

Explanation

To complete tasks involves planning, which usually requires procedural self-talk. Because the executive functions of the brains of children in poverty tend to be less developed, planning and self-talk can be directly taught.

When students plan their grades they are keeping "the end in mind" (Covey, 1989). Planning controls impulsivity. In this particular example, when students plan their grade and review their current progress every Friday, they generally do much better academically.

Directions

At the beginning of the grading period, the teacher asks students to answer questions about the kinds of grades they want. Then each Friday the teacher gives 15 minutes for the students to record their grades from the week, calculate their averages, and identify what they must do to maintain or bring up their grades.

The strategy is effective with retakes as well: Identify for students how many questions they need to get right in order to pass. Then have students count how many questions are in each category and predict what their performance will be when the test is retaken. At that point they retake the test or a similar one and compare their performance with their prediction.

1. What work have I done well in my English class?

    a.

    b.

    c.

    d.

2. What work have I done poorly in my English class?

    a.

    b.

    c.

    d.

3. I was/was not satisfied with my grade in English III last semester.

    1st _____ 2nd _____ 3rd _____ Exam _____ Average _____

4. What grade do I realistically believe that I can earn this semester in English III?

5. What will I do in my English class to earn that grade?

    a.

    b.

    c.

Fourth Grading Period   I want to earn _____.

    Test 60%   Daily 10%   Quiz 30%

Fifth Grading Period   I want to earn _____.

    Test 60%   Daily 10%   Quiz 30%

Sixth Grading Period   I want to earn _____.

    Test 60%   Daily 10%   Quiz 30%

I am/am not satisfied with my grade in English III this semester.

1st _____   2nd _____   3rd _____   Exam _____   Average _____

Directionality

Academic
Strategy

Researchers

Feuerstein, R. (1980).
Gunzelmann, G. (2008).
Gyselinck, V., Meneghetti, C., De Beni, R., & Pazzaglia, F. (2009).
Hattie, J. (2015).
National Research Council. (2006).
Seligman, M. E. P., et al. (2005).

Effect Size

Cognitive task analysis: .87

Added Effect of Poverty

Students who have traveled very little often have limited experiences with directionality. Students who were inadequately mediated as children often have an inability to conceptualize, structure, and organize space.

Explanation

Spatial orientation is needed for organization and math (rotate this object). Spatial orientation is how objects are represented in space, e.g., a map represents objects in space.

Directions

A. Directionality with Arrows and Dots

This is one way in which we diagnose, ascertain, and teach space.

Directions for Students

Stand up and put the end of your pencil or pen on the end of your nose. (Demonstrate.) Face me. The tip of your pencil is the tip of the arrow. This dot is your arm. Now the question is as follows: To which side of the tip of the arrow is the dot? And the answer to your first box (upper-left-hand corner) is left.

This is called directionality. If you cannot do this, you have serious problems in math and problems on IQ tests.

On which side of the tip of the arrow is the dot?

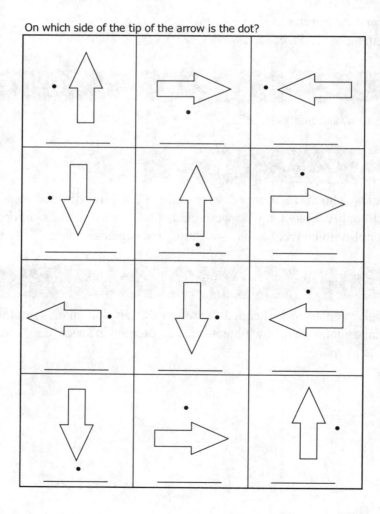

B. Mental Model for Directionality

To extend students' understanding of space and directionality, post essential information somewhere in the room with directions for students to locate the information.

For example: The answer to a test question is posted on the left-hand side of the filing cabinet on your right.

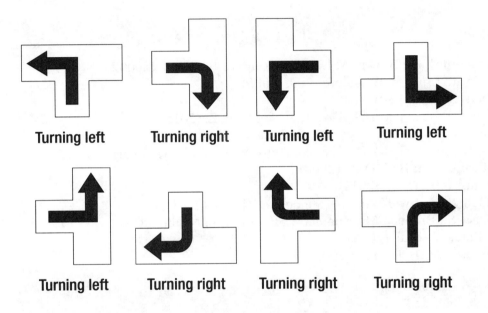

| Turning left | Turning right | Turning left | Turning left |

| Turning left | Turning right | Turning right | Turning right |

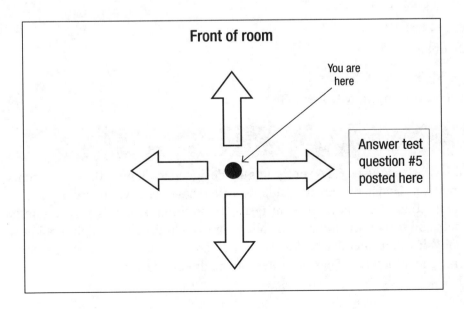

Strategy 25

Content Comprehension: Teaching the Purpose, Patterns, Structures, and Processes of Disciplines

Academic
Strategy

Researchers

Bransford, J. D., Brown, A. L., & Cocking, R. R. (Eds.). (2000).
Donovan, M. S., & Bransford, J. D. (2005).
Feuerstein, R. (1980).
Gürses, A., Cetinkaya, S., Dogar, C., & Sahin, E. (2015).
Hattie, J. (2015).
Hill, H. C., Blunk, M. L., Charalambous, Y., Lewis, J. M., Phelps, G. C., Sleep, L., & Ball, D. L. (2008).
Hollins, E. R. (Ed.). (2015).
Kilpatrick, J., Swafford, J., & Findell, B. (Eds.). (2001).
Krauss, S., Brunner, M., Kunter, M., Baumert, J., Neubrand, M., Blum, W., et al. (2008).
Seligman, M. E. P., et al. (2005).

Effect Size

Piagetian programs: 1.28

Cognitive task analysis: .87

Teacher clarity: .75

Concept mapping: .64

Prior achievement/knowledge: .63

Added Effect of Poverty

Cognitive task analysis (CTA) programs are designed to identify the components of expertise. Under-resourced students often have less exposure to expert knowledge than their more affluent peers. In addition, students whose family members and friends did not attend college or even high school might not know what physics and chemistry classes are all about, much less their purpose, patterns, and structures. These features can be directly taught.

Explanation

All content has a purpose, as well as structures, patterns and processes. That is the basis for determining what is and is not important in the discipline. These can be represented by concept maps, mental models, and visual representations.

It also can be stated that if teachers don't understand their content against these four criteria—purpose, structures, patterns, and processes—they can't facilitate or develop high achievement. It's impossible to teach what you don't know.

Directions

Step 1: Post purpose statements for each discipline (purpose statements must be developmentally appropriate, yet maintain as much consistency as possible throughout the grade levels, kindergarten through college)

Knowing the purpose of a discipline provides the incentive needed for individuals to focus on and care about its contents. For example, millions of people tune in to TV presentations (lessons) about meteorology every day because they understand and care about the purpose of this discipline—to predict the weather—and how it affects their lives. Weather forecasters emphasize this purpose consistently throughout their "lessons."

The Purpose of Meteorology is to predict the weather

The Purpose of Language Arts is communications
(using language to influence a reader or listener)

The Purpose of Social Studies is to
understand how people interact over time

Step 2: Teach the patterns of the disciplines

Experts see patterns

Expert chess players can look at a chess game in progress for seconds and can then recall where various chess pieces were located. Non-experts, however, can recall very few positions after observing the board for the same length of time. Why? They could not recognize patterns. The experts recognized patterns and could use this information to recall data and predict outcomes.

When chess pieces were randomly placed on a board, however, the experts were able to recall fewer positions than they could when patterns were visible, whereas novices' performance did not change, regardless of how the positions were set up.

Expert teachers teach patterns

Meteorologists invest considerable time explaining past patterns of weather and forecasting future weather: temperature, humidity, pressure, wind, clouds, and precipitation. Without this organizational schema, students and viewers of presentations about the weather would struggle to understand and to later retrieve meteorological data.

Weather patterns include:

- Air masses
- High- and low-pressure systems
- Wind
- Convection
- Cloud formation
- Precipitation

Patterns in math include:

- Fractions
- Decimals
- Measurement

Step 3: Teach the structures of the disciplines

The principal structures of meteorology are energy, moisture, and temperature.

The structures of language arts are the genres (short story, drama, poetry, biography, novels, nonfiction, etc.) grammar, syntax, organizational patterns of text, phonics, etc.

Structures of math include:

- Numbers
- Space
- Time

The principal purpose of math is assigning order and value to the universe.

Step 4: Teach purpose, patterns, and structures of the disciplines for retrievability

Retrievability

"Experts not only have more knowledge … but also their knowledge is organized more effectively" (Hollins, 2015). Students who store abstract data according to purpose, structures, and patterns are better equipped to retrieve it when it is needed.

Retrieval and expertise are enhanced and quickened by framing new information in terms of patterns, structures, and mental models.

Directions

Begin a lesson by saying (for example), "Go inside your head to your Social Studies file cabinet and open the drawer labeled Religion. Also open the folder labeled War. Inside it you will find …"

End the lesson by saying (in effect), "We learned five things about … File them in your mental Social Studies cabinet. Where in your head is your Social Studies filing cabinet? And where in your mental Social Studies cabinet should these five things you learned be stored?"

Bulletin Board

The primary purpose of math is assigning order and value to the known universe:

Patterns in math include:

- Fractions
- Decimals
- Measurement

Structures in math include:

- Numbers
- Space
- Time

Step 5: Create and teach mental models of the disciplines

This is the fifth component of your bulletin board for the year. Your discipline's purpose statement, patterns, structures, processes, and mental models are now available for quick reference with every lesson.

Mental Model for Social Studies

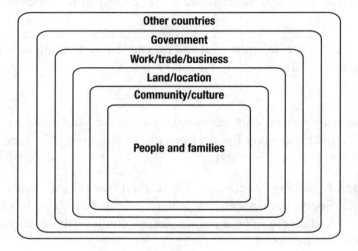

Step 6: Teach the tools and processes of the disciplines

A meteorologist's processes would include the use of radar, satellites, barometers, weather maps, computers, etc., and aspiring meteorologists are given specific directions in how to use them.

Explanation

Any process requires a systematic approach in order to do it. Without a systematic approach, it is possible, according to Feuerstein (as noted in Strategy 18), to miss as much as 50% of the data. What this process for math problem solving does is provide a systematic approach.

Directions

Teach process skills, then post the steps for ready reference and review.

Language Arts: Tools and Processes

- Reading
- Writing
- Listening

- Speaking
- Viewing (filmmaking)
- Using nonlinguistic mental models

Social Studies: Tools and Processes
- Evaluating sources
- Researching and developing positions on current Social Studies issues
- Using information acquired from a variety of sources, including technology, photographs, first-person accounts, diaries, historical documents

Strategy 26

Problem-Solving Process: Instructions in Mathematics

Academic
Strategy

Researchers

Boulware-Gooden, R., Carreker, S., Thornhill, A., & Joshi, R. M. (2007).

Feuerstein, R. (1980).

Fuchs, L. S., Fuchs, D., Prentice, K., Hamlett, C. L., Finelli, R., & Courey, S. J. (2004).

Gürses, A., Cetinkaya, S., Dogar, C., & Sahin, E. (2015).

Hattie, J. (2015).

Morrison, J. A., & Young, T. A. (2008).

Schraw, G., Brooks, D., & Crippen, K. J. (2005).

Seaton, D. T., Reich, J., Nesterko, S. O., Mullaney, T., Waldo, J., Ho, A. D., & Chuang, I. (2014).

Singh, C. (2008).

Star, J. R., & Rittle-Johnson, B. (2008).

Effect Size

Piagetian programs: 1.28

Cognitive task analysis: .87

Teacher clarity: .75

Concept mapping: .64

Added Effect of Poverty

Cognitive task analysis (CTA) programs are designed to identify the components of expertise.

Under-resourced students often have less exposure to expert knowledge than their more affluent peers. For example, a student from a wealthy family in Chicago where I was principal matter-of-factly told me one day that the previous summer he had gotten pitching lessons from Hall of Fame great Nolan Ryan.

In addition, students whose family members and friends did not attend high school or college might not know what Physics and Chemistry classes are all about, much less their purpose, patterns, and structures. These features can be directly taught.

Explanation

As stated previously, any process requires a systematic approach in order to do it. Without a systematic approach, it is possible, according to Reuven Feuerstein (1980), to miss half the data.

Directions

Teach this process, then post the steps for students' ready reference.

Problem-Solving Process

Step 1:   **READ THE PROBLEM**
- Read the problem through completely to get a general idea of what the problem is asking.

Step 2:   **REREAD THE PROBLEM AND QUESTION**
- Reread to visualize the problem.
- Highlight or mark the question with a wavy line.

Step 3:   **MARK YOUR INFORMATION**
- Mark the important information and eliminate unnecessary information.

- Box the action or important words.

- Circle needed information.

- Loop out extra information. *eeeeeee*

Step 4:   **CHOOSE AN APPROPRIATE STRATEGY**
- Choose an operation (+ - x ÷).
- Solve a simpler problem.
- Make an organized list.
- Look for a pattern.
- Use logical reasoning.
- Guess and check.
- Make a table.
- Use objects.
- Draw a picture.
- Act it out.
- Work backwards.

Step 5:   **SOLVE**
- Solve the problem.

Step 6:   **IS THE QUESTION ANSWERED?**
- Read the question again.
- Does the solution answer the question?
- Does it make sense? Is it reasonable?
- Check by using a different strategy if possible.

Source: J. Sain, 2004.

Strategy 27

Process Selection

Academic
Strategy

Researchers

Bandura, A. (1997).

Gürses, A., Cetinkaya, S., Dogar, C., & Sahin, E. (2015).

Hattie, J. (2015).

Seaton, D. T., Reich, J., Nesterko, S. O., Mullaney, T., Waldo, J., Ho, A. D., & Chuang, I. (2014).

Effect Size

Cognitive task analysis: .87

Added Effect of Poverty

Self-regulation skills are learned skills. Inadequate mediation results in underdeveloped self-regulatory skills.

Explanation

The ability to choose behavior is referred to as self-regulation (Bandura, 1997).

Directions

Teach self-regulatory skills, and draw students' attention to specific self-regulatory strategies. Guide students in selecting the most effective strategies prior to beginning tasks.

Self-Regulation Skills

Self-monitoring
Self-instruction
Self-consequences
Self-evaluation
Help seeking
Information seeking
Memorizing
Considering choices

Identifying task strategies
Time management
Environmental structuring
Organizing
Rehearsing
Reviewing notes
Evaluating results
Goal setting

Strategy 28

Managing Cognitive Load: External Task Aids

Academic
Strategy

Researchers

Clark, R. C. (2008).

Davelaar, E. J., Goshen-Gottstein, Y., Haarmann, H. J., Usher, M., &
Usher, M. (2005).

Hattie, J. (2015).

Koppenaal, L., & Glanzer, M. (1990).

Seaton, D. T., Reich, J., Nesterko, S. O., Mullaney, T., Waldo, J., Ho, A. D., &
Chuang, I. (2014).

Effect Size

Cognitive task analysis: .87

Added Effect of Poverty

Students who are novice learners are hearing much information that is "new,"
thereby quickly filling up available slots in their short-term memory. External
task aids enable information to bypass working memory, allowing former
information to be stored.

Explanation

Short-term memory can hold four or five chunks of new information. This new
information must be processed or it will disappear. This strategy allows content
to bypass working memory by providing external task aids (Clark, 2008).

Stress (sometimes termed allostatic load) fills some of those available spaces,
reducing capacity to three, two, or even one slot available for receiving new
information. This section offers suggestions for strategies for managing short-
term memory limits and cognitive load.

Directions

Post memory charts so that students can easily refer to them while completing tasks. Automaticity (see Strategy 29) allows for information to be processed without filling short-term memory space.

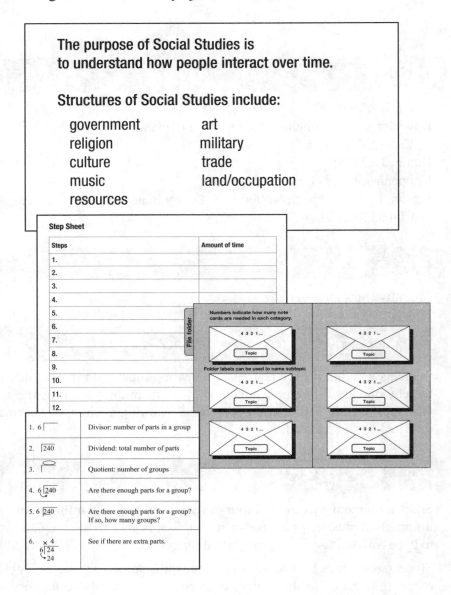

The purpose of Social Studies is to understand how people interact over time.

Structures of Social Studies include:

government	art
religion	military
culture	trade
music	land/occupation
resources	

Step Sheet

Steps	Amount of time
1.	
2.	
3.	
4.	
5.	
6.	
7.	
8.	
9.	
10.	
11.	
12.	

1. 6⟌	Divisor: number of parts in a group
2. ⟌240	Dividend: total number of parts
3. ⟌	Quotient: number of groups
4. 6⟌240	Are there enough parts for a group?
5. 6⟌240	Are there enough parts for a group? If so, how many groups?
6. ×4 / 6⟌24 / 24	See if there are extra parts.

Numbers indicate how many note cards are needed in each category.

4 3 2 1... Topic

4 3 2 1... Topic

Folder labels can be used to name subtopic

4 3 2 1... Topic

4 3 2 1... Topic

4 3 2 1... Topic

4 3 2 1... Topic

Strategy 29

Automaticity

Academic
Strategy

Researchers

Bloom, B. (1976).
Clark, R. C. (2008).
Hattie, J. (2015).
Therrien, W. J. (2004).

Effect Size

Piagetian programs: 1.28

Teaching process skills (Piagetian programs) has an effect size that is more than three times the effect of the average influence.

Added Effect of Poverty

Novice learners require additional time to acquire automaticity, which allows information to bypass short-term memory.

Explanation

Once skills or processes become automatic, they can bypass short-term memory. The student then has more available "slots" in which to store more new information.

A meta-analysis of repeated-readings research by William Therrien (2004) found the following elements to be critical for developing reading automaticity, for example:

- Efforts are more efficacious when students read passages to an adult (ES * = 1.37) rather than a peer (ES = .36).

- Results are more pronounced when followed immediately with direct, corrective feedback.

- Readings are most powerful when students practice until they reach a rate and accuracy criterion (ES = 1.78) rather than a set number of times reading the material (ES = .38).

* effect size

117

Strategy 30

Activating Prior Knowledge

Academic
Strategy

Researchers

Ausubel, D. P., & Youssef, M. (1963).
Brooks-Gunn, J., Duncan, G. J., & Maritato, N. (1997).
Clark, R. C. (2008).
Corcoran, M., & Adams, T. (1997).
Dewey, E. (1938).
Hart, B., & Risley, T. R. (1995).
Hattie, J. (2015).
Marzano, R. J. (2004).
Mayer, R. E. (2003).
Schmidt, H., & Moust, J. (2000).

Effect Size

Prior achievement/knowledge: .63

Added Effect of Poverty

Linking new information to stored knowledge, so that students have less need to process, enables novice learners to store more new information.

Explanation

Strategies for activating prior knowledge are most effective when students work in groups rather than individually. This is particularly true for students whose background knowledge stems from experiences that are valid, yet very different from those of middle-class teachers and peers. In some studies, students with limited prior knowledge gained no advantage from KWL-type activities (know, want to know, learned) when they worked alone, but the strategy effect was very powerful when implemented with groups.

Information given to students prior to teaching can help students organize their thoughts during instruction (Mayer, 2003). Advance-thought organizers, such as the ones illustrated below, contribution to activation of prior knowledge and the organization of new information.

Directions

Mind Map

Before beginning a unit, the teacher asks students to tell anything they know about a topic. As students offer ideas that they remember, the teacher or other students make connections, add to, clarify, or correct misunderstandings.

Example:

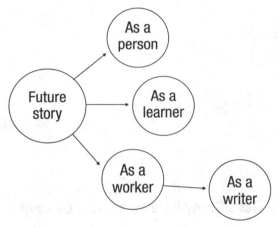

Cueing Technique

Alert students to content importance: Pick up your pencils!

KWL

What I know	What I want to know	What I learned

Source: D. Ogle, 1986.

Group Discussion About a Case Study Related to New Content

"… [A] combination of reviewing a problem
and discussing it in a group [has]
independent positive effects …"

–H. Schmidt & J. Moust, 2000, p. 31

Comparative Advanced Organizer

Example:

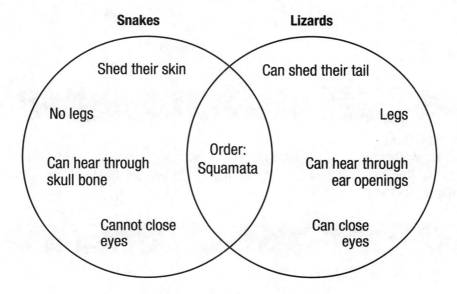

Source: Adapted from D. Ausubel & M. Youssef, 1963.

Strategy 31

Compensating for Missing Prior Knowledge

Academic
Strategy

Researchers

Clark, R. C. (2008).

Head, M. H., & Readence, J. E. (1986).

Seaton, D. T., Reich, J., Nesterko, S. O., Mullaney, T., Waldo, J., Ho, A. D., & Chuang, I. (2014).

Effect Size

Prior achievement/knowledge: .63

Added Effect of Poverty

Linking new information to stored knowledge, so that students have less need to process, enables novice learners to store more new information.

Explanation

This strategy is for providing background knowledge for students whose experience is different from that required for content comprehension.

Directions

At the beginning of a unit give students:

- An outline of unit content
- A list of key points
- Vital vocabulary

Engage students in group discussions of a problem or case study related to the content of the lesson.

Anticipation Guide

1. Write several thought-provoking statements related to an upcoming topic or text. Beside each statement, provide a block in which students indicate whether they agree or disagree with the statements.

2. Students then read the text, jotting down notes that either support or discount their initial reactions.

3. Have a class discussion after reading, during which students defend either their positions or how their minds changed based on evidence from the text (Head & Readence, 1986).

Additional Strategies

- Picture books (for all ages)
- Textbook scavenger hunts
- Wide reading

Strategy 32

Minimizing Activation of Irrelevant Prior Knowledge

Academic
Strategy

Researchers

Clark, R. C. (2008).
Hattie, J. (2015).
Seaton, D. T., Reich, J., Nesterko, S. O., Mullaney, T., Waldo, J., Ho, A. D., & Chuang, I. (2014).

Effect Size

Teacher clarity: .75

Added Effect of Poverty

Novice learners have difficulty sorting important from unimportant data. Irrelevant information complicates this issue.

Explanation

The introduction of irrelevant information can interfere with students' ability to recognize and sort important from unimportant information.

- Omit unnecessary details.
- Omit tangential stories and visuals.

"This is my least favorite topic ..."

"My children like to talk about ..."

"On an unrelated note ..."

Using Worked Examples: Replacing Some Practice with Worked Examples for Students to Analyze

Academic
Strategy

Researchers

Clark, R. C., Nguyen, F., & Sweller, J. (2006).

Hattie, J. (2015).

Paas, F., Renkl, A., & Sweller, J. (2003).

Renkl, A. (2005).

Renkl, A., Atkinson, R. K., & Grosse, C. S. (2004).

Schwonke, R., Renkl, A., Krieg C., Wittwer, J., Alven, V., & Salden, R. (2009).

Seaton, D. T., Reich, J., Nesterko, S. O., Mullaney, T., Waldo, J., Ho, A. D., & Chuang, I. (2014).

Sweller, J., & Cooper, G. A. (1985).

Effect Size

Worked examples: .57 for K–12 and .37 for college/university

Added Effect of Poverty

Having an actual example to analyze potentially benefits students less familiar with the content; many of these students are under-resourced.

Explanation

Once skills or processes become automatic, they can bypass short-term memory. The student then has more available "slots" in which to store more new information.

Strategy 34

Increased Time on Task

Academic
Strategy

Researchers

Behrmann, M., & Jerome, M. K. (2002).
Bloom, B. (1976).
Champaign, J., Colvin, K. F., Liu, A., Fredericks, C., Seaton, D., &
    Pritchard, D. E. (2014).
Farbman, D., & Kaplan, C. (2005).
Farmer-Hinton, R. L. (2002).
Gladwell, M. (2008).
Hattie, J. (2015).
Mattox, K., Hancock, D., & Queen, J. A. (2005).
Rocha, E. (2008).
Swan, K., van't Hooft, M., Kratcoski, A., & Unger, D. (2005).
Williams, A., Rouse, K., Seals, C., & Gilbert, J. (2009).
Wright, J. C., & Huston, A. C. (1995).

Effect Size

Earlier research analyses by John Hattie (2015) and others rated time on task at the .38 level, but Hattie's most recent and most exhaustive analysis, which includes higher education, elevates this influence to the .62 level.

Added Effect of Poverty

Research is clear that students unfamiliar with typical course content are more likely than others to benefit from additional time on task.

Explanation

Numerous studies link time on task with success. Benjamin Bloom (1976) found in his research that the amount of time a student spends engaged in a topic has a high correlation with mastery learning. Malcolm Gladwell (2008) adds that to become an expert in just about anything requires 10,000 hours working in that occupation, pursuit, or knowledge base.

Extra time is one of four variables that impact student learning. Numerous studies link time on task in a classroom to achievement in that classroom.

Directions

Extra time on task can be accomplished by:

- Examining the "pacing guide" and adjusting the amount of time needed for learning based on the needs of the current students.

- Opening the library before or after school to accommodate a learning space for students and parents to meet and learn from tutors—flexing the schedule of the staff for time to be with students.

- Recording lessons for upcoming or struggling students to listen to. Using mobile-phone video cameras, lessons can be recorded and uploaded to the "cloud" to be visited again by students.

- Scheduling double periods back to back to increase learning time; tutors also may be used to provide extra learning time.

In addition, the "flipped classrooms" movement has increased quality time on task as a major goal.

Strategy 35

Teaching Another Student

Academic and
Behavioral
Strategy

Researchers

Andrade, H. G. (1999a).
Andrade, H. G. (1999b).
Andrade, H. L., Du, Y., & Wang, X. (2008).
Bloom, B. (1976).
Bransford, J. D., Brown, A. L., & Cocking, R. R. (Eds.). (1999).
Goddard, Y. L., & Sendi, C. (2008).
Hafner, J. C., & Hafner, P. M. (2003).
Hattie, J. (2015).
National Institute of Child Health and Human Development. (2000).
Ross, J. A., & Starling, M. (2008).

Effect Size

Peer tutoring: .55

Added Effect of Poverty

Teaching another student improves metacognitive skills, which are needed especially among under-resourced students.

Explanation

Peer tutoring:

- Encourages higher-level thinking
- Improves self-esteem
- Fosters independence
- Offers opportunities for choice of strategies

Directions

A. Key Points

Students are given a list of key points of the lesson and told that during the last 10 minutes of class they will explain one of the key points to other members of their group.

B. Peer Teaching with Model Examples

In pairs, student A has question A and student B has question B. All are given model answers to their questions.

Students study their own question and model answers individually, then explain their question and answer to their partner.

Strategy 36

Structured Academic Controversy

Academic and
Behavioral
Strategy

Researchers

Clark, R. C. (2008).
Hattie, J. (2015).
Johnson, D. W., Johnson, R. T., & Smith, K. A. (1998).
Feuerstein, R. (1980).

Effect Size

Metacognitive strategies: .53

Added Effect of Poverty

In poverty, issues are often seen and presented in polarities—right or wrong. This strategy, on the other hand, helps students consider more than one lens through which to view reality.

Explanation

Structured academic controversy (SAC) teaches and reinforces a number of the input skills from the work of Reuven Feuerstein (1980)—primarily planning, organizing, and considering more than one source of information.

Directions

Prepare statements about a topic with which students can take pro or con positions. Provide class time for groups to research and prepare key points for their position, then present a 10-minute argument for the group's position. Provide guidelines for group listening and participation. Groups then take the opposite viewpoint, using the previously stated rules. Finally, have each student write an expository essay presenting both viewpoints.

Physical Activity

Researchers

Bailey, R., Armour, K., Kirk, D., Jess, M., Pickup, I., & Sandford, R. (2009).

Bandura, A., & Wood, R. E. (1989).

Burton, L. J., & VanHeest, J. L. (2007).

Chomitz, V. R., Slining, M. M., McGowan, R. J., Mitchell, S. E., Dawson, G. F., & Hacker, K. A. (2009).

Ericsson, I. (2008).

Hattie, J. (2015).

Ratey, J., & Hageman, E. (2008).

Sibley, B. A., Ward, R. M., Yazvac, T. S., Zullig, K., & Potteiger, J. A. (2008).

Tomporowski, P. D., Davis, C. L., Miller, P. H., & Naglieri, J. A. (2008).

Tremarche, P. V., Robinson, E. M., & Graham, L. B. (2007).

Effect Size

Exercise/relaxation is low on John Hattie's effect-size list (.22). He comments in an interview, however, that physical activity normally is studied separately from cognitive influences.

Added Effect of Poverty

Because children and teenagers in poverty generally spend more time in sedentary activities, including watching television, this strategy is even more critical for this population.

Explanation

Harvard research indicates that 45 minutes of exercise at the beginning of the school day significantly raises reading and math scores. The exercise activates brain activity.

Directions

In addition to planning activities that require movement during Physical Education sessions, ask students to "Stand if you agree ..." and "Stand and give your neighbor a high five" after they have been sitting for 20 minutes. You also might come up with other simple exercises for the students to do in class in order to illustrate the thrust of this strategy.

Strategy 38

Bowtie Feedback

Academic
Strategy

Researchers

Alderfer, C. P. (1972).
Bandura, A., & Wood, R. E. (1989).
Clark, R. C. (2008).
Dweck, C. S. (2006).
Feuerstein, R. (1980).
Hattie, J. (2015).
Lucas, J. H., & Stallworth, J. R. (2003).
Mueller, C. M., & Dweck, C. S. (1998).
Quilligan, S. (2007).
Sadler, D. R. (1989).
Sadler, D. R. (2013).

Effect Size

Feedback: .73

Added Effect of Poverty

Research of Reuven Feuerstein (1980) reveals that under-resourced students often receive inadequate mediation—being told the *what, why,* and *how* of task completion. Inadequately mediated students benefit greatly from detailed feedback about *what* they are doing well or incorrectly, *how* they can make maximum progress, and *why* the task is important.

Explanation

Feedback is required about where the student was, the student's present position, the desired learning goal, and how the student can further close the gap (Sadler, 1989).

Bowtie Feedback

Bowtie feedback uses the bowtie shape as a reminder of the components of effective feedback.

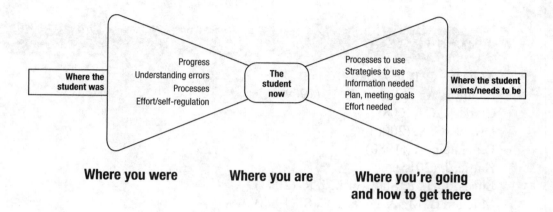

Where You Were

Task Performance Feedback

- "Good; all the commas are in exactly the right place."
- "You are really concentrating well now."
- "The presentation of the data is crystal-clear."

Effort Feedback

In a research project Claudia Mueller and Carol Dweck (1998) gave students a solvable task, then praised them for their success. Some were praised for their intelligence ("You are really smart") while others received effort praise ("You worked hard"). Later, on a set of harder problems, those who had been praised for being smart were reluctant to attempt more challenging tasks and performed significantly worse than the other groups, in fear of appearing not so smart after all. They also rated the problems as not enjoyable.

Ninety percent of those in the group that was praised for working hard, however, chose more challenging tasks to perform. They reported thinking the difficulty meant that they should try harder and that the harder problems were more fun than the easier ones, for example: "I see that you're working (trying) hard. You stuck with this until you got it done." Here are some other helpful comments by teachers:

- "It was a hard project, but you worked through it one step at a time, and it turned out great!"
- "I like how you chose the tough problems to solve."
- "Just imagine what would happen if you worked this hard on everything!"
- "Sometimes, when effort does not achieve the results we want, we need to find more effective ways to study. Let's talk about how you studied for this test."
- "We all have trouble sometimes. We learn from our mistakes. What would you do differently next time?"
- "Good job. Perhaps you could do even better if you ..."
- "You said you're dumb, but you're not. You're very capable. In fact, you can do even better on the next test."
- "Next time, instead of staying up late the night before the test ..."
- "If you take notes and study them regularly, you'll do better on the next test."

Process Feedback

- "You got the right answer. What process did you use here?"
- "How did you do this? It looks like you used a process that worked for you."
- "Why did this process work?"
- "That's a good way of solving that problem."
- "Why did you select that approach?"
- "What other approaches have you considered?"
- "What else could you consider?"
- "What are you doing now?"

Source: Adapted from R. C. Clark, 2008.

Error Feedback

Explain to students that learning from mistakes is a way of getting smarter. Scientists are famous for this form of thinking. For example, finding cures for diseases happens through much trial and error before they achieve success. Inventor Thomas Edison once said that genius is 1 percent inspiration and 99 percent perspiration, adding (with regard to his invention of the electric light bulb), "I have not failed; I've just found 10,000 ways that won't work."

We can give feedback by pointing out which answers are wrong and which are not.

- "The first three are correct. The next two need some work."
- "Your major weakness lies in your support. You need to find at least one more source. But your effort thus far has paid off."

Students learn and recall more from feedback about errors they made than they learn from getting answers right. There's a saying in chess: "It's more fun to win, but you can learn more from your losses."

Where You Are

Ask students to respond to five questions that address key points of the previously taught lesson(s).

Collect the cards and separate correct from incorrect (correct, partially correct, incorrect).

Review the lesson from the note cards—explaining which responses are correct, as well as which could not be correct and why.

Growth Feedback

Make students aware of their personal growth: "Look at what you can do now that you could not do last week."

Clayton Alderfer (1972) reviewed literature showing that when people do not have sufficient opportunities to experience growth, they will likely redouble efforts in the survival and relationship-building arenas in order to compensate for unrealized growth needs.

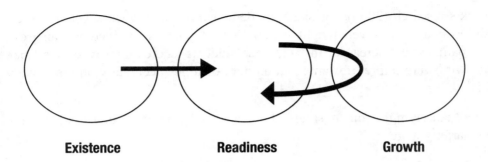

Existence	Readiness	Growth

Growth Awareness Strategy

Have students record their initial understanding of new topics at the beginning of a unit, then record their understanding following multiple exposures to the topic.

Initial understanding	Multiple exposures

Where You're Going

Dynamic, Brain-Growth Feedback

Researchers told some individuals that their performance on a certain task would measure their intelligence, while others were told that the task required skills that could be learned. Those who were told that their performance would reflect their intelligence behaved erratically, and their confidence plummeted. The students who were told that the skills required to complete that task could be learned maintained a high sense of personal efficacy (Bandura & Wood, 1989).

Multiple studies show that students benefit greatly from the understanding that intelligence is not fixed but developmental. They are much more interested in learning than in just looking smart, and they are more likely to approach new challenges rather than avoid them.

Dweck's research (2006), for example, demonstrates that when seventh-graders with low math scores were taught that one's intelligence is not fixed but can grow, their math scores increased. In fact, these students' scores improved more than those who were tutored for an equal amount of time specifically on math study skills.

Rather than saying, "You are smart," tell students, "The more you use your brain, the smarter you get."

For additional examples, see the book *Mindset* (2006) by Dweck.

Activity A

Have students keep a "success journal" in which they record successes and list the skills, talents, and strategies that they used to bring about positive outcomes.

Activity B

Add "yet" to students' ambivalent statements:

- "I don't earn a good income … yet."
- "I don't understand this … yet."

Adding "yet" to the end of these sentences encourages the speakers to think about the next step rather than perceiving themselves to be at a dead end (Dweck, 2006).

Process/Goal Feedback

Your goal is to convince your audience of your position. Correct these errors, find someone to read your argument to, then ask for feedback. Look at the process chart; seeking feedback is high on the list.

What do you think about this approach?

Transcendence Feedback

Where else could you use this strategy?

Feuerstein identifies transcendence as an essential cognitive principle. Transcendence involves explaining experiences so that the benefit extends beyond the student's immediate needs.

Show students on a rubric: "This is where you were, this is where you are, this is where you want to be, and this is what you need to do to get there: _____ _____."

Assessment of a Skilled Historian

	Beginning historian	Developing historian	Competent historian	Expert historian
Identifies repeat patterns in history (e.g., migration, war, etc.)	Has no idea there are repeat patterns.	Recognizes that a couple of patterns happen frequently, such as war.	Articulates multiple patterns in history and can explain some of the reasons.	Can predict current happenings based upon historical patterns and the synthesis of those patterns.
Understands historical interpretation and bias	Believes whatever the book says.	Knows that there is more than one side to the story. Knows that some sources are more credible than others.	Can distinguish between primary and secondary sources. Explains the role of the victor in history.	Can distinguish primary and secondary sources, as well as the victor role. Can identify the prevailing ideologies of the time and the influence on what is recorded and observed.
Identifies and integrates canons of history (e.g., military, religious, governmental, arts, social, cultural, country, world, etc.)	Thinks history is only one canon and one country.	Knows there is more than one canon but does not integrate them as part of cause and effect.	Integrates the canons and explains the influence of one on the other for a particular country.	Integrates the canons and explains the influence of one on the other for the world. Can explain the influence of a country on world events.

(continued on next page)

(continued from previous page)

	Beginning historian	Developing historian	Competent historian	Expert historian
Explains cause and effect, generational linkages, role of personality and timing, chronological sequence	Knows only chronological sequence.	Identifies chronological sequence. Can explain cause and effect of some events.	Can explain cause and effect and role of intergenerational interactions. Recognizes that personality and timing play a role.	Explains the chronological sequence of interlocking personality, timing, precedents, and events. Identifies the places where another choice might have been made.
Understands accuracy of interpretation, sources, conclusions	Thinks the written document is accurate.	Realizes that historical interpretation is based upon the victor.	Believes that accuracy is possible by careful documentation of sources.	Articulates the nebulous and even nefarious difficulties of accuracy. Identifies the methodologies most probable to approximating historical accuracy.

Strategy 39

Student Self-Assessment

Academic
Strategy

Researchers

Andrade, H. G. (1999a).
Andrade, H. G. (1999b).
Andrade, H. L., Du, Y., & Wang, X. (2008).
Bloom, B. (1976).
Bransford, J. D., Brown, A. L., & Cocking, R. R. (Eds.). (1999).
Brink, J., Capps, E., & Sutko, A. (2004).
Gladwell, M. (2008).
Goddard, Y. L., & Sendi, C. (2008).
Hafner, J. C., & Hafner, P. M. (2003).
Hattie, J. (2015).
Hoffman, A. (2003).
Kirby, N. F., & Downs, C. T. (2007).
Mistar, J. (2011).
National Institute of Child Health and Human Development. (2000).
Po-ying, C. (2007).
Ross, J. A., & Starling, M. (2008).
Thompson, D. D., & McDonald, D. M. (2007).

Effect Size

Student self-reported grades: 1.33

Added Effect of Poverty

John Hattie (2015) explains that "self-reported grades" means for students to predict the grade they think they will earn on a task or test, then compare their actual performance with their prediction. Such a step is critical for moving novice learners to expertise.

Explanation

When students self-assess their own resources, they learn to view their struggles less as personal weaknesses and more as opportunities for resource development.

Directions

A. Taking Control of Your Own Learning Tools

To help students pass the state assessment, a teacher did the following and was very successful. All of her students took a mock test in math. Then they scored their own papers. They made a grid like the one that follows.

In the top row, for each category, students wrote the numbers of the test questions and the objectives they went with. Then they identified strategies that could be used with each objective. As they went through the questions, in the second row of boxes, they identified where they would put it, e.g., "no clue" got moved to "I know I could get it right."

The teacher identified for students how many questions they had to get right in order to pass. The students then went back and counted how many questions were in each category and recalculated what they thought their performance would be. Whereupon they took another sample or mock test and refigured how they actually did. This self-advocacy also provides tools for addressing a task.

Questions I got right and could get right again	Questions I did or did not do correctly but am not sure how to do	Questions where I had no clue
Question # _____ Objective _____ Strategy _____	Question # _____ Objective _____ Strategy _____ Move to _____	Question # _____ Objective _____ Strategy _____ Move to _____
Question # _____ Objective _____ Strategy _____	Question # _____ Objective _____ Strategy _____ Move to _____	Question # _____ Objective _____ Strategy _____ Move to _____
Question # _____ Objective _____ Strategy _____	Question # _____ Objective _____ Strategy _____ Move to _____	Question # _____ Objective _____ Strategy _____ Move to _____

B. Self-Assessment Using Model Answers

- Students do an exercise, then they're given model exemplars that have been graded.

- The students mark their own work against the model answers.

Students also can self-assess by highlighting their papers to reflect their performance compared with worked examples.

C. Peer Assessment with Model Answers or Worked Examples

Students complete worksheets and sign them with code names known only to the teacher who collects the papers and redistributes them to different students who assess them by comparing with the model answers.

Return the work to the owner. All students keep the model answers so they can check the quality of their peer's feedback.

D. Rubric for Self-Assessment and Teacher Assessment

Have students highlight where they think their performance lies on a rubric (e.g., the historian rubric of Strategy 38). Later they will compare their self-assessments with the teacher's highlights on the same or similar rubric.

E. Green, Red, and Amber Highlights

- Students self-mark their paper using worked examples provided by the teacher.
- They highlight topics and sections within their papers as follows:

    –Green if they can understand how to do them (ignoring careless slips)

    –Red if they don't understand how to do them

    –Amber if they aren't sure

- The teacher looks through the papers to identify topics or sections highlighted red by a number of students, then uses this information for reteaching.
- Students also use their highlights to guide their review, listing specific strategies to relearn, as is possible.

Younger students can be instructed to "traffic light" a list of key words or topics on a paper or test.

Strategy 40

Formative Assessment

Academic
Strategy

Researchers

Bandura, A. (1991).

Bandura, A., & Cervone, D. (1983).

Baumeister, R. F., Hutton, D. G., & Cairns, K. J. (1990).

Black, P., & Wiliam, D. (1998).

Brophy, J. E. (1981).

Cleary, T. J., Gubi, A., & Prescott, M. V. (2010).

Dweck, C. S. (1986).

Dweck, C. S., & Leggett, E. L. (1988).

Epstein, M. L., Lazarus, A. D., Calvano, T. B., Matthews, K. A., Hendel, R. A., Epstein, B. B., et al. (2002).

Fedor, D. B. (1991).

Goodman, J., Wood, R. E., & Hendrickx, M. (2004).

Hartman, H. (2002).

Hattie, J. (2015).

Kulhavy, R. W. (1977).

Kulik, J. A., & Kulik, C. C. (1988).

Malone, T. W. (1981).

Mason, B. J., & Bruning, R. (2001).

Merrill, J. (1987).

Moreno, R. (2004).

Mory, E. H. (1994).

Narciss, S., & Huth, K. (2004).

Paas, F., Renkl, A., & Sweller, J. (2003).

Schwartz, F., & White, K. (2000).

VanLehn, K., Lynch, C., Schulze, K., Shapiro, J. A., Shelby, R., Taylor, L., et al. (2005).

Vygotsky, L. S. (1987).

Williams, S. E. (1997).

Effect Size

Providing formative feedback: .68

Added Effect of Poverty

Novice and under-resourced learners need more specific directions than competent or expert learners. Formative feedback helps provide this support.

Explanation

Formative evaluation refers to any activity used as an assessment of learning progress before or during the learning process itself.

"Written feedback is much more useful for students than grades or points. Studies indicate that comments rather than grades lead to significant improvement, while grades by themselves and even comments combined with grades did not improve performance" (Cleary, Gubi, & Prescott, 2010).

Directions

A. Use two steps to assess student work: formative (comments, no grade) and summative (grade) _____ .

In first return of papers, give comments; in second return, give grades.

B. Use step sheets to guide formative assessment.

Give feedback (no grades, though points can be awarded) to each step of the step sheet.

Require students to check off each step as it is completed—a simple action that contributes to students acquiring achievement as a driving force.

Steps	Amount of time
1. Choose author	1 day
2.	
3.	
4.	
5.	

Strategy 41

Question Making

Academic
Strategy

Researchers

Abernathy, C. (2003).
Campbell, T. (2006).
Chin, C., & Kayalvizhi, G. (2002).
Chin, C., & Osborne, J. (2008).
Dermody, M. M., & Speaker Jr., R. B. (1999).
Hattie, J. (2015).
Martin, M. M. B., Rosselle, C., & Tarrida, A. (2007).
McManus, D. O., Dunn, R., & Denig, S. J. (2003).
National Institute of Child Health and Human Development. (2000).
Palincsar, A., & Brown, A. L. (1984).
Parker, M., & Hurry, J. (2007).
Ross, T. (2003).
Texas Assessment of Knowledge and Skills. (2003).
Walberg, H. (1990).
Whalon, K., & Hanline, M. F. (2008).

Effect Size

Self-questioning: .64

Added Effect of Poverty

This strategy is particularly effective for students who are discouraged from asking questions at home, as is often the case in under-resourced environments.

Explanation

Students trained to prepare for examinations by generating and then answering their own questions outperformed comparable groups who prepared in conventional ways.

Directions

Twice a week, instead of having students answer the questions the end of at the chapter, have them work in groups to write questions, following the rules below. Questions can be multiple-choice, higher-order, true/false; all sorts of question making has strong effect size.

Once the questions are complete, collect papers with no names visible. Using an overhead projector, show the questions, one at a time, and ask the class to critique them:

- Is this a question?
- What is it asking?
- Is it clear?
- Is there one correct answer—or more than one?
- Do we need a qualifier?

Questions are returned to groups for corrections. When one or more student-generated questions are included on teacher-made tests, student motivation and ownership are enhanced.

Writing Multiple-Choice Questions

Question:

a.

b.

c.

d.

Three rules:

1. Only one answer choice can be right.
2. One wrong-answer choice must be funny.
3. May not use "all of the above" or "none of the above."

Math Questions

1. Stems need to use the terminology.

2. Distracters are:

   - Incorrect operation

   - Incorrect order

   - Decimal in wrong place

   - Answer in wrong form, for example: percentage instead of number

   - Missed step

   - Unnecessary information included

   - Computational errors

Science Question-Writing Stems

How for the student	Question stem
Defining and describing	**Knowledge** • What is (are) _____? • Where is (are) _____? • Which is (are) _____? • How is (are) _____? **Comprehension** • What conclusions can you draw from _____? • What observations did you make? **Application** • Why does _____ work? • Sketch your mental model of _____. • Explain how _____. **Synthesis** • How could you explain _____ to your friend? • Design a model of _____ to represent _____. • Write a letter to _____ giving a summary of _____. • What facts can you compile about _____? • Rewrite the definition of _____ in your own words. **Evaluation** • Describe the importance of _____.

(continued on next page)

(continued from previous page)

How for the student	Question stem
Representing data and interpreting representations	**Knowledge** • Describe what happens when _____. **Comprehension** • Construct a model to explain your data. **Application** • How could you organize your data to help you draw your conclusion(s)? • How could you change the process/procedure to increase/decrease the _____? **Analysis** • How can you sort the parts of _____? • What order can you place the data in to make them easier to interpret? **Synthesis** • How could you compile the data/facts for _____? • What plan do you have for collecting your data? • What format will you use to represent your data? **Evaluation** • What data will you use to evaluate _____? • How could you verify the interpretation of your graph/table/map? • What is your interpretation of your data?
Identifying and classifying	**Knowledge** • How could you recognize _____? **Comprehension** • How could you differentiate between _____ and _____? **Application** • Determine what characteristics/properties you can use to identify _____? **Analysis** • Identify the characteristics of _____ and compare them to the characteristics of _____. **Synthesis** • Devise a new way to classify _____. • What other ways can _____ be identified? **Evaluation** • What criteria would you use to assess the _____ classification system?

(continued on next page)

(continued from previous page)

How for the student	Question stem
Measuring: ordering/comparing along a continuum	**Knowledge** • What qualitative data did you record? **Application** • When compared along the continuum of _____, how can _____ be ordered? **Synthesis** • Develop a plan/grid to record your observations for _____. • How could you arrange your groups differently? **Evaluation** • What qualitative data were used to evaluate _____? • What is your interpretation of the data gathered when _____?
Measuring: qualifying	**Knowledge** • What qualitative data did you record? **Application** • How can you organize your data? **Synthesis** • What properties remained constant when _____? • What properties changed when _____? **Evaluation** • Develop a plan/table to record your observations for _____. • How could you arrange your data differently?
Designing and conducting investigations	**Knowledge** • Identify the materials you would need to conduct your investigation. **Comprehension** • What is the responding/dependent variable in your investigation? **Application** • How will you organize your data for _____? **Analysis** • What did you observe during your investigation? **Synthesis** • What changes could you make to your investigation in order to _____? **Evaluation** • What data were most important to prove or disprove your hypothesis?

(continued on next page)

(continued from previous page)

How for the student	Question stem
Constructing evidence-based explanations	**Knowledge** - What scientific theories/models/principles are related to your explanation? **Comprehension** - How could you explain _____? **Synthesis** - What alternative hypotheses are there for _____? **Evaluation** - How will you assess all the hypotheses to verify or dispute?
Analyzing and interpreting data	**Knowledge** - What data would you choose to analyze? - Comprehension - Translate the data in your table to a graph. **Application** - What do the collected data mean? **Analysis** - How do the data help you answer your question? - What patterns do you find in _____? Synthesis - What other factors could be measured for _____? Evaluation - How could you verify your interpretation?
Predicting/ inferring	**Knowledge** - What do you know about _____? **Comprehension** - What clues do you have about _____? **Application** - What would be the result of _____? **Analysis** - What do you think happened from the data about _____? **Synthesis** - Predict the outcome of _____ if _____. **Evaluation** - What choices would you have made if you could _____? - What changes could be made to alter _____? - How could you verify what you have inferred?

(continued on next page)

(continued from previous page)

How for the student	Question stem
Evaluating/ reflecting/ making an argument	**Knowledge** ▪ What data do you have to support your argument? **Comprehension** ▪ Explain your argument. **Application** ▪ How could you develop _____ to represent _____? **Analysis** ▪ Do your data support your argument? **Synthesis** ▪ How could this model of _____ be revised to represent _____? **Evaluation** ▪ Does this model follow or "obey" the theory or argument?
Posing questions	**Knowledge** ▪ How is (are) _____? ▪ What is (are) _____? ▪ Where is (are) _____? ▪ Which is _____? ▪ When did _____? ▪ Who is (are) _____? **Comprehension** ▪ List what you know and what you want to learn about. ▪ Using the CPR (capitalization, punctuation, restatement) model, write a question about _____? **Application** ▪ What actions would you have to take to test your question? ▪ Where can you find more information concerning your question? **Analysis** ▪ Explain how your questions ask about causes and effects. ▪ How is _____ in your question connected to _____? **Synthesis** ▪ What changes would you make to revise _____? **Evaluation** ▪ What criteria could you use to assess if your question is testable?

Source: Adapted from training materials developed by T. Ross, 2003.

Question Stems for Fifth- and Ninth-Grade Reading

1. In paragraph _____, what does _____ mean?
2. Paragraph _____ is mainly about _____.
3. From the article, the reader can tell _____.
4. From the passage, the reader can tell _____.
5. From the paragraph, the reader can tell _____.
6. From what the reader learns about _____, which statement does not make sense?
7. How does _____ feel?
8. Why is it important?
9. Which of these is the best summary of the selection?
10. Look at this web (flow chart, graph, charts, etc.). Which detail belongs in the empty space?
11. An idea present in both selections is _____.
12. One way these selections are alike is _____.
13. One way these selections are different is _____.
14. Paragraph _____ is important because it helps the reader understand _____.
15. How does _____ feel?
16. In paragraph _____, why is _____ sad? (happy, confused, angry, etc.)
17. What is this article mainly about?
18. What can the reader tell about _____ from information in this article?
19. The author builds suspense by _____.
20. One way this story resembles a fable is that _____.
21. In paragraph _____, the author uses the word _____ to emphasize _____.
22. Which of the following words is a synonym (and antonym) for the word _____ in paragraph _____?
23. What is the overall theme expressed in this article?
24. Which of the following sentences from the article explains the author's primary conflict?
25. The audience that would probably relate most to the article's central message would be _____.

Source: Adapted from TAKS (Texas Assessment of Knowledge and Skills), 2003.

Social Studies Question-Stem Starters
Elementary (K–4)

1. What does the map (chart, drawing, timeline, graph) illustrate?
2. Which statement best explains (summarizes) _____?
3. What was the main cause of _____?
4. One advantage of _____ is _____.
5. The primary function (purpose, goal, objective) of _____ is _____.
6. Which of the following were consequences of _____?
7. What is the best definition of _____?
8. Which of these is a past (current) trend in _____?
9. Approximately when did _____ occur?
10. Which date is associated with _____?
11. Which of these statements explains how _____?
12. What is an example of _____?
13. Which of these would be the best solution to _____?
14. What was (person's) major accomplishment?
15. Who is best known for _____?
16. Which best explains what happened in _____?
17. Who was _____?
18. What person (event, element, condition) was responsible for _____?
19. What happened when _____?
20. What can be concluded from the visual aid?
21. Who made a factual statement about the _____?
22. What document includes the ideas represented in the diagram?
23. What happened at the beginning, middle, end of the story/event?
24. What picture or event goes first, second, next, last?
25. What happened first, second, next, last on the timeline?
26. How are you alike or different from the character in the story or historical event?
27. What happened long ago, yesterday, or today on the timeline, in the story/event?
28. How many days, weeks, months, years, decades, centuries did it take to _____?

29. What natural and/or man-made features played a role in _____?

30. What natural and/or man-made features were near, next to, north, south of _____?

31. What features/characteristics can you identify in the picture, on the map?

32. What would you see, taste, hear, touch, smell if you were "in the shoes" of the person/character?

33. What questions would you like to ask the person about _____?

34. How would things have turned out differently if the character in a historical story, legend, myth, or narrative had acted differently?

35. What was a problem people had in _____ and how is that alike or different from a problem we have today?

36. What characters, events, or dates should be grouped together and why should they be grouped together?

37. What words help you understand where, when the story, event happened?

Remember: Many of the above questions can be reconfigured into negative questions, e.g., #18: What person (event, element, condition) was *not* responsible for _____?

Source: Adapted from training materials developed by C. Abernathy, 2003.

Strategy 42

Possible Selves

Academic and
Behavioral
Strategy

Researchers

Adelabu, D. H. (2008).
Amyx, D., & Bristow, D. (2004).
Bowles, T. (2008).
Dweck, C. (2006).
Farson, R. (1996).
Giota, J. (2006).
Greene, B. A., & DeBacker, T. K. (2004).
Greene, B. A., Miller, R. B., Crowson, H. M., Duke, B. L., &
    Akey, K. L. (2004).
Hattie, J. (2015).
Hock, M. F., Schumaker, J. B., & Deshler, D. D. (2003).
Horstmanshof, L., & Zimitat, C. (2007).
Kaylor, M., & Flores, M. M. (2007).
Kerpelman, J. L., Eryigit, S., & Stephens, C. J. (2008).
Leondari, A. (2007).
Malka, A., & Covington, M. V. (2005).
Malmberg, L.-E., Ehrman, J., & Lithen, T. (2005).
Phalet, K., Andriessen, I., & Lens, W. (2004).
Robbins, R. N., & Bryan, A. (2004).
Ryken, A. E. (2006).
Seginer, R. (2008).
Tabachnick, S. E., Miller, R. B., & Relyea, G. E. (2008).

Effect Size

Motivation: .44

Added Effect of Poverty

Research related to future stories is not specifically included in the effect-size research of John Hattie (2015). A sense of future, however, is an integral component of motivation and is heavily impacted by family and community expectations, both of which can be impacted by socioeconomic class.

Explanation

Possible selves are the ideal selves that we would like to become. They are also the selves that, paradoxically, we could become and are afraid of becoming.

The possible selves that are hoped for might include the successful self, the creative self, the rich self, the thin self, and/or the loved and admired self. The possible selves we run from could include the alone self and/or the depressed self (Hock, M. F., Schumaker, J. B., & Deshler, D. D., 2003).

Directions

The possible-selves program (Hock et al., 2003) guides students through sketching a tree with three major branches labeled Learner, Person, and Worker. Students are encouraged to add enough details to each branch so that their future selves are well-balanced. At that point they identify elements that could threaten their trees, as well as ways to enrich the soil in which their possible-selves trees are planted.

Academic and
Behavioral
Strategy

Researchers

Barnett, R. C., Gareis, K. C., James, J. B., & Steele, J. (2001).
Berzonsky, M. D., Branje, S. J. T., & Meeus, W. (2007).
Bianchi, A. J., & Lancianese, D. A. (2005).
Britsch, B., & Wakefield, W. D. (1998).
Burke, P. J., Owens, T. J., Serpe, R., & Thoits, P. A. (Eds.). (2003).
Cinamon, R. G., & Rich, Y. (2002).
Diemer, M. A. (2002).
Erikson, E. (1988).
Gianakos, I. (1995).
Hattie, J. (2015).
Kashima, Y., Foddy, M., & Platow, M. (Eds.). (2002).
Marcia, J. E. (1966).
Pasley, K., Furtis, T. G., & Skinner, M. L. (2002).
Perrino, T., Gonzalez-Soldevilla, A., Pantin, H., & Szapocznik, J. (2000).
Pilavin, J. A., & Callero, P. L. (1991).
Razumnikova, O. M. (2005).

Effect Size

Peer influences: .53

Home environment: .52

Parental involvement: .49

Added Effect of Poverty

First-generation high school students are often in greater need of encouragement than their more affluent peers whose family members expect academic achievement.

Explanation

From elementary school through adulthood, individuals move back and forth among the following stages of identity formation:

Stage 1: No sense of or desire to clarify future story (students report to class simply because this is "the place to be").

Stage 2: Most students tend to mirror and accept the identities imposed on them by parents, friends, and teachers (Marcia, 1966). Students in this stage generally don't question the values and beliefs they have heard or seen, such as "Real men take care of their families," "Real men fight," "Real men are lovers," or "Real men play sports."

Stage 3: This stage is called moratorium by Erik Erikson (1988) and others—explore options, but do not commit. The more independence adolescents are afforded and the more they are encouraged to think for themselves, the more productive this stage will be.

Stage 4: Students actively pursue careers and self-identities that they chose, based on their own research and values (Pilavin & Callero, 1991).

Socioeconomic status, along with group and gender identity, interface with role identity throughout each stage. Adolescents whose relationships with parents are positive tend to develop a more coherent and integrated sense of identity, whereas those adolescents whose family relationships are distant or conflicted tend to develop a more fragmented sense of identity (Perrino, Gonzalez-Soldevilla, Pantin, & Szapocznik, 2000).

Role identity is what you want to do or be. It is, for example, one of the most effective tools to prevent early pregnancy.

When students learn a new skill, say to them, "This qualifies you to study _____ and perhaps become a _____." This feedback is intensely personal, yet it doesn't conflict with whatever stage the student might be in.

When appropriate, you might follow up with "You'd be good at that because _____."

Strategy 44

Future Self/Future Story

Academic and
Behavioral
Strategy

Researchers

Adelabu, D. H. (2008).

Amyx, D., & Bristow, D. (2004).

Bowles, T. (2008).

Dweck, C. (2006).

Farson, R. (1996).

Giota, J. (2006).

Greene, B. A., & DeBacker, T. K. (2004).

Greene, B. A., Miller, R. B., Crowson, H. M., Duke, B. L., & Akey, K. L. (2004).

Hattie, J. (2015).

Hock, M. F., Schumaker, J. B., & Deshler, D. D. (2003).

Horstmanshof, L., & Zimitat, C. (2007).

Kaylor, M., & Flores, M. M. (2007).

Kerpelman, J. L., Eryigit, S., & Stephens, C. J. (2008).

Leondari, A. (2007).

Malka, A., & Covington, M. V. (2005).

Malmberg, L.-E., Ehrman, J., & Lithen, T. (2005).

Phalet, K., Andriessen, I., & Lens, W. (2004).

Robbins, R. N., & Bryan, A. (2004).

Ryken, A. E. (2006).

Seginer, R. (2008).

Tabachnick, S. E., Miller, R. B., & Relyea, G. E. (2008).

Effect Size

Socioeconomic status: .54

Motivation: .44

Added Effect of Poverty

Research related to future stories is not specifically included in the effect-size research of John Hattie (2015); however, a sense of future is an integral component of motivation and is heavily impacted by family and community expectations, both of which can be affected by socioeconomic class.

Explanation

A future story is a plan for the future. Without it, neither schooling nor work has much purpose.

Effective, positive future stories provide a sense of:

1. What the individual would like to do or become in the future

2. Why this future story is desirable to the person

3. When the future story might be realized

4. How to get there

Directions

A. Give each student a copy of this exercise.

Future Story	Name
You are 10 years older than you are now. You are the star of a movie. What are you doing? Who is with you?	
Circle any of the following that are in your future story: children, job, career, marriage/partnership, health, wealth, travel, living in a city, living in a town, living in a rural area, living in another country, a vehicle, hobbies, sports, music, movies, college, technical school, military, church, religion, Internet, video games, friends, family, other.	
For which of these reasons do you want to graduate from high school? To keep track of money, to know I am getting paid correctly, so I can go to college or military or technical school, to get a good job, to take care of my parents or siblings, to afford my hobbies, to pay for my vehicle, to take care of my children, other.	
What do you enjoy doing and would do even if you did not get paid for it? What do you need to do so you can do that and get paid for it?	
Who are the friends and adults who will help you achieve your future story?	
Write out your future story, including how education will help you get it.	
Signature	Date

B. Carol Dweck (2006) recommends that students write a letter to you from 10 years in the future telling you about an obstacle they faced while trying to reach their goals—and how they surmounted that hurdle.

C. Have students write a Future Story Book as a semester-long, yearlong, or multi-year project.

  1. Students design a book cover for a future-self book.

  2. Students write an introduction to their book telling why they want to pursue their career or goal.

  3. Students dedicate their book to someone who supports their efforts (supportive people can trigger goals).

  4. Students estimate the year or date they hope to accomplish their designated goal, mark that date on a calendar, and plan backward.

  5. Each major step (grade level, etc.) becomes a chapter in the book.

  6. Students create an index of tools for succeeding with step sheets, planning backward forms, graphic organizers, resource-assessment forms, self-assessment forms, and organization drill-down sheets.

  7. Students create a listing of references (people who can help).

  8. Students compile the glossary with a list words that can help their future selves to communicate clearly.

A future story involves role identity and a future plan that almost always includes education.

D. Have students write a letter to a child or grandchild describing themselves and giving advice for the future. Have them put the letter in an envelope marked "To My Child (Grandchild et al.)" and store it in a safe place.

Strategy 45

Anticipating and Accepting Challenges and Changes

Academic and Behavioral Strategy

Researchers

Austin, J., & Bartunek, J. (2004).
Chen, H. T., Mathison, S., & Chen, H. T. (2005).
Clark, H., & Taplin, D. (2012).
Collins, E., & Clark, H. (2013).
Connell, J., Kubisch, A., Schorr, L., & Weiss, C. (Eds.). (1998).
Coryn, C., Noakes, L., Westine, C., & Schroter, D. (2011).
Dweck, C. (2006).
Earl, S., Carden, F., & Smutylo, T. (2001).
Farson, R. (1996).
Funnell, S., & Rogers, P. (2011).
Hattie, J. (2015).
Jackson, E. (2013).
Mackinnon, A., & Amott, N., with McGarvey, C. (2006).
Taplin, D., Clark, H., Collins, E., & Colby, D. (2013).

Effect Size

Conceptual-change programs: 1.16

Added Effect of Poverty

Programs that clarify concepts have a hugely positive impact on students. Those with few role models from high school likely have more misconceptions than those whose family members are familiar with the high school community.

Explanation

"The healthier you are psychologically, or the less you may seem to need to change, the more you can change." –R. Farson, 1996

As Carol Dweck (2006) notes in Strategy 38, when students say, "I don't understand," have them add the word "yet" to their statement.

For example:

- "I don't understand this … yet."
- "I don't know … yet."
- "I don't like math … yet."

Strategy 46

Reframing

Behavioral
Strategy

Researchers

Andreas, S., & Faulkner, C. (1994).

Chagnon, F. (2007).

Elliott, M., Gray, B., & Lewicki, R. (2003).

Elliott, M., Kaufman, S., Gardner, R., & Burgess, G. (2002).

Fox, J. E. (1999).

Hattie, J. (2015).

Jaser, S. S., Fear, J. M., Reeslund, K. L., Champion, J. E., Reising, M. M., & Compas, B. E. (2008).

Mills, A. (1999).

Nelson, M. (2000).

Peters, G. (2002).

Rapee, R. M., Gaston, J. E., & Abbott, M. J. (2009).

Reddy, L. A., De Thomas, C. A., Newman, E., & Chun, V. (2009).

Riley, L. P., LaMontagne, L. L., Hepworth, J. T., & Murphy, B. A. (2007).

Scherff, L., & Singer, N. R. (2008).

Effect Size

Conceptual-change programs: 1.16

Added Effect of Poverty

Reframing for educators enables us to see the world through the lens of students. Reframing for students enables them to view the world through the lens of the school campus, which often operates on hidden rules that are different from those learned by many students from poverty.

Explanation

Reframing is a neuro-linguistic programing technique used to help individuals view the content or context of an event through a new frame of reference that changes or broadens the meaning of the event. Reframing allows the process of metacognition to develop; it moves from the concrete to the abstract. It also allows for thinking without a power struggle between teacher and student or student and student.

Directions

Strategy

This application of reframing uses the adult voice (see Strategy 60) to reframe behaviors that are inappropriate in the classroom in terms of what the student wants or needs—respect, control, desire to win, being tough, metacognitive functioning, etc.

Issue	Reframing (use adult voice)
Talking back to the teacher	How does that help you win?
Physical fighting	It takes more strength to stay out of a fight than get into a fight. How strong are you?
I can't do it.	Are you tough? I think you're tough enough to do this, and I'm here to assist you as you develop your skills to conquer this challenge.
I don't like you.	I don't like everything you do either. But I care about you a great deal. Sometimes when I'm frustrated, I don't like the person who frustrates me, but as I look deeper, it may be *the situation that frustrates me more than the person.*
Another student calls the student a name, and the student reacts.	Who's in control here? You or him? What are they saying about your behaviors? Are they trying to manipulate you? Do they envy the control or knowledge you have when you don't react?
I'm going to quit.	How will you have control? How will you be respected if you don't know if you're being cheated or not?

NOTE: Reframing moves the mind from *reacting* into the beginning stages of "becoming *proactive.*" This allows the student to maintain dignity. There are no right or wrong answers in reframing—only cognitive development.

Strategy 47

Mediating to Change Behavior

Behavioral
Strategy

Researchers

Hattie, J. (2015).
Payne, R. K. (2013).

Effect Size

Conceptual-change programs: 1.16

Added Effect of Poverty

Students who were inadequately mediated (not told *what, why,* and *how* regarding behavior) as children often have gaps in understanding expectations of others.

Explanation

Mediation takes discipline beyond mere punishment, turning incidents into learning opportunities. Imagine that two children break a rule. The first child is given a slap on the hand and told, "Stop that!" She learns very little except not to get caught next time. The second child is asked the questions listed below, which are aimed at mediating to change behavior and creating positive self-talk.

Directions

Mediating to Change Behavior

When a student demonstrates inappropriate behavior, ask the following four questions:

1. "What did you do?" Legally, you have now given the student due process.

2. "When you did that, what did you want?" Teachers get better, more reflective answers with this than with "Why did you do that?"

3. "What are four other things you could have done instead?" (Younger students might only be able to provide one or two alternative behaviors and might need prompting.) This question helps students realize they have options and can control their behavior.

4. What will you do next time?" This question helps students develop a plan and think toward the future.

Strategy 48

Story Book to Improve Behavior

Behavioral
Strategy

Researchers

Andreas, S., & Faulkner, C. (1994).
Hattie, J. (2015).
Hsu, J. (2008).
Seebaum, M. (1999).

Effect Size

Classroom behavior: .63

Added Effect of Poverty

Inadequately mediated students, many of whom are under-resourced, need behavioral mediation in order to function successfully in the school environment. This strategy allows students to own the behaviors they have acquired through mediation.

Explanation

The story in the student-created book compensates for inadequate mediation, enhances self-talk, and creates a mental model of appropriate behavior at school.

Directions

Strategy: Story Book to Improve Behavior

Start with a blank book.

1. Identify the student with a stick figure.
2. Identify what the student did.
3. Identify student's feelings when doing the behavior.
4. Identify what the student did.
5. Identify how the victim felt.
6. Identify what the student could have said or done.
7. Identify how the student would feel.
8. Identify how the victim would feel.

Strategy 49

Classroom Management/ Procedures Checklist

Researchers

Hattie, J. (2015).
Schamberg, M. (2008).
Simonsen, B., Fairbanks, S., Briesch, A., Myers, D., & Sugai, G. (2008).
Stichter, J. P., Lewis, T. J., Whittaker, T. A., Richter, M., Johnson, N. W., & Trussell, R. P. (2009).
Walberg, H. J. (1990).
Wong, H. K., & Wong, R. T. (1998).

Effect Size

Teacher clarity: .75

Added Effect of Poverty

A detailed list of procedures fosters a sense of fairness among teachers and a sense of security among students.

Explanation

The story in the student-created book compensates for inadequate mediation, enhances self-talk, and creates a mental model of appropriate behavior at school.

Good classroom management allows for more time to be spent on tasks. It also reduces the "allostatic load" in the brain. Allostatic load is the response of the body's systems to stress (Schamberg, 2008). The more chaotic the environment, the greater the stress. Allostatic load interferes with working memory, which in turn reduces learning.

According to Herbert Walberg (1990), up to 65% of achievement can be attributed to classroom management. Ninety-five percent of discipline referrals come the first or last five minutes of class because of the lack of procedures.

Procedures Checklist

The following checklist is adapted from "Guidelines for the First Days of School," from the Research Development Center for Teacher Education, Research on Classrooms, University of Texas, Austin.

Starting class	My procedure
Taking attendance	
Marking absences	
Tardy students	
Giving makeup work for absentees	
Enrolling new students	
Un-enrolling students	
Students who have to leave school early	
Warm-up activity (that students begin as soon as they walk into classroom)	

Instructional time	My procedure
Student movement within classroom	
Use of cellphones and headphones	
Student movement in and out of classroom	
Going to restroom	
Getting students' attention	
Students talking during class	
What students do when their work is completed	
Working together as group(s)	
Handing in papers/homework	
Appropriate headings for papers	
Bringing/distributing/using textbooks	
Leaving room for special class	

(continued on next page)

(continued from previous page)

Instructional time	My procedure
Students who don't have paper and/or pencils	
Signal(s) for getting student attention	
Touching other students in classroom	
Eating food in classroom	
Laboratory procedures (materials and supplies, safety routines, cleaning up)	
Students who get sick during class	
Using pencil sharpener	
Listing assignments/homework/due dates	
Systematically monitoring student learning during instruction	

Ending class	My procedure
Putting things away	
Dismissing class	
Collecting papers and assignments	

Other	My procedure
Lining up for lunch/recess/special events	
Walking to lunch/recess	
Putting away coats and backpacks	
Cleaning out locker	
Preparing for fire drills and/or bomb threats	
Going to gym for assemblies/pep rallies	
Respecting teacher's desk and storage areas	
Appropriately handling/using computers/ equipment	

(continued on next page)

(continued from previous page)

Student accountability	My procedure
Late work	
Missing work	
Extra credit	
Redoing work and/or retaking tests	
Incomplete work	
Neatness	
Papers with no names	
Using pens, pencils, colored markers	
Using computer-generated products	
Internet access on computers	
Setting and assigning due dates	
Writing on back of paper	
Makeup work and amount of time for makeup work	
Use of cellphones, headphones, iPods, etc., during class	
Letting students know assignments missed during absence	
Percentage of grade for major tests, homework, etc.	
Explaining your grading policy	
Letting new students know your procedures	
Having contact with all students at least once during week	
Exchanging papers	
Using Internet for posting assignments and sending them in	

(continued on next page)

(continued from previous page)

How will you ...	My procedure
Determine grades on report cards (components and weights of those components)?	
Grade daily assignments?	
Record grades so that assignments and dates are included?	
Have students keep records of their own grades?	
Make sure your assignments and grading reflect progress against standards?	
Notify parents when students are not passing or having other academic problems?	
Contact parents if problem arises regarding student behavior?	
Keep records and documentation of student behavior?	
Document adherence to IEP (individualized education plan)?	
Return graded papers in timely manner?	
Monitor students who have serious health issues (peanut allergies, diabetes, epilepsy, etc.)?	

Source: Adapted from "Guidelines for the First Days of School," Research Development Center for Teacher Education, Research on Classrooms, University of Texas, Austin, n. d.

Strategy 50

Planning Behavior

Behavioral
Strategy

Researchers

Agran, M., Blanchard, C., Wehmeyer, M., & Hughes, C. (2001).
Coyle, C., & Cole, P. (2004).
Feeney, T. J., & Ylvisaker, M. (2008).
Feuerstein, R. (1980).
Greene, J. A., Moos, D. C., Azevedo, R., & Winters, F. I. (2008).
Hamilton, J. L. (2007).
King-Sears, M. E. (2008).
Kishiyama, M. M., Boyce, W. T., Jiménez, A. M., Perry, L. M., & Knight, R. T. (2009).
Mithaug, D. K. (2002).
Moore, D. W., Prebble, S., Robertson, J., Waetford, R., & Anderson, A. (2001).
Peterson, L. D., Young, K., Richard, S., Charles, L., West, R. P., & Hill, M. (2006).

Effect Size

Teacher clarity: .75

Added Effect of Poverty

Students with few role models demonstrating behaviors that mirror classroom expectations require explicit, ongoing instruction regarding classroom expectations and procedures.

Explanation

Planning is related to controlling impulsivity. Also, individuals tend to honor their own plans and not the plans that others make for them.

Plan, Do, Review

Plan for the day	Steps to do	Review (how did I do?)

Strategy 51

If You Choose

Behavioral
Strategy

Researchers

Carlson, J. I., Luiselli, J. K., Slyman, A., & Markowski, A. (2008).
Carr, E. G., & Carlson, J. I. (1993).
Dyer, K., Dunlap, G., & Winterling, V. (1990).
Hattie, J. (2015).

Effect Size

Classroom behavior: .63

Added Effect of Poverty

Under-resourced students often are less aware of choices and consequences than their more affluent peers.

Explanation

This strategy guides students through the critical steps of:

1. Realizing they do have choices

2. Determining what those choices might be

3. Determining the consequences of each choice

4. Selecting the most appropriate choice for the circumstances at hand

If you choose _____, then you have chosen _____.

Strategy 52

Metaphor Story

Behavioral
Strategy

Researchers

Andreas, S., & Faulkner, C. (1994).
Freedman, J., & Combs, G. (1996).
Hsu, J. (2008).

Effect Size

Self-questioning: .64

Added Effect of Poverty

Students whose lives are different from the norm sometimes are more fearful of sharing details about influences in their environments than more economically and socially stable students tend to be.

Explanation

The Metaphor Story Strategy is a technique from neuro-linguistic programming (NLP) that uses metaphor story to identify causation behind a particular behavior. See Payne (2013) for more information.

Directions

Using Metaphor Stories

Another technique for working with students and adults is to use a metaphor story. A metaphor story will help an individual voice issues that affect subsequent actions.

A metaphor story does not have any proper names in it and goes like this.

A student keeps going to the nurse's office two or three times a week. There is nothing wrong with her. Yet she keeps going. Adult says to Jennifer, the girl, "Jennifer, I am going to tell a story and I need you to help me. It's about a fourth-grade girl much like yourself. I need you to help me tell the story because I'm not in fourth grade.

"Once upon a time there was a girl who went to the nurse's office. Why did the girl go to the nurse's office? (Because she thought there was something wrong with her.) So the girl went to the nurse's office because she thought there was something wrong with her. Did the nurse find anything wrong with her? (No, the nurse did not.) So the nurse did not find anything wrong with her, yet the girl kept going to the nurse. Why did the girl keep going to the nurse? (Because she thought there was something wrong with her.) So the girl thought something was wrong with her. Why did the girl think there was something wrong with her? (She saw a TV show …)"

The story continues until the reason for the behavior is found, and then the story needs to end on a positive note. "So she went to the doctor, and he gave her tests and found that she was OK."

This is an actual case. What came out in the story was that Jennifer had seen a TV show in which a girl her age had died suddenly and had never known she was ill. Jennifer's parents took her to the doctor, he ran tests, and he told her she was fine. So she didn't go to the nurse's office anymore.

A metaphor story is to be used one on one when there is a need to understand the existing behavior and motivate the student to implement the appropriate behavior.

Strategy 53

Building a Reward System Based on Implementing Your Own Plan

Behavioral
Strategy

Researchers

Butera, L. M., Giacone, M. V., & Wagner, K. A. (2008).
Caine, R. N., & Caine, G. (1991).

Effect Size

Feedback: .73

Added Effect of Poverty

Students who are discouraged from asking questions in general often develop fewer self-regulatory skills, including the strategy of self-rewarding.

Explanation

Extrinsic rewards work if they are used to start a behavior. Once the behavior is established, extrinsic rewards interfere with the behavior and lessen the behavior. If you tie rewards to the students' ability to complete their own plans, then you have established behaviors you want. Once those behaviors are established, then a new plan is made for additional behaviors.

Directions

- Have students make a list of validating experiences. That list can be anything: an adult who talked to them, a friend, something they did well, etc.

- Lists can be group lists, but it's also important for individual students to have their personal lists as well. Group self-rewards must be subject to teacher approval. Examples can include a five-minute dance break, extra reading time, etc.

- Have students draw from the list to self-reward when warranted.

Strategy 54

Registers of Language

Academic
Strategy

Researchers

Adger, C. (1994).
Godley, A. J., & Minnici, A. (2008).
Hattie, J. (2015).
Koch, L. M., Gross, A. M., & Kolts, R. (2001).
Montaño-Harmon, M. R. (1991).
Olmedo, I. M. (2009).
Skipper, J. I., Goldin-Meadow, S., Nusbaum, H. C., & Small, S. L. (2007).
Wheeler, R. S. (2008).

Effect Size

Conceptual-change programs: 1.16

Added Effect of Poverty

The major goals of this strategy are for those who know primarily only formal register to understand casual register and to code-switch when appropriate, and for those who know primarily casual register to understand formal register and to code-switch when appropriate.

Explanation

To build formal register, one must use the current vocabulary and build upon it. One way to build it is to translate casual register (what is known—current schema) to formal register.

Directions

A. Registers of Language

Write words and phrases that students use in the classroom that are casual in the "casual" column on a chart like the one above. Then have students work in groups to translate the casual expressions into formal ones.

Register	Explanation
Frozen	Language that is always the same. For example: Lord's Prayer, wedding vows, etc.
Formal	The standard sentence syntax and word choice of work and school. Has complete sentences and specific word choice.
Consultative	Formal register when used in conversation. Discourse pattern not quite as direct as formal register.
Casual	Language between friends, characterized by a 400- to 800-word vocabulary. Word choice general and not specific. Conversation dependent upon nonverbal assists. Sentence syntax often incomplete.
Intimate	Language between lovers or twins. Language of sexual harassment.

Source: M. Joos, 1967.

Casual register (language of close friends)	Formal register (language of school and business)
This sucks.	There's no longer any joy in this activity.

Also, have students write a radio talk show, with the interviewer using formal language and the interviewee using casual language.

B. Teach and Require Use of Complete Sentences

Give students the format for complete sentences and require them to use them at appropriate times.

Examples:

- "Yes, I am buying lunch," rather than, "I'm buying."
- "Yes, I would like to go," rather than, "Yes."
- "No, I am not hungry," rather than "Yes" or "Yeah."
- "My preference for breakfast is _____" rather than "Cereal."

C. Teach Use of Words as Opposed to Nonverbals to Express Feelings

In casual register, emotions are often unlabeled; instead they are shown through actions/nonverbals. Making the shift from the nonverbal body movements to the use of words to express feelings takes time, practice, and explicit instruction in the use of words to express feelings.

Give students the words for their nonverbal. Say, for example, "I think I know how you feel, and the word for it is_____."

Words are abstract, and at least initially they will feel like a "weak" replacement for the physical gesture. As vocabulary grows, however, the use of nonverbals in the classroom will decrease, and metacognitive skills will increase.

Strategy 55

Chronological Story Structure

Academic
Strategy

Researchers

Ausubel, D. P., Novak, J. D., & Hanesian, H. (1968).
Chomsky, C. (1972).
Dreher, M. J., & Singer, H. (1980).
Gordon, C., & Braun, C. (1982).
Hattie, J. (2015).
McConaughy, S. H. (1982).

Effect Size

Comprehension programs: .53

Added Effect of Poverty

Beginning a story at the most exciting point and inviting feedback that says, "I'm with you; I'm listening" is a way to compete for attention in crowded, noisy, or busy environments.

Explanation

Casual story structure is characterized by emotional rather than chronological order and interactive teller/listener roles.

Directions

Story Structure

A. In casual register, students tell stories starting at the most emotional point, hoping to gain the listener's attention. Although interesting, stories told in emotional order lack continuity. One strategy is to jot down students' key story points on sticky notes, then ask, "Which of these happened first?" Move that sticky note to the top, then ask what happened second, third, etc., until the stickers are in chronological order. Have the student retell the story following the order of the sticky notes. For older students, paragraphs can be cut apart and reordered for retelling.

B. Casual story structure is often interactive, with the listener asking questions and adding comments as a way of saying (as noted), "I'm listening to you." Students must learn that in more formal conversations these reactive comments could be misunderstood as rude interruptions.

Formal-Register Story Structure

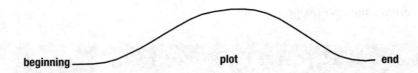

Casual-Register Story Structure

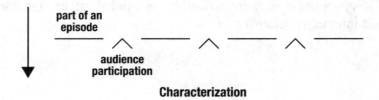

Strategy 56

Formal Discourse

Academic
Strategy

Researchers

Chomsky, N. (2002).
Hattie, J. (2015).
Howatt, A. P. R., & Widdowson, H. G. (2004).
Leech, G. N. (2008).
Smith, G., & Kurthen, H. (2007).
Thornton, S. (2008).

Effect Size

Conceptual-change programs: 1.16

Added Effect of Poverty

Making points through storytelling is a characteristic of casual discourse, which is often the expected mode of communication in communities of poverty.

Explanation

Formal discourse involves getting to the point rather quickly in a conversation. In casual discourse, on the other hand, individuals tend to approach the topic circuitously, often making major points in story format.

Directions

It's possible to communicate more effectively with students who use primarily casual discourse by:

1. Expecting stories to reveal key points and allowing ample time for these stories to be told

2. Teaching students how to engage in formal discourse when they need or choose to, such as during job interviews

Patterns of Discourse

Formal

Casual

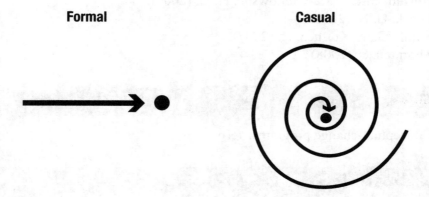

Strategy 57

Folder Activity (Mental Model for Part to Whole): Language Arts Example

Academic
Strategy

Researchers

Ellis, K. D. (2004).
Hattie, J. (2015).

Effect Size

Piagetian programs: 1.28

Teaching process skills (Piagetian programs) has an effect size with more than three times the impact of the average influence.

Added Effect of Poverty

The folder strategy reinforces organization, impulse control, and procedural self-talk, skills that often are inadequately developed among under-resourced students.

Explanation

Models are necessary for the systematic gathering of data. The folder system is for the facilitation of the part to whole of tasks. Twenty percent of the grade is based on using the process. Eighty percent of the grade is based on the final report. While this strategy is applicable to many topics, it is particularly beneficial for the teaching of writing skills and is especially critical for students unfamiliar with the part-to-whole task.

Directions

Have students take a manila folder and glue six envelopes onto the inside of it, with the flaps on the outside. This helps them visually see part to whole, especially when they have to divide a report into parts. When you first teach this you may need to give students some of the topics, but after several attempts most of them will be able to complete this step independently.

Using this strategy to collect research helps students:

- Understand part to whole of tasks
- Understand the research process and complete it effectively
- Practice an organizational structure
- Sort more important from less important information
- Control impulsivity
- Pull information from multiple sources

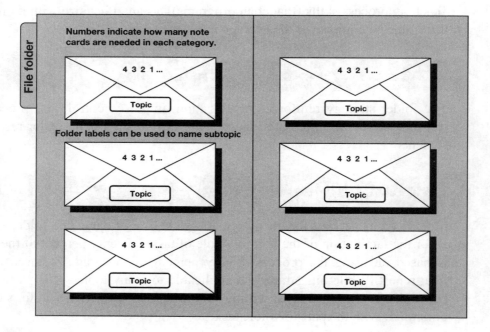

Strategy 58

Writing Organizers

Academic
Strategy

Researchers

Chalk, J. C., Hagan-Burke, S., & Burke, M. D. (2005).
Feuerstein, R. (1980).
Guastello, E. F., Beasley, T. M., & Sinatra, R. C. (2000).
Hattie, J. (2015).
Idol, L., & Jones, B. F. (Eds.). (1991).
Lin, H., & Chen. T. (2006).
Mason, L. H., & Shriner, J. G. (2008).
National Institute of Child Health and Human Development. (2000).
Williams, J. P. (2005).
Williams, J. P., Hall, K. M., & Lauer, K. D. (2004).

Effect Size

Piagetian programs: 1.28

Teaching process skills (Piagetian programs) has an effect size with more than three times the impact of the average influence.

Added Effect of Poverty

Teaching students text structures and mental models for those structures helps them organize their thoughts, an input skill that Reuven Feuerstein (1980) identified as inadequately developed among many under-resourced students.

Explanation

To write, one must organize against purpose for writing and structure of text. Teaching text patterns and organizers facilitates this process.

Directions

Students will get much higher comprehension if they use one of the following five techniques for sorting. In nonfiction there are basically five kinds of text. Each icon represents the five types of text and gives students a quick memory tool.

1. Descriptive Topical

The hand is topical or descriptive. Use each finger to sort topics or descriptive details.

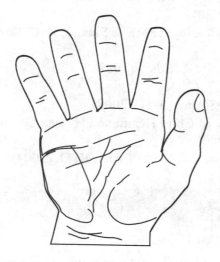

2. Sequence/How-To

Label sequential steps on a ladder.

3. Story Structure

Use the car as a mental model (front, middle, back) to sort and remember components of a story. For example, in a work of fiction there are characters; the beginning, middle, and end; the episode; the problem; the goal; and the setting.

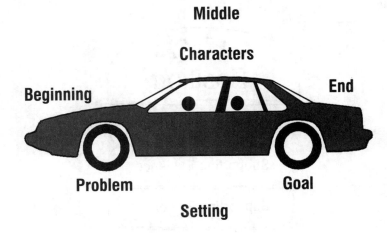

4. Compare/Contrast

Advantages/disadvantages

Cause/effect

Use the two sides of the T-shape to compare and contrast.

5. Persuasive Reasoning

If you use a hamburger, the top bun represents the person's position. Each layer in the sandwich is a piece of supporting evidence. The bottom bun is the conclusion. Also see Strategy 3 for another mental model for persuasive reasoning and techniques—and Strategy 11 for a step sheet on persuasive writing.

Strategy 59

Mental Model for Formal Written Expression

Academic Strategy

Researchers

Bruce, C., Snodgrass, D., & Salzman, J. A. (1999).
Enfield, M., & Greene, V. (2004).
Hattie, J. (2015).
"The Proof." (2017).
Schacter, J. (2001).
Wolff, J. (2002).

Effect Size

Piagetian programs: 1.28

Teaching process skills (Piagetian programs) has an effect size with more than three times the impact of the average influence.

Added Effect of Poverty

Under-resourced students often have less-well-developed concepts of the characteristics of formal written expression.

Explanation

It isn't unusual for you to get students who have only casual register and who cannot write very much.

Writing fluency is based on formal register. The following mental model from Project Read enhances fluency and sentence composition. The research data of William Swan (2007) on the work of aha! Process indicate that if the mental model is used consistently, the result is extraordinary writing scores.

Now let's look at sentence development and expansion.

Directions

A sentence starts with a capital letter and ends with a punctuation mark. It has a subject and a verb. A straight line is the subject, and a wavy line is the verb. A rectangle describes the subject, and a triangle expands the predicate. A triangle also answers one of four questions: *how, when, where,* or *why.*

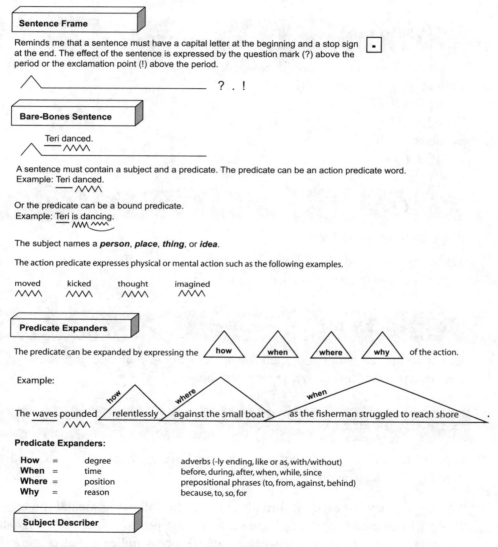

Sentence Frame

Reminds me that a sentence must have a capital letter at the beginning and a stop sign at the end. The effect of the sentence is expressed by the question mark (?) above the period or the exclamation point (!) above the period.

? . !

Bare-Bones Sentence

Teri danced.

A sentence must contain a subject and a predicate. The predicate can be an action predicate word.
Example: Teri danced.

Or the predicate can be a bound predicate.
Example: Teri is dancing.

The subject names a **person**, **place**, **thing**, or **idea**.

The action predicate expresses physical or mental action such as the following examples.

moved   kicked   thought   imagined

Predicate Expanders

The predicate can be expanded by expressing the   how   when   where   why   of the action.

Example:

The waves pounded / *how* relentlessly / *where* against the small boat / *when* as the fisherman struggled to reach shore .

Predicate Expanders:

How	=	degree	adverbs (-ly ending, like or as, with/without)
When	=	time	before, during, after, when, while, since
Where	=	position	prepositional phrases (to, from, against, behind)
Why	=	reason	because, to, so, for

Subject Describer

Words that describe physical characteristics, personality, numbers, and ownership.

Source: Project Read® (The Proof Is in the Classroom) excerpt reprinted with permission of copyright holder, Language Circle Enterprises, Inc., and its creators, M. L. Enfield, Ph.D., & V. Greene, 1973. Contact: (800) 450-0343. www.projectread.com

Strategy 60

Voices

Academic
Strategy

Researchers

Berne, E. (1996).
Hattie, J. (2015).
Steiner, C. (1994).

Effect Size

Metacognitive strategies: .53

Added Effect of Poverty

Many times students from under-resourced environments play the role of parent for younger siblings and learn to use the negative parent voice. When students use that voice with teachers who also use the negative parent voice, conflict usually ensues.

Explanation

Eric Berne (1996) identified three voices that one uses inside the head to direct one's behavior: child voice, parent voice, and adult voice. Claude Steiner (1994) found that if individuals become their own parent quite young, or if the primary caregiver is unsympathetic, those individuals typically develop only two voices—the child and the negative parent. Without an adult voice, it is very difficult to resolve conflicts or maintain healthy relationships.

Directions

Practice using the adult voice and teach students adult-voice phrases. As noted, however, if you are forced to become your own parent while quite young, you tend to have just two voices:

- Child voice
- Negative parent voice

The adult voice allows one to resolve a conflict, yet still maintain the relationship.

If you have only two voices (child and negative parent), everything is about power and control.

The voice you start in is usually the voice that determines the outcome.

Three Voices

The Child Voice *

Defensive, victimized, emotional, whining, losing attitude, strongly negative nonverbal

- ☐ Quit picking on me.
- ☐ You don't love me.
- ☐ You want me to leave.
- ☐ Nobody likes (loves) me.
- ☐ I hate you.
- ☐ You're ugly.

- ☐ You make me sick.
- ☐ It's your fault.
- ☐ Don't blame me.
- ☐ She, he, _____ did it.
- ☐ You make me mad.
- ☐ You made me do it.

* The child voice also is playful, spontaneous, curious, etc. The phrases listed often occur in conflictual or manipulative situations and impede resolution.

The Parent Voice * **

Authoritative, directive, judgmental, evaluative, win/lose mentality, demanding, punitive, sometimes threatening

- ☐ You shouldn't (should) do that.
- ☐ It's wrong (right) to do _____ .
- ☐ That's stupid, immature, out of line, ridiculous.
- ☐ Life's not fair. Get busy.
- ☐ You are good, bad, worthless, beautiful (any judgmental, evaluative comment).

- ☐ You do as I say.
- ☐ If you weren't so _____ , this wouldn't happen to you.
- ☐ Why can't you be like _____ ?

* The parent voice also can be very loving and supportive. The phrases listed usually occur during conflict and impede resolution.

** The internal parent voice can create shame and guilt.

The Adult Voice

Not judgmental, free of negative nonverbals, factual, often in question format, attitude of win/win

- ☐ In what ways could this be resolved?
- ☐ What factors will be used to determine the effectiveness, quality of _____ ?
- ☐ I would like to recommend _____ .
- ☐ What are choices in this situation?
- ☐ I am comfortable (uncomfortable) with _____ .
- ☐ Options that could be considered are _____ .
- ☐ For me to be comfortable, I need the following things to occur _____ .
- ☐ These are the consequences of that choice/action _____ .
- ☐ We agree to disagree.

Source: Adapted from work of E. Berne, 1996.

Strategy 61

Generative Vocabulary Instruction

Academic
Strategy

Researchers

Aronoff, M. (1994).
Biemiller, A., & Boote, C. (2006)
Educational Epiphany. (2012).
Hattie, J. (2015).
Nagy, W. E., & Anderson, R. C. (1984).

Effect Size

Vocabulary instruction: .62

Added Effect of Poverty

According to Andrew Biemiller and Catherine Boote (2006), on average children from 1 year old to second grade acquire approximately 860 root-word meanings per year—or 2.4 root words per day (about 6,000 root-word meanings). However, 25% of children with the smallest vocabularies acquire approximately 1.6 root words a day (about 4,000 root-word meanings).

Explanation

Generative vocabulary instruction involves teaching about word formation, including word parts—prefixes, suffixes, and base words. Knowledge of word-formation processes enables students to decode word meanings.

Most Commonly Used Prefixes

Prefix: a word part that can be added to the beginning of a root or base word that changes the meaning of a root or base word.

anti = against	auto = self	bi = two
circum = around	co, con, com = with	contra = against
de = opposite	dis = reverse/opposite	e, ex = out
en, em = cause to	in, im, il, ir = not	inter = between
macro = large	micro = small	mid = middle
mis = wrongly	mono = one	non = not
poly = many	post = after	pre = before
re = back/again	semi = partly	sub = under
super = above	syn = same time	trans = across
tri = three	un = not	uni = one

Source: © Educational Epiphany. Reprinted with permission. www.educationalepiphany.com, 2012.

Most Commonly Used Root Words

Root: a word part to which affixes (prefixes and suffixes) may be added to create related words.

audi = hear	auto = self	bene = good
bio = life	chrono = time	cred = believe
dict = say	duc = lead	fid = truth, faith
flex = bend	gen = give birth	geo = earth
graph = write	greg = group	jur, jus = law
log = thought	luc = light	man = hand
mand = order	mis, mit = send	omni = all
path = feel	phil = love	phon = sound
photo = light	port = carry	scrib = write
sens, sent = feel	spec, spect, spic = look	tele = far off
terr = earth	vac = empty	vid, vis = see

Source: © Educational Epiphany. Reprinted with permission. www.educationalepiphany.com, 2012.

Most Commonly Used Suffixes

Suffix: a word part added to the end of a root or base word that changes the meaning of a root or base word.

able, ible = can be done	acy = state or quality of	al = act or process of
al, ial = pertaining to	ate = become	dom = place or state of
ed = past tense	el, er, or = one who	er = comparative
en = become	ess = female	ful, ous = full of
ic, ical = pertaining to	ify, fy = make or become	ing = present participle
ion, tion, ation, = act, process	ish = somewhat like or near	ism = characteristic of
ist = one who	ity, ty = quality of	ize, ise = make or become
less = without	ly = characteristic of	ment = act of, result of
ness = state of	ology = study, science	s, es = more than one, plural
ship = position held	ward = in the direction of	y = having the quality of

Source: © Educational Epiphany. Reprinted with permission. www.educationalepiphany.com, 2012.

Prefixes and Suffixes

In order to understand and analyze across genres, determine the meaning of grade-level, technical, and academic English words in multiple content areas (Science, Math, Social Studies, the Arts) derived from Latin, Greek, or other linguistic roots and affixes. Adapted from Educational Epiphany.

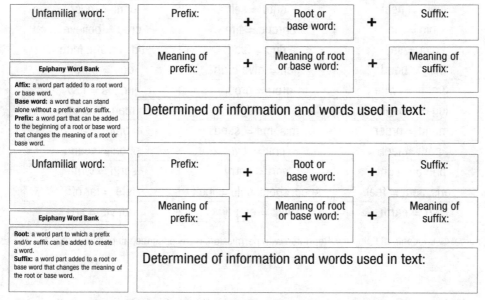

Source: © Educational Epiphany. Reprinted with permission. www.educationalepiphany.com, 2012.

Example of Generative Vocabulary Instruction

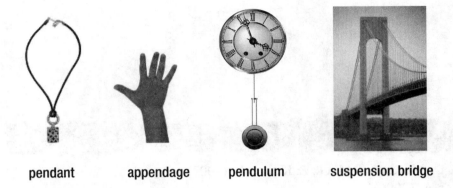

pendant   appendage   pendulum   suspension bridge

- To suspend something is to hang it.
- To depend on something is to rely on it, or hang onto it.
- A pendant hangs around one's neck.
- Hands, feet, and other appendages hang from one's body.
- A clock's pendulum hangs from the clock.
- A book's appendix hangs onto the end of a book.

Strategy 62

Language: Vocabulary Development

Academic
Strategy

Researchers

Beck, I. L., McKeown, M. G., & Kucan, L. (2002).
Biemiller, A. (2006).
Carrell, C. (1987).
Hattie, J. (2015).
Joshi, R. M. (2005).
Neuman, S. B. (2006)
Ryan, R., Fauth, R., & Brooks-Gunn J. (2006).
Skipper, J. I., Goldin-Meadow, S., Nusbaum, H. C., & Small, S. L. (2007).
Templeton, S., Invernizzi, M., Johnston, F., & Bear, D. (2008).

Effect Size

Vocabulary programs: .62

Added Effect of Poverty

"First-grade children from higher-SES [socioeconomic status] groups knew about twice as many words as lower-SES children" (Beck, McKeown, & Kucan, 2002).

Explanation

Vocabulary is the principal tool the brain uses for thinking. Formal register is the vocabulary or ideas and abstract representational systems. Playful, relational, associative activities build vocabulary, as well as sketching.

Directions

1. Knowledge Ratings

Using a graph like the one below, have students list the words in the first column to be studied. They evaluate their knowledge level of each word and check the appropriate box. If they have some idea of the meaning, they write in their guess. Following discussion or study, they write the definition in their own words. This activity is particularly useful in helping students develop metacognitive (being able to think about one's own thinking) awareness.

Example:

Word	Know	Think I know	Have heard	Guess	Definition
saline			X	A liquid for contact lenses	A salt solution

Activity:

Word	Know	Think I know	Have heard	Guess	Definition
torsade					
lurdane					
macula					

2. Word Dangles

Students read a novel or story and then, on a piece of construction paper, illustrate it and write a summary of it. From the selection, they choose approximately five words that interest them, then write and illustrate each word on a separate card. They write a definition of the word on the reverse side of the card. The cards subsequently are attached to the bottom of the construction paper and "dangle" from it. The finished product can be hung as a mobile.

By using "word dangles," students enhance their comprehension. The illustrations also help them with conceptualization. They learn how vocabulary, reading, and writing are connected. The strategy is adaptable for all content areas, including fine arts. For example, in math, students might write a summary of a process and write, define, and illustrate several key words for that process. "Word dangles" also provide a word-rich environment and stimulate student interest in vocabulary study.

Example:

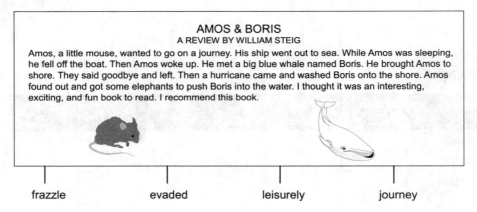

Activity:

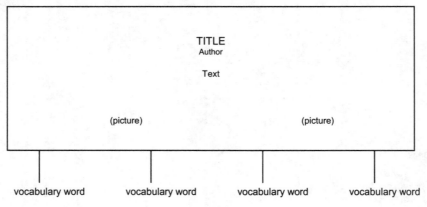

3. Picture It

With each new story/reading, assign each student one vocabulary word. Students are expected to:

- Find the word in the story/reading and record the page number (see form below).

- Find the word in the dictionary and record the pronunciation, number of syllables, part of speech, and definition used in the story.

- Create a picture of the word (on the second form below) to represent the word.

- Present the word to the class using the definition and picture.

Example:

(word)	(page number)
(pronunciation)　　(# of syllables)　　(part of speech)	
Definition from story_____	

Activity:

Word picture

4. Word Web

Students write the target word in the box, then write a synonym, an antonym, a definition, and an experience to complete the web.

Example:

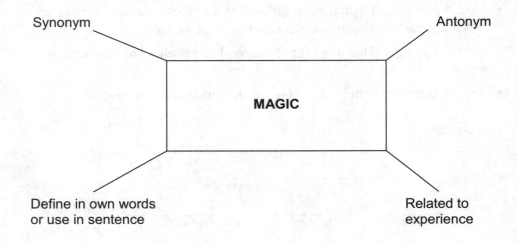

Activity:

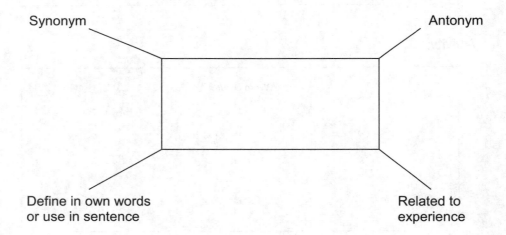

5. Concept Building

Guessing opposites or seeing relationships

To a small group, the teacher says:

1. Candy is sweet, but pickles are _____

2. An airplane is fast, but a horse is _____

3. The sky is above; the ground is _____

This type of procedure also can be used to elicit analogies.

Examples:

1. Pies are made by a baker; clothes are made by a _____

2. A cat runs on its legs, but a car runs on _____

3. In the morning the sun rises; at night the sun _____

The level at which this exercise can be done will vary widely with different children.

Activity:

1. _____

2. _____

3. _____

6. Intermediate Adaptation

With each text reading, assign each student one vocabulary word. Students are expected to do the following ...

Find the word in the text, then:

- Copy the text definition (taken directly from the book)
- Write the definition (in the student's own words)
- Use discriminating/distinguishing characteristics (information that helps give more details about the word)
- Draw illustration (drawing that gives a visual representation of the word)

Example:

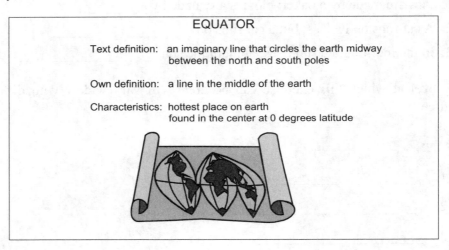

Activity:

7. Vocabulary Word Map

Have the students write a vocabulary word in the box in the middle of the page under the vocabulary word. Then have the students write the definition or synonym for the word in the box labeled DEFINITION or SYNONYM. Have the students then write on the line an antonym for the word. Next the students should able to use the word in a sentence. Finally, have the students sketch a mental model for the word. If the word is love, they might draw a heart. If the word is religion, they might draw a cross, crescent moon, or six-pointed star.

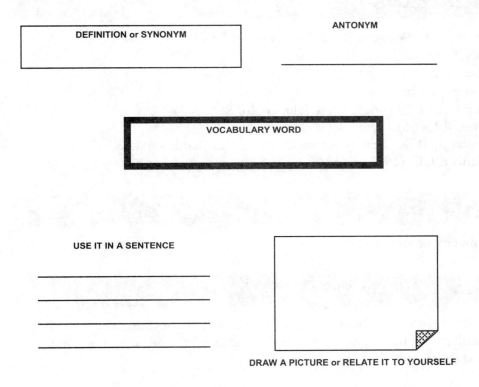

8. Vocabulary Chief

When assigning student roles for cooperative learning groups, consider assigning the role of "vocabulary chief" to one student in each group. Responsibilities (depending on the ages of the students) could include devising a "glossary" of terms in a text or chapter for group members, finding answers to peers' questions about technical vocabulary, and/or writing vocabulary words on one side an index card—with definitions or sample sentences on the other side for group members to use when preparing for tests.

Strategy 63

Sketching Vocabulary

Academic
Strategy

Researchers

Apperly, I. A., Williams, E., & Williams, J. (2004).
Fields, C. (2003).
Hattie, J. (2015).
Marzano, R. (2007).
Paquette, K. R., Fello, S. E., & Jalongo, M. R. (2007).
Rohrer, T. (2006).
Tanenhaus, M. K., Spivey-Knowlton, M. J., Eberhard, K. M., &
    Sedivy, J. C. (1995).

Effect Size

Vocabulary programs: .62

Added Effect of Poverty

Sketching vocabulary helps make abstract concepts concrete, which can be particularly useful to under-resourced students who tend to struggle more with abstractions.

Explanation

Visual memory precedes verbal memory. Linguistic definitions are preceded by a visual representation in the brain.

Directions

Sketching Vocabulary

Divide a paper into two columns. Have the students write a word in the first column, then draw a picture (a visual representation of the word) in the second column. If students cannot draw a visual representation of the word, they probably don't know the word. One of the fastest ways to teach vocabulary in any subject is to have students sketch. If they can't sketch the word, they likely don't know it.

Examples of Sketching

These are student examples of sketching activities using certain biology and math terms.

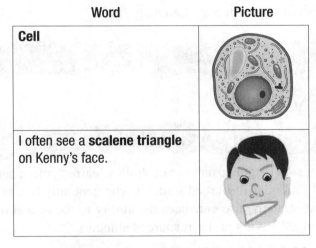

Word	Picture
Cell	
I often see a **scalene triangle** on Kenny's face.	

Source: Adapted from training materials developed by C. Fields, 2003.

Strategy 64

Sign Language for Comprehension

Academic
Strategy

Researchers

Daniels, M. (1994).
Daniels, M. (1996).
Daniels, M. (2001).
Hattie, J. (2015).
Penn State University Center for Sign Language. (2017).

Effect Size

Teaching strategies: .60

Added Effect of Poverty

The iconic nature of sign language makes vocabulary learning more concrete, which is beneficial for under-resourced students who generally live in a non-abstract world. This strategy also enhances the ability to focus, a skill often inadequately developed among under-resourced students.

Explanation

A Penn State University associate professor has this to say about the benefits of signing (often with American Sign Language):

> Subject areas other than reading or spelling also can be enhanced with sign language. ASL is routinely used in many schools from first grade through fifth grade for social studies, history, music, science, geography and even math. In these settings, it clearly supports content by defining concepts and aiding memory.

> –M. Daniels, 2001

Additional Research

It isn't necessary to become expert in the use of American Sign Language in order to teach a number of basic words and phrases. The benefits, especially to vocabulary development, are many, including:

- In one particular research study at Penn State, elementary students' retention of vocabulary words jumped from 55% to 80% when signing was added to the learning program.

- Showing students the corresponding sign for a word can give them clues to its meaning.

- There is evidence that children using signing pay better attention because they must watch the teacher when a lesson is being presented.

- A variety of studies demonstrates that there is a common neurological foundation between the areas of the human brain responsible for language development and the areas responsible for motor coordination.

Source: Penn State University, 2001.

Strategy 65

Teaching Students Their
Lexile Measures

Academic
Strategy

Researchers

Hattie, J. (2015).
Stenner, A. J., & Smith III, M. (1989).

Effect Size

Direct instruction: .60

Added Effect of Poverty

Teaching students their Lexile levels gives them control over their learning, which is highly motivational for under-resourced students.

Explanation

A Lexile measure serves two functions: It is the measure of how difficult a text is *and* a student's reading level.

The Lexile framework was developed by MetaMetrics©, an educational assessment and research team, funded originally by the National Institute of Child Health and Human Development.

Students receive their Lexile measure by taking a school-administered SRI (scholastic reading inventory) test, which is designed to measure Lexile or reading ability or by taking a standardized reading test that converts the reader's results to a Lexile measure.

If a student's measure is 550, then 550L is the measure of that student's readability level. The levels are marked on the back cover of many library books. Lexile levels range from 5L (beginning reader) to 2000L.

Directions

After explaining the Lexile concept to students, tell them their Lexile measure, then teach them how to find books and other reading materials at that level.

Parents and teachers also can use the Lexile database to search by Lexile level, title, or subject to find books that each student will enjoy and be able to read.

In the absence of Lexile measures, have students count the number of words they cannot read on a page. Once the student reaches five unfamiliar words (all the fingers on one hand) it can be assumed that the book is possibly too difficult for the student at that point.

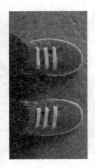

Strategy 66

Tucker Signing Strategies for Reading

Academic
Strategy

Researchers

Cole, C., & Majd, M. (2003).
Hattie, J. (2015).
Thompson, R. L., Vinson, D. P., & Vigliocco, G. (2009).

Effect Size

Phonics instruction: .52

Added Effect of Poverty

Inadequately mediated students often struggle with strict concepts, such as written letters on paper. This mental model makes letter/sound associations concrete.

Explanation

A student must be able to decode in order to comprehend. Decoding means you know that a symbol (e.g., *sh*) represents a sound. Tucker Signing has identified 44 sound chunks used in English and has developed a hand movement for each. When the student makes the movement, that movement translates a sound to an associated symbol.

The Center on Education and Lifelong Learning at Indiana University, in its evaluation of this decoding strategy, found the following growth: With the progress score being the difference between the number of words students could read on the pre- and post-tests, the mean progress score for the control group—no Tucker reading instruction—was only 5.30 points, as compared with 36.75 points for the experimental group.

Example: Tucker Signing Strategies Movement Mental Model

Sign for the /e/. The long /e/ is signed by making the *e*-shape and stretching the arm out long.

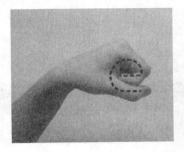 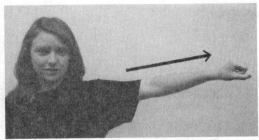

(always use left hand)

The short /e/ is signed by holding the *e*-shape close to the face.

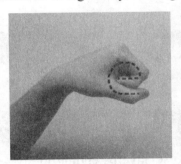 

Benefits of the Tucker Signing strategy include:

- The strategy reduces the amount of time required to learn letter/sound associations.
- The mental model utilizes minimal movement.
- The signs are visible to and meaningful for the learner.
- The strategy contains no extraneous information.
- It is effective with all learners, but it's especially effective with boys, students with ADHD (attention-deficit hyperactivity disorder), and adults.
- The strategy shifts more responsibility from teacher to students.
- It requires little effort.
- It's fun!

NOTE: As alluded to above, an effective movement mental model:
- Uses the least amount of movement necessary
- Is visible to and meaningful for the student
- Has no extraneous data

For more information, contact www.ahaprocess.com.

Strategy 67

Teaching Adverbs and Prepositions

Academic
Strategy

Researchers

Delfitto, D. (2006).
Hattie, J. (2015).
Macaulay, R. (2002).
Shenk, D. S. (1962).

Effect Size

Vocabulary programs: .62

Added Effect of Poverty

Studies have shown that middle-class speakers use adverbs ending in "ly" more than twice as frequently as working-class speakers (Macaulay, 2002). Students with limited formal register often lack adverbs and prepositions in their spoken and written vocabulary.

Explanation

A large portion of syntactical and writing errors involve prepositions and adverbs. Adverbs are most frequently omitted. Prepositions are often misspelled, misplaced, misused, or omitted.

While researchers don't necessarily agree on how prepositions are best taught, they do agree that multiple approaches are necessary for enabling students to discover patterns in the ways prepositions are used. But first … adverbs.

Directions

A. Teaching Adverbs

Adverbs add "spice" to verbs, adjectives, and other adverbs. List the types of adverbs on spice-container images, and encourage students to thereby add a certain "spice" to writing assignments.

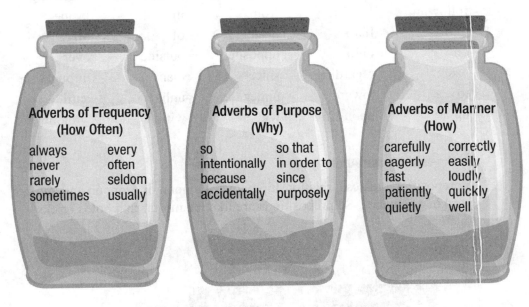

Adverbs of Frequency (How Often)

always	every
never	often
rarely	seldom
sometimes	usually

Adverbs of Purpose (Why)

so	so that
intentionally	in order to
because	since
accidentally	purposely

Adverbs of Manner (How)

carefully	correctly
eagerly	easily
fast	loudly
patiently	quickly
quietly	well

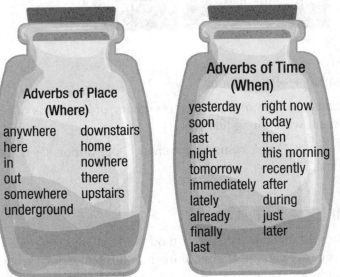

Adverbs of Place (Where)

anywhere	downstairs
here	home
in	nowhere
out	there
somewhere	upstairs
underground	

Adverbs of Time (When)

yesterday	right now
soon	today
last	then
night	this morning
tomorrow	recently
immediately	after
lately	during
already	just
finally	later
last	

B. Teaching Prepositions

about	above	across	after	against
along	among	around	as	at
before	behind	below	beneath	beside
between	beyond	but	by	concerning
considering	despite	during	except	excluding
following	for	from	in	inside
into	like	near	of	off
on	onto	opposite	outside	over
past	regarding	since	than	through
to	toward	under	unlike	until
up	upon	with	within	without

Bricks-and-Mortar Analogy

A preposition creates a relationship between a noun or pronoun and another word in a sentence. So prepositions are like the mortar that holds bricks together.

Example:

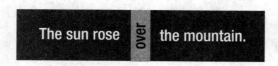

'Simon Says—Prepositions'

Use the game "Simon Says" for reviewing prepositions of place and movement with young learners:

"Simon says, 'Look behind your chair,'" or "Simon says, 'Look under your desk.'"

'I Went _____ the Building'

This simple sentence can often, though not always, indicate when a word is a preposition. If a word fits into the sentence "I went [blank] the building," it's a preposition. There are, of course, a few exceptions like "of" and "until."

Source: Attributed to D. S. Shenk, 1962.

Strategy 68

Teaching Words for Feelings

Academic and
Behavioral
Strategy

Researchers

Antonakis, J. (2004).
Ashkanasy, N. M., & Dasborough, M. T. (2003).
Barbuto, J. E., & Burbach, M. E. (2006).
Dulewicz, V., & Higgs, M. (2000).
Hattie, J. (2015).
Lee, S. Y., & Olszewski-Kubilius, P. (2006).
Slaski, M., & Cartwright, S. (2002).

Effect Size

Vocabulary programs: .62

Added Effect of Poverty

Emotional intelligence contributes to students' ability to control their behavior, a skill often inadequately developed among under-resourced students.

Explanation

Emotion perception is the ability to perceive emotions in yourself and others. Understanding emotions involves knowledge of emotions and emotional vocabulary; managing emotions involves the ability to manage your own emotions and connect at an emotional level with people around you.

Directions

Teach "words for feelings" as a way to label emotions and to replace nonverbals in casual register. Boys in particular are often "at a loss for words" when it comes to expressing their feelings—and tuning in to the feelings of others.

Have students download emojis and match them with words for feelings.

Surprised

Hostile

Sad

Sample List of Words for Feelings

afraid	aggravated	alarmed	alienated	amazed
amused	angry	anguished	annoyed	anxious
awkward	bored	calm	cheerful	comfortable
concerned	confident	confused	contented	curious
defeated	delighted	disliked	depressed	disappointed
disgusted	disturbed	eager	elated	embarrassed
enthusiastic	envious	exasperated	excited	exhausted
exhilarated	fearful	frustrated	grumpy	guilty
happy	helpless	hesitant	hopeful	hopeless
horrified	hostile	humiliated	hurt	indifferent
insecure	insulted	interested	intrigued	irritated
isolated	jealous	joyful	lonely	neglected
nervous	optimistic	outraged	overwhelmed	panicky
pleased	powerless	proud	regretful	rejected
relaxed	relieved	resentful	restless	sad
safe	satisfied	scared	self-conscious	shamed
shocked	sorrowful	stunned	suspicious	uncertain
uncomfortable	worried			

The next list of *feeling words* is adapted from the Nonviolent Communication organization, founded by Marshall Rosenberg.

Affectionate
compassionate
friendly
loving
open-hearted
sympathetic
tender
warm

Confident
empowered
open
proud
safe
secure

Engaged
absorbed
alert
curious
engrossed
enchanted
entranced
fascinated
interested
intrigued
involved
spellbound
stimulated

Excited
amazed
animated
ardent
aroused
astonished
dazzled
eager
energetic
enthusiastic
giddy
invigorated
lively
passionate
surprised
vibrant

Exhilarated
blissful
ecstatic
elated
enthralled
exuberant
radiant
rapturous
thrilled

Grateful
appreciative
moved
thankful
touched

Hopeful
expectant
encouraged
optimistic

Inspired
amazed
awed

Joyful
amused
delighted
glad
happy
jubilant
pleased
tickled

Peaceful
calm
clear-headed
comfortable
centered
content
equanimous
fulfilled
mellow
quiet
relaxed
relieved
satisfied
serene
still
tranquil
trusting

Refreshed
enlivened
rejuvenated
renewed
rested
restored
revived

Source: *Nonviolent Communication: A Language of Life* (3rd ed.), 2015, by M. B. Rosenberg. Reprinted with permission.

The Feelings Wheel

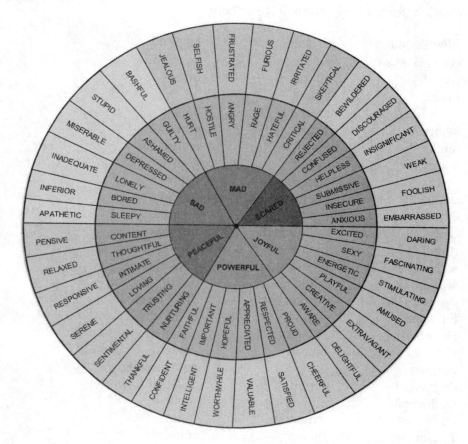

Source: Adapted from resource
developed by G. Willcox, 1982.

Strategy 69

Karpman Triangle

Researchers

Karpman, S. B. (1968).

Effect Size

Conceptual change: 1.16

Added Effect of Poverty

Under-resourced individuals tend to protect their "people," whom they often think of as possessions. They are, therefore, frequently drawn into the Karpman Triangle and find it difficult to find their way out.

Explanation

Especially when there's a crisis, individuals are often pulled into the triangle. Someone is the rescuer, one is the victim, one is the abuser. The same person can take on all three roles in different situations. Further, some of the bullies are victims at home.

Directions

The Karpman Triangle is effective for faculty development. Explain to faculty and staff that if you participate in the triangle you already have created another one!

The best way to stay out is to ask questions. You don't have to fight with your students or children. If you ask questions, they will begin to illuminate what is going on. When a student says, for example, "I'm bored," we can ask, "Whose problem is it?" The student wanted to be the victim and thought a rescuer was needed.

The recommended "rule" regarding the Karpman Triangle is this: Stay out of it! Or, if you're in one, ask questions and work your way out.

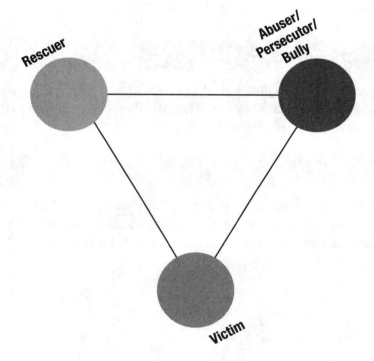

Source: Adapted from S. B. Karpman, 1968.

Strategy 70

Setting Appropriate Boundaries

Behavioral
Strategy

Researchers

Bagby, J. H., Rudd, L. C., & Woods, M. (2005).

Burts, D. C., Schmidt, H. M., Durham, R. S., Charlesworth, R., & Hart, C. H. (2007).

Covey, S. (1989).

Fraser, M. W., Galinsky, M. J., Smokowski, P. R., Day, S. H., Terzian, M. A., Rose, R. A., et al. (2005).

Louv, R. (2006).

Petermann, F., & Natzke, H. (2008).

Vestal, A., & Jones, N. A. (2004).

Effect Size

Classroom behavior: .63

Added Effect of Poverty

The closer one is to survival and "the tyranny of the moment," the fewer the boundaries.

Explanation

Appropriate boundaries are a factor in emotional health. These include boundaries in behavior, relationships, verbal comments, judgments, accusations, physical space, physical touch, bullying, and questions. These concepts can and must be directly taught.

Stephen Covey (1989) states that one goes from dependence to independence to interdependence. In the field of addiction, the term codependence is used. Boundaries are linked to emotional health, decision making, power, autonomy, and self-governance. As a child, one is dependent—i.e., the adults tell you which behaviors are acceptable, establish boundaries, etc.

When the adult is inappropriate (sexual abuse, physical abuse, bullying, using the child to meet the adult's needs), then the child does not learn appropriate boundaries and behaviors. In adolescence, students tend to be increasingly independent ("I will do what I want to do"). As adults, it's important to be interdependent—i.e., have your own autonomy, yet still be able to work with others. The way this is taught in school tends to be through discipline. Teaching appropriate boundaries is necessary for groups of people, including students, to live together in peace.

Directions

Establishing Boundaries

- The closer one is to the culture of survival, the fewer the boundaries.
- A typical response to a lack of boundaries is to become over-controlling, manipulative, and rigid.
- Options generally are not considered; thinking tends to become polarized.

To Help Establish Boundaries

- Start the discussion from the perspective of physical boundaries—why we need our own space, privacy, etc.
- Move the discussion to other boundaries: choices, criticism, flattery, decisions, feelings.

Bracketing Distracting Thoughts

Researchers

Chödrön, P. (2012).
Hattie, J. (2015).
Wenzlaff, R. M., & Wegner, D. M. (2000).

Effect Size

Classroom behavior: .63

Added Effect of Poverty

The stress rate is higher in poverty; therefore, students from poverty need strategies for dealing with stress.

Explanation

Bracketing, in the educational sense, is a strategy that students and adults can use to identify and deal with distracting thoughts, some of which induce stress.

Directions

Step 1: Students examine their current thoughts and categorize them as:

- Appropriate *now* for the task at hand
- Appropriate *later*
- *Never* appropriate

Step 2: Have students use their imaginations to draw a box into which they can place their "later" thoughts until a time in the future—and a trash can into which they can toss their "never" thoughts.

Step 3: When students' attention begins to drift from the task at hand, they decide if the distracting thoughts are "now," "later," or "never." The latter two are placed in the appropriate container!

Strategy 72

Self-Affirmations

Academic and
Behavioral
Strategy

Researchers

Dweck, C. (2006).
Hattie, J. (2015).
Marzano, R., & Arredondo, D. (1986).
Scott, E. (2016).
Steiner, C. (1994).

Effect Size

Self-concept: .47

Added Effect of Poverty

Poor self-concepts are often observed among students from poverty.

Explanation

Brain scans show promise that self-affirmations are most effective when future-oriented: "Think about how you will feel next week when you do well on your test" rather than "Remember a time that you did well on a test … Had fun with your family," etc. Also avoid evaluative statements like: "You are a good test taker."

There is brain-scan evidence that another promising approach is to have students engage in "self-affirming" exercises, such as writing about things or people they like.

Three explanations as to why self-affirmations are beneficial include:

- It's enjoyable to dwell on what we like and value.

- Self-affirmations radiate immediate, positive thoughts into our whole being and sense of self-worth.

- The exercise can help individuals learn to regulate their emotions.

Directions

A. Have students write about things they like. (Thinking about things we like is self-affirming.)

B. Have students engage in future-oriented success affirmations. (Such affirmations tend to be more effective than those expressed in the present.)

C. Instruct students to choose a computer password that reminds them about a goal or positive attitude that they would like to strengthen.

   Examples:
   iamstrong
   forgiveothers
   icanstaycalm
   iamawinner
   iamworthit
   futureinvestor

Source: E. Scott, 2016.

Strategy 73

Gratitude Journals

Behavioral
Strategy

Researchers

Emmons, R. A., & McCullough, M. E. (2003).
Hattie, J. (2015).
Positive Psychology Program. (2017).
Sansone, R. A., & Sansone, L. A. (2010).

Effect Size

Self-concept: .47

Added Effect of Poverty

In the culture of survival, individuals often have difficulty identifying elements of their hard life for which they feel grateful.

Explanation

It has been shown that keeping a "gratitude journal" shifts individuals' focus toward more positive environmental influences, actually strengthening brain synapses associated with these positive thoughts. Research studies indicate that writing in a gratitude journal also can improve sleep and psychological health in general.

Directions

- Provide all students with their own blank notebook or journal in which they will record daily notes about events or things for which they are grateful.

- Occasionally require students to write about a mistake they have made— and why they're thankful for that learning opportunity.

- Encourage students to enhance their journal entries with photos, personal notes, quotes, verses, etc.

- Ask students to list in their journal (as part of their homework) at least one thing daily for which they are grateful.

Strategy 74

Harsh Environments and Self-Expression: Language Skills

Researchers

Ellis, B. J., Figueredo, A. J., Brumbach, B. H., & Schlomer, G. L. (2009).
Hart, B., & Risley, T. R. (1995).
Hattie, J. (2015).
Shenk, D. W. (2017).

Effect Size

Self-concept: .47

Added Effect of Poverty

Living in a harsh environment often prompts harsh language.

Explanation

Most under-resourced students are unaware as to how often they hear or say negative or harsh words.

When students live in negative environments (Hart & Risley, 1995) and hear people say, for example, "I'll kill you!" they tend to unthinkingly repeat these words and expressions, not realizing the toxic nature of such verbalizing—unless this is pointed out to them.

Moving from the negative to the positive is a method of developing more abstract thinking. It assumes there are options for solving problems or expressing feelings other than physical aggression.

Dan Shenk, coeditor of this book, offers an example of this principle:

> One of my favorite stories from 30 years ago—when our son Tim was 7 and Jason was 5—happened at supper one evening (and mother Vera gets much of the credit for Jason's response). Tim said, "Jason, it really irritates me when you slurp your soup like that." Little brother didn't miss a beat. He smiled and said, "Thank you for using *words,* Timothy." Blew me away then … and now. By the way, both brothers (now in their 30s) are very close and supportive of each other.

Stating our ideas in a positive way—at any age!—is more acceptable behavior for those who live in the middle-class and professional worlds. In fact, it's a hidden rule.

Directions

Create awareness of words and expressions that have negative connotations and create negative feelings—and teach students to replace negative expressions with positive ones.

I can't do it.	I can do the first step. I can't do this yet.
I'll never lose weight.	I'll lose just one pound to start with.

Service Learning

Researchers

Billig, S. H. (2002).
Brooks, R. (1991).
Haskitz, A. (1996).
Hattie, J. (2015).
Vanderbilt University. (2017).

Effect Size

Service learning: .58

Added Effect of Poverty

Although doing for others is a motivator, many under-resourced individuals rarely have the opportunity to engage in service learning.

Explanation

Giving back to the community in service has very high payoffs in developing resilience and adult capacity.

The Vanderbilt University Center for Teaching lists many additional benefits of service, including:

- Reduced stereotypes and greater intercultural understanding
- Improved social responsibility and citizenship skills
- Greater involvement in community service after graduation from high school and/or college

Directions

There are many ways to integrate community engagement into an existing course (even in elementary school), including:

- One-time group projects or requirements
- Community engagement as a course or project option
- Action research projects

Strategy 76

Six-Step Process

Academic
Strategy

Researchers

Hattie, J. (2015).
Payne, R. K. (2008).
Payne, R. K. (2017).

Effect Size

This multi-step process reflects many of the influences on the list of John Hattie (2015), including Teacher estimates of teacher performance (1.62), which was determined by research to be the most effective influence on a student's life—because, as noted in the Introduction, teacher performance has a direct impact on student achievement.

Added Effect of Poverty

Many of the influences reflected in the six-step process directly impact the lives of under-resourced students.

Explanation

Response to intervention (RTI) is the federally mandated approach for regular education to address Special Education student needs. The RTI process is embedded as a form of intervention in the six-step process.

Six-Step Process

The six-step process involves the following:

1. Gridding students against the class chart

2. Aligning time and content grids against standards

3. Quality instruction

4. Formative assessments

5. Interventions using the RTI process

6. Assigning relevant activities to the annual school calendar

John Hattie (2015) says the influence that has the most powerful impact on campuses, kindergarten through college, is teacher estimates of teacher performance (which includes self-analysis) with a 1.62 effect size. The preceding six-step process guides such self-analysis and campuswide analysis.

For more information about the six-step process, see Strategy 6 in the book *Under-Resourced Learners* (2017) by Ruby K. Payne.

Additional Support Strategies

Art and Music

Both art and music teach students to translate between an abstract symbol (a note, a drawing) and the sensory sound or object it represents. As noted in Strategy 10, music also is beneficial in teaching math, language and input skills.

Art

April, A. (2001).
Asbury, C., & Rich, B. (Eds.). (2008).
Heath, S. B. (2001).
Richards, A. G. (2003).
Roscigno, V. J. (2009).

Music

Cox, H. A., & Stephens, L. J. (2006).
Gouzouasis, P., Guhn, M., & Kishor, N. (2007).
Harris, M. (2008).
Kinney, D. W. (2008).
Piro, J. M., & Ortiz, C. (2009).
Rauscher, F. H. (1999).
Southgate, D. E., & Roscigno, V. J. (2009).

Additional Support Material

Putting the Pieces Together

- Strategies to help students move between concrete and abstract concepts
- Designed for elementary-level educators and core-subject secondary-level educators

For more information about this support material, visit www.ahaprocess.com.

Sample Mental Models

Social Studies/History Grades 6–12

Includes mental models on geographical themes, economic patterns, political patterns, historical patterns, conflicts—even historians and history itself.

English/Language Arts: Grades 1–6 and 6–12

Includes structures and patterns of language arts, development of a thesis, patterns of written text, logic, and proof in written and oral persuasion, grammar, word meaning, and conventions of writing.

Mental Models for Math: Grades 6–12

Includes mental models on rational numbers, geometry, and algebraic structures.

For more information about these support materials, visit www.ahaprocess.com.

Appendixes

Appendix A

How to Calibrate Student Work and Use It to Drive Achievement

What if the National Football League functioned the way many schools do? They would shoot video of the coach, give the players a paper/pencil test on the subject of football, but never watch them play. We would all say, "How stupid!!" You gauge the quality of the coach based upon the players' performance—what they can actually do. Knowledge means next to nothing if you cannot do something with it.

Yet that is what we are doing in the school business. We are scrutinizing the teacher (Georgia has a 24-page teacher evaluation instrument, Memphis is videoing their teachers), giving batteries of state assessments (paper/pencil tests) to the students, and paying precious little attention to actual student work.

And then we wonder why achievement is so low, why the business community complains that graduates are so unprepared, and why the graduation rate in the United States is only 70%. (It's boring to only accumulate knowledge but not do anything with it. Can you imagine how many players a football coach would have left if he only "tested" players and did drills, but they never got to play a game?!)

Dual systems

Furthermore, we have a dual system going on in most schools—particularly secondary. We tie standards to lesson plans to formative assessments to state assessments. Then we have another separate system that ties standards to lesson plans to assignments to grades to credits. The two are often not connected. Rarely are assignments tied or calibrated to standards.

What does it mean to be calibrated?

Calibration means that the assignments are actually leveled to the difficulty of the grade-level standard. For example, I was in a sixth-grade classroom in a low-performing middle school. The sixth-grade teacher had written on the board that the standard was to "understand character development in literature." The assignment that the sixth-graders were doing was coloring in a coloring book. When I asked the teacher what was going on, she told me that most of the students couldn't read. She said coloring was one of the few things they could do in relation to the subject matter.

In a study in California, researchers gathered 18,000 assignments from low-performing schools. They found that in kindergarten 100% of assignments were on grade level. By fifth grade, only 2% of assignments were on grade level.

How do you calibrate assignments?

First: At the high school, you have each teacher take either the SAT or ACT practice test in either verbal or math (whichever is most applicable to what they teach) to identify the level of difficulty that students will need to perform to get into college. Then assignments are tied to the SAT or ACT in 11th and 12th grades and leveled down for ninth and 10th grades.

At the middle level, each teacher takes either the end-of-course test (or state assessment) for either math or language arts that is used in the ninth grade. Eighth-grade assignments are tied to the ninth-grade level of difficulty. Sixth- and seventh-grade assignments are leveled in relation to eighth grade.

In the elementary grades, teachers take the sixth-grade state assessment test in reading and math and repeat the process stated above.

Second: The second piece of calibration is to identify the amount and kind of work that should be done at that level. How much writing should the student be doing? How much reading? How many math problems? How many projects? How much homework? I cannot tell you how many schools I have been in where the amount has been insufficient for high achievement. I worked with one high school that did no writing in the ninth grade, none in 10th grade, and only second semester of 11th grade. School officials there could not understand why 50% of the students in 11th grade failed the writing assessment. The amount was insufficient.

And the other piece of this is the kind of work students are being asked to do. To every day answer the questions at the end of the chapter?? The attached checklist provides a list of ways to assess the value of the assignment.

Teacher and student artifact analysis

Artifacts are the products of the classroom. They often reflect the pedagogy and/or curriculum.

Teacher artifacts	Student artifacts
Examples: Lesson plans, project guidelines, classroom guidelines/procedures, rubrics, tests, homework assignments	**Examples:** Completed projects, research papers, tests, homework, writing samples, rubrics used for self-assessment, student notes
Questions to ask about the teacher artifacts	**Questions to ask about the student artifacts**
1. Is the process clearly identified (procedures, steps)?	1. Did the student complete the assignment?
2. Are student evaluation tools given (rubrics, grading guidelines, etc.)?	2. What was the level of difficulty of the assignment for the student?
3. Is the assignment relevant to the student in any way? (linked to a personal experience, a future story, a creative option)	3. Was the quality of the student work sufficient to assess student understanding of the task/content?
4. Is the purpose of the assignment to develop automaticity? If so, how much automaticity is required?	4. Was the finished project/assignment on grade level?
5. Is the assignment tied to grade-level standards and expectations?	5. Is the student able to demonstrate the use of the self-evaluation tool?
6. How often is the same kind of assignment given? is there variation in the week?	6. Did the student follow directions?
7. Does the assignment require thought?	
8. Is it a "beginning learning" assignment? If so, what are the opportunities to do the assignment with a peer or a group?	
9. Does it involve media/technology? If so, is that accessible to the student?	
10. Is the time frame given to do the assignment reasonable for the majority of students?	
11. What is the motivation for the student? (tied to a future story, a work environment, a personal interest, an understanding of the content, the relationships with the teacher, personal expertise/knowledge)	
12. Does the assignment provide any choice(s) for demonstrating understanding?	

Third: The third piece of calibration is tying the work to expertise. What does that mean? Experts think differently from novices. Experts tend to "chunk" information in patterns. For example, please note the gradations from novice (1) to expert (4) in the Skilled Musician Rubric that follows.

Skilled Musician Rubric (in Band and Orchestra)

Criteria	1	2	3	4
Accuracy	Not in time Several wrong notes Wrong key	Mostly in correct time Misses notes Key is correct Fingerings are off	In correct time Mostly uses correct fingerings Notes are correct	Timing is virtually always correct Fingerings are correct Notes are virtually always correct
Articulation	No variation in tempo Markings not observed No contrast in sound	Some variation in tempo but not correct Some contrast but incorrect for piece Random use of markings	Tempo mostly correct Mostly correct use of markings Dynamic contrast thin but correct	Markings are virtually always observed and followed Wide range of dynamic contrast Tempo is correct
Sound quality	Thin timbre High and low notes are off Too loud or too soft for note or section Unpleasant to ear	Timbre for most notes is fuller All difficult notes have some timbre Use of sound markings is random	Timbre is mostly full Sound markings are used but not advantageously	Timbre is full Sound markings are correctly interpreted and followed

(continued on next page)

(continued from previous page)

Criteria	1	2	3	4
Interpretation	No meaning assigned to piece No understanding of intent or purpose of composer	Playing indicates emotion but little understanding of meaning Understands that piece has climax but does not know where it is	Playing mostly conveys meaning and always conveys emotion Understands role of climax Can talk about intent and purpose	Playing conveys meaning and emotion Climax can be identified Plays truly to intent and purpose
Ensemble contribution	Does not pay attention to conductor Listens only to own playing Too loud/soft for group	Periodically pays attention to conductor Is mostly in balance with group Listens to own section Has little understanding of own contribution to melody	Mostly follows conductor's interpretations In balance with group Mostly listens to piece as whole Can verbally articulate contribution to melody but does not always reflect that in playing	Follows conductor's interpretation In balance with group Listens to piece as whole Understands own contribution to melody

Conclusion

My team and I have raised achievement scores in many schools. Once there is order, time management, and relationships of mutual respect, the key factor in student achievement is the calibrated work we ask students to do. There is no substitute for it. To ignore it, to put the emphasis in places that don't have high payoff, is to jeopardize the future of our children—indeed, the very future of our country.

First published in *AMLE Magazine* in January 2014. AMLE is the Association of Middle Level Education. Reprinted with permission.

Appendix B

Understanding Learning: the How, the Why, the What
by Ruby K. Payne

Introduction
Teaching vs. Learning

Teaching is outside the head and the body; learning is inside the head and the body.

This book will look at learning—what is inside the head and the body.

Let's make a simplified analogy to a computer. The brain is the hardware; the mind is the software. Learning is about the development and use of the software. Just as hardware and software must have each other in order to function, so the brain must have a mind. So must teaching and learning go together. But they are not the same thing. In order to teach, one must know what needs to go on inside a student's head. That's what this book is.

[For those of you familiar with brain research and cognitive studies, this book is a synopsis of those findings. Please do not be offended by this effort to offer the fruits of that research to a wider audience.]

Chapter One
The Brain and the Mind

> It is possible to have a brain
> and not have a mind.
> A brain is inherited;
> a mind is developed.
>
> —Feuerstein

To begin our discussion, a distinction will be made between the brain and the mind. Truth be told, it is all one and the same. But for the purposes of this book, the brain is going to mean what you inherited and the mind will be what was developed by your environment. Cognitive scientists have concluded that it's about a 50-50 arrangement. About half of who an individual becomes is developed by his/her genetic code and about half by his/her environment.

All functions of the brain are either a chemical or electrical interaction. A chemical interaction occurs on the face of the cell and continues down the tail (axon) of the cell as an electrical impulse. When the electrical impulse enters the dendrites and synapses, causing their structure to permanently change, learning has occurred.

Therefore, learning is physiological. That's why it takes so long to "unlearn" something that has been learned incorrectly.

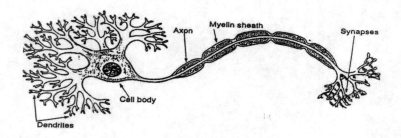

Chemicals in the brain come from four sources: what the genetic code indicates will be made, hormonal fluctuations, external experience (you get frightened and produce adrenaline), and what you eat and breathe.

This book is going to concentrate on the development of the mind. What is the mind as it's being defined here? It's the part that was learned in the environment. But more importantly, it is the abstract replication/representation of external reality. What does that mean?

As human beings, we are very limited. We cannot communicate telepathically. Wouldn't it be nice if we could communicate by, say, rubbing heads? Well, we can't. So we use abstract representational systems, which illustrate common understandings, in order to communicate. Numbers, language, drawings, etc. ... all are forms of this.

For example, in the winter, "cold" is measured by a thermometer. However, the sensory reality of cold is not the same as the measured reality of cold. After the temperature gets 10 below zero, it's hard to tell the difference between 10 below zero and 40 below zero. Both are cold. The measurement system is the abstract overlay of the sensory-based reality.

How did we get this abstract structure? We got it from the interplay of language and experience in our environment. When we were young, we were mediated by the adults in our life. What they did when they mediated us was to give us the what, the why, and the how. In other words, they pointed out the stimulus (what we were to pay attention to), gave it meaning (the why), and gave us a strategy (how).

Mediation

Point out the stimulus (what)	Give it meaning (why)	Provide a strategy (how)

For example, a parent says to a child:

- "Don't cross the street without looking" (what).
- "You could be killed" (why).
- "Look both ways twice before you cross the street" (how).

This mediation builds an abstract architecture inside the child's head. That architecture acts as an abstract replication of external reality, just as the blueprint acts as an abstract replication of a house.

Chapter Two
Learning (Mediation): How, Why, What

The mediation of the mind happens when an individual is taught the what, the why, and the how. Just as a computer has a programmer for the software, so a student has individuals who help develop the mind. Reuven Feuerstein studied under Jean Piaget and asked him how he accounted for individual differences. Piaget, a biologist, was more interested in accommodation and assimilation. Feuerstein believed that when a caring adult intervened using mediation, significant learning occurred.

Mediation is particularly required when an individual is a new learner to a skill, process, content … whatever.

Research on new learners (Bloom and Berliner) indicates that there is a process that an individual goes through.

Novice	Has no experience with information, skill, process, etc. Needs terminology, models, and procedures. Needs context-free rules.
Advanced Beginner	Has some experience and begins to collect episodic knowledge (stories) and strategic knowledge (strategies). Begins to see similarities across contexts or situations that he/she is in.
Competent	Can make conscious choices about what will and will not work. Can distinguish important from unimportant. Takes personal responsibility for his/her learning because he/she knows what he/she did to make a difference.
Proficient	Sees hundreds of patterns and sorts information quickly by pattern. Uses intuition and know-how to make judgments. Has wealth of experience from which to make generalizations and judgments.
Expert	Makes his/her own rules because of extensive experience. Performance is so fluid it can happen virtually without conscious thought; this is called automaticity.

A beginning learner in anything needs the three components of mediation—the what, the why, and the how. Often the expert has difficulty helping a novice because so many of the expert's actions are at the level of automaticity, and the expert has a great deal of difficulty articulating what he/she is doing. This dynamic is frequently seen in sports.

There is a rule in cognitive research that goes like this:

The more complex the process an individual is involved in, the more parts of that process need to be at the level of automaticity.

For example, when a child learns to ride a bicycle, training wheels are often used. But a skilled rider would never use training wheels. What the training wheels allow the child to do is learn to steer, guide, pedal, and brake. When those are more at the level of automaticity, then the training wheels are taken off, and additional skills are developed.

So it's a mistake to teach beginners in the same way one would teach a skilled individual.

Second, the brain processes things differently when one is a new learner.

In the book *Making Connections* (1991) by Caine and Caine, the authors describe two different kinds of memory functions in the brain. One is used by beginning learners (taxon), while the other is used by individuals who have more experience with it (locale).

Taxon	Locale
No context (experience)	Context (experience)
Memory capacity: about five things	Unlimited memory
Requires continuous rehearsal to remember	Remembers quickly but has loss of accessibility over period of time
Is in short-term memory	Is in long-term memory
Limited to extrinsic motivation	Motivated by novelty, curiosity, expectation (intrinsic)
Specific, habit-like behaviors that are resistant to change	Updated continuously, flexible
Isolated items	Interconnected, spatial memory
Not connected to meaning	Has meaning that is motivated by need to make sense
Acquisition of relatively fixed routes	Forms initial maps quickly and involves sensory activity and emotion; generates personal maps through creation of personal meaning
Follows route	Uses map

What this means is that a beginning learner must be mediated in order to learn. He/she must be given the what, the why, and the how.

Often in schools, the focus is on the content; the why and how are seldom if ever mentioned, so the student is unable to do the work.

Chapter Three
Abstract Representational Systems

One of the reasons you and I are successful is that we have been mediated, not only in sensory data, but also in abstract data. What does that mean?

Just as a computer has icons to represent the software, so does the mind.

A Dutch linguist, Martin Joos, has researched language and has found that no matter which language in the world one speaks, there are five registers.

Registers of Language

Register	Explanation
Frozen	Language that is always the same. For example: Lord's Prayer, wedding vows, etc.
Formal	The standard sentence syntax and word choice of work and school. Has complete sentences and specific word choice.
Consultative	Formal register when used in conversation. Discourse pattern not quite as direct as formal register.
Casual	Language between friends and is characterized by a 400- to 800-word vocabulary. Word choice general and not specific. Conversation dependent upon non-verbal assists. Sentence syntax often incomplete
Intimate	Language between lovers or twins. Language of sexual harassment.

The research indicates that there is a strong relationship between the amount of vocabulary an individual has and social class. In generational poverty, it is not unusual for individuals to know only casual register. An individual who has only casual register does not have many abstract words. The abstract words are in formal register.

Hart and Risley in *Meaningful Differences in the Everyday Experience of Young American Children* (1995) found the following patterns in children between the ages of 1 and 4 in stable households.

Economic group	Number of words exposed to
Welfare households	13 million words
Working-class households	26 million words
Professional households	45 million words

Language or words are the tools of ideas. Abstract words represent those ideas, concepts, processes, etc., that do not have sensory-based representations.

What Are These Abstractions or Representations?

A few summers ago it was so hot in Fort Worth, Texas, that the railroad tracks warped. We keep butter out in our house, and it kept melting. One day I said to my husband, "The thermometer says it's 72 degrees in here, but the butter is melting. In the winter, it says 72 degrees and the butter does not melt." He said, "Do not confuse real heat with measured heat."

You see, Anders Celsius and Gabriel Fahrenheit decided they wanted a better way to talk about heat, so each designed a system to do so. But the systems are abstract representations and measurements of a sensory-based reality.

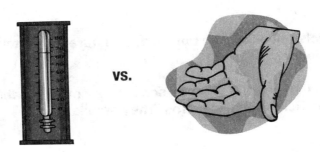

VS.

Language is the tool we use to create and acknowledge those abstract systems. Abstract systems are learned. If a student comes from an environment where there is a heavy reliance on casual register, and there isn't much formal education, often the student has few abstract representational systems. **To survive in poverty, one must be very sensory-based and non-verbal. To survive in school, one must be very verbal and abstract.**

Furthermore, abstractions are stored in the mind in either visual or auditory rhythmic memory. Abstractions are kept in mental models. **Mental models are in the form of a story, a metaphor, an analogy—or, perhaps, a two-dimensional drawing.**

For example, when a house is being built, blueprints are used. The blueprints become the abstract representational system for the final sensory-based object, the house.

Another example: A lawyer I know got a call from a colleague who was in court and needed a piece of paper from his desk. She said, "Your desk is a mess. No one could find it." And he said to her, "Go stand in front of my desk. Picture an overlay of the map of the United States. That paper is somewhere around Vermont." And she found it. He had given her an abstract representational system.

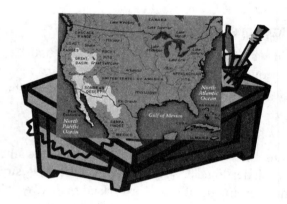

Mental models tell either the purpose, structure, or pattern of a subject area or discipline.

To survive in the world of work or school, one must be able to use abstract representational systems. They are learned.

Chapter Four
Abstract Processes (the How)

Abstract processes are "the how" and accompany all learning. Jerome Bruner says all learning is connected to the task and context of the learning. In other words, the process and the content are interwoven. To teach one without the other is to have incomplete learning.

Just as one must follow steps in software, i.e., double-click the icon, then do this … so the mind must have procedures.

Often in schools, we do not direct-teach the process. We direct-teach the content. Reuven Feuerstein describes the abstract processes that must be used to learn.

Input Strategies

Input is defined as "quantity and quality of the data gathered."

1. Use planning behaviors.
2. Focus perception on specific stimulus.
3. Control impulsivity.
4. Explore data systematically.
5. Use appropriate and accurate labels.
6. Organize space with stable systems of reference.
7. Orient data in time.
8. Identify constancies across variations.
9. Gather precise and accurate data.
10. Consider two sources of information at once.
11. Organize data (parts of a whole).
12. Visually transport data.

Elaboration Strategies

Elaboration is defined as "use of the data."

1. Identify and define the problem.
2. Select relevant cues.
3. Compare data.
4. Select appropriate categories of time.
5. Summarize data.
6. Project relationships of data.
7. Use logical data.
8. Test hypotheses.

9. Build inferences.
10. Make a plan using the data.
11. Use appropriate labels.
12. Use data systematically.

Output Strategies

Output is defined as "communication of the data."

1. Communicate clearly the labels and process.
2. Visually transport data correctly.
3. Use precise and accurate language.
4. Control impulsive behavior.

Where does an individual get these strategies? Mediation builds them! Typically in school we start teaching at the elaboration level, i.e., the use of the data. When students don't understand, we reteach these strategies but don't revisit the quality and quantity of the data gathered—namely, the input strategies.

In order to better understand input strategies, each is explained in more detail. Typically, input strategies are not directly taught, because we don't know how to teach them. The assumption is that everyone has them. For those students who don't have these strategies, however, the strategies can be directly taught to students.

Input Strategies

Using planning behaviors includes goal setting, identifying the procedures in the task, identifying parts of the task, assigning time to the task(s), and identifying the quality of the work necessary to complete the task.

Focusing perception on a specific stimulus is the strategy of seeing every detail on the page or in the environment. It is the strategy of identifying everything noticed by the five senses.

Controlling impulsivity is the strategy of stopping action until one has thought about the task. There is a direct correlation between planning and impulse control.

Exploring data systematically means that a strategy is employed to procedurally and systematically go through every piece of data. Numbering is a way to go systematically through data. Highlighting important data is another way.

Using appropriate and accurate labels (vocabulary) is the precise use of words to identify and explain. If a student does not have specific words to use, then his/her ability to retrieve and use information is severely limited. It's not enough that a student can do a task, he/she also must be able to label the procedures, tasks, and processes so that the task can be successfully repeated each time and analyzed at a metacognitive level. Metacognition is the ability to think about one's thinking. To do so, labels must be attached. Only when labels are attached can the task be evaluated and, therefore, improved.

Organizing space with stable systems of reference is crucial to success in math. It means that up, down, across, right, left, horizontal, vertical, diagonal, east, west, north, south, etc., are understood. It means that an individual can identify with words the position of an item. It means an individual can organize space. For example, he/she can find things on a desk. It means that a person can read a map. If an individual does not have this ability, then it's virtually impossible to tell a *p* from a *b* from a *d*. The only differentiation is the orientation to space.

Orienting data in time is the strategy of assigning abstract values to time and the use of the measurements of time. Without an abstract sense of time that includes a past, present, and future, a student cannot plan, he/she cannot sequence, and he/she cannot match time and task (and, therefore, doesn't get work done).

Identifying constancies across variations is the strategy of knowing what always remains the same and what changes. For example, if you don't know what always makes a square a square, you cannot identify constancies. This strategy enables the individual to define things, to recognize a person or an object, and to compare and contrast. This strategy also allows cursive writing to be read in all its variations.

Gathering precise and accurate data is the use of specific vocabulary and word choice, identifying precisely when something occurred in time and where it occurred in space, knowing the constancies, and exploring the data systematically.

Considering two sources of information at once means that the mind can hold two objects simultaneously and compare and contrast the two objects. To do this, the individual must be able to visually transport data accurately, identify the constancies and variations, and go through the data systematically. When those processes are completed, the student must be able to assign new vocabulary (if things have changed) and reassign existing vocabulary.

Organizing data (parts of a whole) involves going through data systematically, organizing space, identifying constancies and variations, and using vocabulary to label both the parts and the whole.

Visually transporting data is when the eye picks up data, then carries it accurately into the brain, examines it for constancies and variations, and labels the parts and the whole. If a student cannot visually transport data, then he/she often cannot read, has difficulty with basic identification of anything, and cannot copy.

What does this mean in the classroom?

When a student cannot:	One will often see this:
Use planning behaviors …	Does not get his/her work done, is impulsive.
Focus perception on a specific stimulus …	Misses parts of the task; cannot find the information on the page.
Control impulsivity …	Cannot plan.
Explore data systematically …	Does not have a method for checking work, for getting all the work done, and for finding complete answers.
Use appropriate and accurate labels (vocabulary) …	Does not have the words to explain; cannot label processes; uses generic words, e.g., "Get that thing."
Organize space with stable systems of reference …	Cannot read a map; cannot use the procedures in math
Orient data in time …	Cannot sequence or plan; cannot follow directions.
Identify constancies across variations …	Cannot make judgments or generalizations; cannot identify patterns.
Gather precise and accurate data …	Cannot tell specifically when, where, and how something happened.
Consider two sources of information at once …	Cannot compare and contrast; does a different assignment the way the first one was done, whether appropriate or not.
Organize data (parts of a whole) …	Cannot explain why; does not recognize when something is missing.
Visually transport data …	Cannot cheat because he/she cannot copy.

How does the teacher embed these processes and develop minds?

One way is to teach these processes with all content to all students. The way I approached it in my teaching career was to use four simple processes—sorting, question making, planning to control impulsivity, and planning and labeling tasks—because these processes embed into all content, use all the input strategies, and are quick and easy.

1. Sorting, Using Patterns

In brain research what is fairly clear is that the information must be sorted or "chunked" in order to be remembered. Details are not remembered over time, but patterns are. So if you teach patterns directly and then teach students to sort what is and is not important in relation to the patterns, the students will learn much more quickly.

In problem solving at work or school, it's very important that the worker or student is able to sort through a great deal of information quickly. He/she does this by going through patterns. For example, if you want to buy shoes at a department store, you don't wander aimlessly through the store. You know that a department store is arranged in predictable patterns. You find the shoe department.

So for any content you're teaching, teach the patterns and mental models of the content. That will help students sort what is and is not important in the learning.

2. Question Making

A quick approach is to give students the question stems and then have them use the rules to develop a multiple-choice question. Developing multiple-choice questions develops critical-thinking skills. Some examples follow.

Reading-Objective Question Stems

Objective 1: Word Meaning
In this story the word _____ means …
The word _____ in this passage means …

Objective 2: Supporting Ideas
What did _____ do after …?
What happened just before _____ …?
What did _____ do first? Last?
According to the directions given, what was _____ supposed to do first?
After _____? Last?
Where does this story take place?
When does the story take place?

Objective 3: Summarizing Written Texts
Which sentence tells the main idea of the story?
This story is mainly about …
What is the main idea of paragraph 3?

What is the story mostly about?

Which statement best summarizes this passage (paragraph)?

Objective 4: Perceiving Relationships and Recognizing Outcomes

Why did __ (name) __ do __ (action) ___?

What will happen as a result of _____?

Based on the information, which is _____ most likely to do?

What will happen to _____ in this story?

You can tell from this passage that _____ is most likely to …

Objective 5: Analyzing Information to Make Inferences and Generalizations

How did _____ feel about _____?

How does _____ feel at the beginning (end) of the story?

According to Figure 1, what … (or where … how many … when …)
    is …?

The ___ (event) ___ is being held in order to …

By ___ (action) ___, ___ (name) ___ was able to show that …

You can tell from this passage that …?

Which word best describes _____'s feelings in this passage?

Objective 6: Distinguishing Between Fact and Opinion

Which of these is a fact expressed in the passage?

Which of these is an opinion expressed in the passage?

Question-Making Stems
(from Texas Assessment of Academic Skills)

1. What does the word _____ mean?
2. What can you tell from the following passage?
3. What does the author give you reason to believe?
4. What is the best summary of this passage?
5. Which of the following is a fact in this passage?
6. What is the main idea of the _____ paragraph?
7. Which of the following is an opinion in this passage?
8. What happens after _____?
9. How did _____ feel when _____?
10. What is the main idea of this passage?
11. Which of these happened (first/last) in the passage?
12. Which of these is not a fact in the passage?
13. Where was _____?

14. When did _____ ?
15. What happens when _____ ?
16. What was the main reason for the following _____ ?
17. After _____, what could _____ ?
18. Where does the _____ take place?
19. Which of these best describes _____ before/after _____ ?

Taken from Julie Ford

More Question-Making Stems

1. From this passage (story), how might _____ be described?
2. Why was _____ ?
3. Why did _____ ?
4. How else might the author have ended the passage (story)?
5. If the author had been _____, how might the information have been different?
6. In this passage, what does _____ mean?
7. How did _____ feel about _____ ?
8. What caused _____ to _____ ?
9. What is _____ ?
10. When _____ happened, why did _____ ?
11. The passage states that _____ .
12. Why is that information important to he reader?

3. Planning to Control Impulsivity

Planning is the key to the tasks that get finished and to the control of impulsivity. Even more importantly, brain research indicates that the primary filter for what gets noticed by the mind is closely correlated with the goals of the person. So when there is no planning, there are no goals. Emotional need or association, then, determines activities.

To teach planning it's important to teach students to plan backwards. Stephen Covey, in *The Seven Habits of Highly Successful People* (1989), says, "Begin with the end in mind." In order to accomplish this "backwards planning," the teacher simply has students go to the end first, then the day or task before that, and so forth.

It's also very important in the planning process that abstract time (minutes, hours, days, weeks) gets assigned to the task.

Planning Backwards

Monday	Tuesday	Wednesday	Thursday	Friday

4. Planning and Labeling Tasks

In addition to controlling impulsivity, planning allows a person to finish tasks. To complete tasks, both labels (vocabulary) and procedures must be used. In addition, teachers need a method for addressing each part of the task, i.e., having a systematic method for getting it all done and checking to see that it has been done.

Process (the how) is crucial to any learning; this must be taught.

In the following example, a battery is made. The left-hand column (on page 271) tells the steps that were followed. The right-hand column tells **why.** In the left-hand column …

Step 1   The student fills a bowl with vinegar.

Step 2   The student puts pieces of cloth in the vinegar and squeezes them out.

Step 3   The student takes a piece of copper and a piece of zinc and puts the squeezed-out cloth between the copper and zinc.

Step 4   The student makes four of the items identified in Step 3.

Step 5   A piece of aluminum foil is put on the bottom of the stack of four and curved to the top of the stack.

Step 6   A small light connects the foil pieces and the stack of four. If the light goes on, the battery is completed.

How (process)	Why (concept)
1.	Electrons, ions
2.	Insulator
3. Copper, cloth, zinc	$\begin{array}{c}+\\ -\end{array}$
4.	Current $\begin{array}{c}+\\ +\end{array}$
5.	Circuit
6.	Closes circuit

On the right-hand side is the label, or the why …

Step 1   Why do we need the vinegar? *Because it provides electrons and ions.*

Step 2   Why do we need the cloth dipped in vinegar? *Because it provides a conductor and insulator.*

Step 3   Why do we need the copper and zinc? *Because they give and take electrons.*

Step 4   Why do we need the stack of four? *Because it makes a current.*

Step 5   Why do we need the aluminum foil? *Because it makes a circuit.*

Step 6   Why do we need the light? *To close the circuit.*

Chapter Five
Mental Models Blueprints of the Subject Matter (the Why)

1. Mental models are how the mind holds abstract information, i.e., information that has no sensory representation.

Each of us carries much abstract information around in our head every day. How do we do this? We carry it in mental models.

Just as a computer has a file manager to represent the structure of the software content, so does the human mind.

2. All subject areas or disciplines have their own blueprints or mental models.

In other words, they have their own way to structure information. For two people to communicate, there must be shared understanding.

This shared understanding comes from the study of subject matter. All occupations and all disciplines have their own mental models. To communicate about that occupation or discipline, an understanding of those mental models (abstract blueprints) is necessary.

3. Mental models tell us what is and is not important in the discipline. They help the mind sort.

4. Mental models often explain "the why" of things working the way they do.

5. Mental models tell the structure, purpose, or pattern.

That's how the mind sorts what is and is not important. The mind can only remember when it can "chunk" and sort information.

6. Mental models are held in the mind as stories, analogies, or two-dimensional drawings.

7. Mental models "collapse" the amount of time it takes to teach something.

8. Mental models of a discipline are contained within the structure of the curriculum.

To illustrate, math is about assigning order and value to the universe. We tend to assign order and value in one of three ways: numbers, space, or time. Fractions, for example, are a part of math curricula because fractions are the shared understanding of parts to whole of *space*. Decimals are studied because decimals tell parts to whole of *numbers*.

Lee Shulman found in his research that the difference between a good and excellent teacher is the depth of understanding the latter has of the discipline.

What are examples of mental models? Teachers have used them forever. But, too often, educators haven't found ways to share them with other teachers. They are the drawings, the verbal stories, the analogies that are given as part of instruction. As one teacher said, "It is how I explain it."

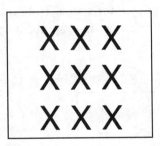

For example, in math a square number is a square number because it physically forms a square. Nine is a square number.

When the root of a square number is discussed, it's very easy to understand. The square root of 9 is 3 because no matter how you draw the lines you will always get 3. In 30 seconds you, the reader, now understand the concept of a square number and a square root.

A mental model to help understand the pattern in the multiplication of positive and negative numbers is found in this short pictorial story.

Multiplying positive and negative numbers

So, for example, the good guys (+) are coming to town (+), which is good. Translated to math, it would read: a positive number (+) multiplied by a positive number (+) yields a positive number (+), and so on.

+ Good guy - Bad guy	+ Coming to town - Leaving town	Get
+ + - -	+ - + -	+ - - +

9. There are generic mental models.

In addition to having mental models for subject areas or disciplines, there also are mental models for occupations. To be successful in work or school one must have four generic mental models. They are: space, time, part to whole, and formal register. These mental models are basic to all tasks.

Space

Space becomes important because your body operates in space. The mind must have a way to keep track of your body. One way is to touch everything. Another way is to assign a reference system to space using abstract words and drawings. For example, we talk about east, west, north, south, up, down, etc. Because math is about assigning order and value to the universe, we tend to do it directionally. Another illustration: We write small to large numbers from left to right. To read a map, one must have a reference for space. To find things in your office or desk, there must be an abstract referencing system for space.

One way to initially teach the concept of space is as follows …

On which side of the tip of the arrow is the dot?

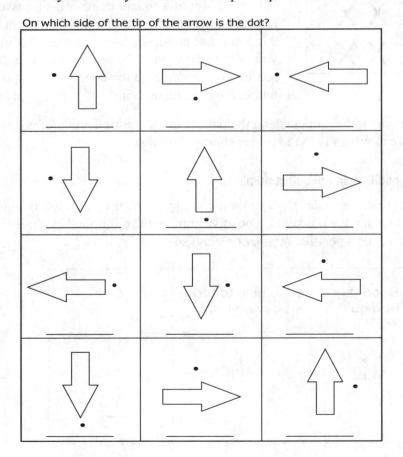

Time

A mental model for abstract time (days, minutes, weeks, hours, etc.) is crucial to success in school and work. One way to keep time is emotionally (how it feels), but another is abstractly with a calendar or a clock. Past, present, and future must be in the mental model because, without these, it isn't possible to sequence.

If you cannot sequence, then …	You cannot plan.
If you cannot plan, then …	You cannot predict.
If you cannot predict, then …	You cannot identify cause and effect.
If you cannot identify cause and effect, then …	You cannot identify consequence.
If you cannot identify consequence, then …	You cannot control impulsivity.
If you cannot control impulsivity, then …	You have an inclination toward criminal behavior.

Part to Whole

Part to whole means that one can identify the parts, as well as the whole. For example, chapters make a book. Words make a sentence. You cannot analyze anything unless you understand part to whole.

Formal Register

Because formal register is the language currency of work and school, it becomes crucial to have an understanding of it. Simple tools have been developed for Project Read® by Language Circle Enterprises, Inc. Some Project Read examples would look like this.

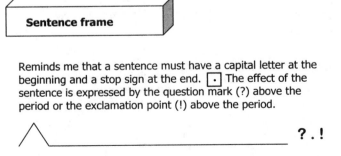

Sentence frame

Reminds me that a sentence must have a capital letter at the beginning and a stop sign at the end. [.] The effect of the sentence is expressed by the question mark (?) above the period or the exclamation point (!) above the period.

? . !

Bare-bones sentence

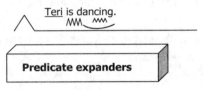

Teri danced.

A sentence must contain a subject and a predicate. The predicate can be an action predicate word.

The subject names a person, place, thing, or idea.

The action of the subject expresses physical or mental action, such as the following examples.

moved   kicked   thought   imagined

Or the predicate can be a bound predicate.

Teri is dancing.

Predicate expanders

The predicate can be expanded by expressing the

how   when   where   why   of the action.

Example:

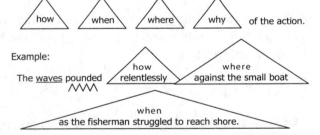

The waves pounded — how relentlessly — where against the small boat — when as the fisherman struggled to reach shore.

Predicate expanders:

How	= degree	adverbs (-ly ending, like or as, with/without)
When	= time	before, during, after, when, while, since
Where	= position	prepositional phrases (to, from, against, behind)
Why	= reason	because, to, so, for

(The opening sentence of each new paragraph should contain four expanders.)

Subject describers

Words that describe physical characteristics, personality, numbers, and ownership.

Source: Project Read® excerpt reprinted with permission of copyright holder, Language Circle Enterprises, Inc., and their creators Victoria Greene and Mary Lee Enfield, Ph.D. Contact: (800) 450-0343. www.projectread.com

10. Sketching is a technique that can be used in the classroom to identify each student's mental models.

Simply ask students to sketch (draw in two dimensions) what a word or concept means to them. If they cannot sketch anything, it probably is not inside their head.

Examples of Sketching:

Same   Same

Different

I saw an <u>isosceles triangle</u> in my refrigerator.

I often see a <u>scalene triangle</u> on Kenny's face.

My friend the <u>rhombus</u> is known as the "Dancing Wonder."

Vertices

TOASTIES

The Cereal of Winners!

I found four <u>vertices</u> on a box of cereal.

Using mental models makes both teaching *and* learning much easier.

Chapter Six
Content (the What)

The content—or "the what" of learning—is the part of instruction that is usually focused on. When the processes (the how) and the blueprints of the subject matter (the why) are direct-taught, the content tends to fall into place.

Just as a computer has files, so does the mind.

Content is organized by the constructs of the disciplines (or the mental models). Here are some examples.

Content	Purpose
Language Arts	Using structure and language to communicate
Math	Assigning order and value to the universe
Biology	Identifying living systems and relationships within and among those systems
Chemistry	Bonding
Algebra	Solving for the unknown through functions
Geometry	Using logic to order and assign values to form and space
Physics	Using matter and energy through math applications
Social Studies	Identifying patterns of people and governments over time
Earth Science	Identifying and predicting physical phenomena

For example, because Language Arts is about using structure and language to communicate, virtually all Language Arts curriculum at the secondary level is divided by genres, i.e., poetry, drama, grammar, etc. Those curriculum divisions end up reflecting the structures of the various disciplines.

Why Is This Important?

The structure of the discipline becomes significant because it identifies what is and is not important. The research indicates that instructional time is a huge factor in learning.

So the questions in this context are: Is it cute or does it count? Does the information presented/explored promote an understanding of the constructs and use of the discipline?

When teachers or other staff persons in a building are deciding "the what" of learning (namely, the content), it's very important to address the amount of time that will be given to learning that chunk of information.

Why is this important to the learner?

If adequate time is not spent on what is important—on what counts—the learner will not have learned enough to sort what is and isn't important in that subject area. Therefore, the learner will not be able to use the information in any competent manner.

Chapter Seven
Motivation for Learning

Probably the most frequently asked question by teachers is this: How can I get my students to want to learn? Dr. James Comer says it best:

> No significant learning occurs without
> a significant relationship [of mutual respect].
> —Comer

What does that mean? Quite simply (going back to the computer analogy), if there isn't someone at the keyboard or entering via voice, nothing happens.

And so it is with learning. It requires human interaction. At the heart of all learning are relationships.

How do you recognize relationships of mutual respect?

Generally, in relationships of mutual respect, three things are present:

Support, insistence, and high expectations

How do support, insistence, and high expectations show up in the classroom? Support becomes the direct-teaching of process and mental models; insistence is the motivation and persistence that comes from the relationship; and high expectations constitute the approach of "I know you can do it, and you will."

When there isn't mutual respect, one person becomes the taker, and the other becomes the giver. Eventually both parties come to dislike or even despise each other.

Many teachers believe that if they are nice to students, students will be nice to them. Not so. Mutual respect is taught, and mutual respect is learned.

All learning is double-coded

In the book *The Growth of the Mind and the Endangered Origins of Intelligence* (1997), Stanley Greenspan and Beryl Benderly say all learning is double-coded, both mentally and emotionally.

It's very important to understand the emotional underpinnings of learning. All learning is in essence emotional, and virtually all learning starts with significant relationships.

The primary motivator for the development of each stage is a significant relationship.

Six developmental stages in the learning process occur when relationships are supportive and nurturing.

These six stages are:

Stage	Explanation
1. Ability to attend	To pay attention to the sensory data in the environment. The earliest sensory data—touch, taste, sound, smell, sight—result from the interplay of relationships.
2. Ability to engage	To experience feelings—joy, pleasure, anger, emotional warmth, disappointment, assertiveness, etc. Intimacy and relating begin at this stage.
3. Ability to be intentional	To create and direct desire. To use non-verbals with purpose and intention. For example, I (as an infant) want you to hold me, so I hold up my arms, and you pick me up.
4. Ability to form complex interactive patterns	To connect and use one's own intentional signals in interaction with another to negotiate and to receive security, acceptance, and approval.
5. Ability to create images, symbols, and ideas	To give abstract mental constructs emotional meaning and significance. This is the basis of reasoning and emotion-based coping strategies. When images, symbols, and ideas don't have emotional investment, they are fragmented.
6. Ability to connect images, symbols, and ideas	To develop the infrastructure and architecture of the mind. To "image" one's own feelings and desires and to understand emotional signals from others.

In discussing the six stages, one overriding reality must be remembered:

Emotion organizes experience and behavior.

STAGE ONE: Ability to Attend

At the very beginning of learning, the infant must sort out what the sensations are and what they mean. Those earliest sensations almost always come through relationships. Someone is holding the child. Someone is feeding the child. The child must stay calm enough to notice the sensations he/she is experiencing. The child must find patterns in the sensations. From these patterns come security and order. From this security and order comes the ability to regulate the mind.

STAGE TWO: Ability to Engage

When young children can attend to the surroundings and actions of the people who are their caretakers, they become engaged. The caretaker smiles, and they smile. In short, the child mirrors the expressions of the caretaker.

Greenspan and Benderly say it well:

> Without some degree of this ecstatic wooing by at least one adult
> who adores her, a child may never know the powerful intoxication
> of human closeness, never abandon herself to the magnetic pull
> of human relationships ... Whether because her nervous system
> is unable to sustain the sensations of early love or her caregiver
> is unable to convey them, such a child is at risk of becoming self-
> absorbed or an unfeeling, self-centered, aggressive individual who
> can inflict injury without qualm or remorse (p. 51).

STAGE THREE: Ability to Be Intentional

At this preverbal stage, a purposeful exchange of signals and responses is used to elicit what the child desires. In this stage the child learns to distinguish between you and me, i.e., from self and other. Boundaries are established. When responses are inappropriate, the child becomes disorganized and eventually loses interest. For example, if a person is talking to someone with a "poker face," eventually the conversation becomes fragmented; the speaker loses interest and gives up.
Interactions become purposeful, and "willful reciprocity" occurs, which also signals a higher developmental level of the central nervous system.

Desires or wishes are tied to actions, not ideas. Desires or wishes also are linked to subjective needs, not objective needs.

STAGE FOUR: Ability to Form Complex Interactive Patterns

At this stage, purpose and interaction become the focus. The child learns to communicate across space, i.e., I am not touching my caregiver. She is in the next room, but I know she is there. This gives a strong sense of emotional security. Imitation is a part of this stage. The child mimics what the adult does. At this stage, a child's emotions are attached to patterns of response. Attitudes and values start here. Meaning is established from patterns of desire, expectation, and intention.

STAGE FIVE: Ability to Create Images, Symbols, and Ideas

Here the child experiences himself/herself in images—and not just in feelings, physical sensations, and behavior. It's important to note that children who haven't mastered the previous stages tend to operate in a concrete, rote manner. At this point in time, individuals can try out behaviors and actions inside their head without actually doing them.

STAGE SIX: Ability to Connect Images, Symbols, and Ideas

At this stage, the individual connects the images, symbols, and ideas that were developed in Stage Five to an architecture in which abstractions are emotionally embedded and interwoven. The individual is able to view emotions abstractly and work through them both at a feeling level and a cognitive one. Sorting occurs both cognitively and through emotion.

Learning the abstract

Because schools and the work setting operate at stages five and six, many individuals are new learners to the abstract. There is a process that a person goes through when he/she is learning something new. That process was discussed in Chapter Two.

How does a student know that a teacher has respect for him/her?

Two pieces of research are particularly instructive. One is from Stephen Covey, and the other is research by TESA (Teacher Expectations and Student Achievement).

Covey states that relationships of mutual respect are like bank accounts. You make emotional deposits to those relationships, and you make emotional withdrawals from the relationships. When the withdrawals are substantially greater than the deposits, the relationship is soon broken.

Deposits	Withdrawals
Seek first to understand	Seek first to be understood
Keeping promises	Breaking promises
Kindnesses, courtesies	Unkindnesses, discourtesies
Clarifying expectations	Violating expectations
Loyalty to the absent	Disloyalty, duplicity
Apologies	Pride, conceit, arrogance
Open to feedback	Rejecting feedback

Chart adapted from *The 7 Habits of Highly Effective People* (1989) by Stephen Covey

The TESA research describes 15 behaviors that teachers use with students when there is mutual respect between teacher and student. The study found that when these behaviors are used with all students, learning jumps dramatically.

Here are the 15 behaviors of mutual respect:

1. Calls on everyone in the room equitably.
2. Provides individual help.
3. Gives "wait time" (allows student enough time to answer).
4. Asks questions to give the student clues about the answer.
5. Asks questions that require more thought.
6. Tells students whether their answers are right or wrong.
7. Gives specific praise.
8. Gives reasons for praise.
9. Listens.
10. Accepts the feelings of the student.
11. Gets within an arm's reach of each student each day.
12. Is courteous to students.
13. Shows personal interest and gives compliments.
14. Touches students (appropriately).
15. Desists (does not call attention to every misbehavior).

TESA copyright is held by Los Angeles Board of Education.

When we asked students in our research how they knew the teacher had respect for them, repeatedly we heard the following:

- The teacher calls me by my name, not "Hey you."
- The teacher answers my questions.
- The teacher cares about me.
- The teacher talks to me respectfully.
- The teacher notices me and says hi.
- The teacher helps me when I need help.

What does this mean in practice?

1. If a student and teacher don't have a relationship of mutual respect, the learning will be significantly reduced and, for some students, it won't occur at all.

2. If a student and teacher don't like each other—or even come to despise each other—forget about significant positive learning. If mutual respect is present, that can compensate for the dislike.

Chapter Eight
Difficult Students, Difficult Classrooms

These questions inevitably come up:

What do I do when more than 40% of the students are difficult? How can learning take place with so many difficult students?

What do I do with a student who habitually breaks relationships with adults?

What do I do with the student who has biochemical issues? Has neurological damage?

To use our analogy to the computer, what do I do when the computer freezes? When the hard drive crashes? When the software doesn't do what it's supposed to?

As you know, just like the computer, not everything can be "fixed." But what we do know are ways to minimize the interruptions and address the learning.

Some suggestions:

1. **Always direct-teach the mental models of the content you are teaching.** Fewer discipline problems occur when students are learning.

2. **Direct-teach the processes and procedures you want to occur in your classroom.** Have students practice those. Remember that 95% of discipline problems in classrooms occur the first five and last five minutes of class. Harry Wong, in his book *The First Day of School* (1998), has a number of excellent suggestions.

3. **Build relationships of mutual respect with the "troublemakers."** Ninety percent of discipline problems come from 10% of the students. Humor (not sarcasm) is one of the best tools for developing mutual respect; students particularly look to see if you have a sense of humor about yourself. Furthermore, students won't respect you unless you are personally strong. So if you show fear, you won't be respected.

4. **Tightly structure tasks by time and procedure.** Do so by giving students the steps—in writing—necessary to do the task, noting specific time frames in which to do it. Then have students work in pairs where they talk to each other while doing the task. More learning usually occurs collaboratively than alone. Typically students are going to talk anyway, so have them talk about their learning. The pair stays together for the duration of that task. And if for some reason the student doesn't like you, he/she may like the person with whom he/she is working.

5. **Use a choice/consequence approach to discipline.** In other words, if a student "messes up" after having heard clear expectations of appropriate behavior, simply express your regret that he/she made a poor choice—and quickly and matter-of-factly establish a natural consequence for the student's misstep.

6. **Have students do a simple planning/goal-setting task each day around their work.** It will significantly lessen impulsivity.

7. **Use a contract system to address individual needs, as well as address different times of finishing work.** I did this with ninth-graders. One day a week the students worked independently; it was 20% of their grade. At the beginning of each grading period, I gave them a list of activities they could choose from. Each activity had points assigned to it, and the student was to identify 100 points toward which he/she would work. The students divided the activities by week and identified what they would finish each week. If a student was particularly weak in a certain area, I would tell him/her to get some points from that area. If a student finished early, I would say, "Go work on your contract." That way students were always busy and always learning.

8. **Separate students who must be separated.** Talk to your administrator about any student combinations that are problematic together and arrange to have them placed in different classrooms.

Conclusion

Learning involves both the physical (the brain) and the environmental influences (the mind). For students who haven't had much exposure to the abstract or to representational systems, they are new learners to the abstract. As new learners, they need three things: the how, the why, and the what. Then they can begin patterning information in order to use it in the long term. Since patterns seem to be related to the structure of the subject matter, it's important to teach mental models.

Because virtually all learning involves emotion, relationships of mutual respect energize, at the most basic level, the motivation to learn.

To close with our computer analogy, the hardware (the brain) needs the software (the mind) to function. Nothing functions without the person at the keyboard or the individual giving voice commands—just as next to nothing in learning occurs without relationships of mutual respect.

Bibliography

Achievement in America 2000. (2001). Retrieved October 2007 from http://www.edtrust.org

Allee, V. (1997). *The knowledge evolution: Building organizational intelligence.* Newton, MA: Butterworth-Heinemann.

Anderson, J. R. (1996). *The architecture of cognition.* Mahwah, NJ: Erlbaum.

Berliner, D. C. (1988, October). *Implications of studies of expertise in pedagogy for teacher education and evaluation.* Paper presented at Educational Testing Service Invitational Conference on New Directions for Teacher Assessment, New York.

Biemiller, A. (2000). Vocabulary: The missing link between phonics and comprehension. *Perspectives, 26*(4), 26–30.

Bloom, B. (1976). *Human characteristics and school learning.* New York: McGraw-Hill.

Brandt, R. (1988). On assessment of teaching: A conversation with Lee Shulman. *Educational Leadership, 46*(3), 42–46.

Bransford, J. D., Brown, A. L., & Cocking, R. R. (Eds.). (1999). *How people learn: Brain, mind, experience and school.* Washington, DC: National Academy Press.

Caine, R. N., & Caine, G. (1991). *Making connections: Teaching and the human brain.* Alexandria, VA: Association for Supervision and Curriculum Development.

Caine, R. N., & Caine, G. (1997). *Education on the edge of possibility.* Alexandria, VA: Association for Supervision and Curriculum Development.

Coles, R. (1989). *The call of stories: Teaching and the moral imagination.* Boston: Houghton Mifflin.

Costa, A., & Garmston, R. (1986). *The art of cognitive coaching: Supervision for intelligent teaching.* Sacramento, CA: California State University Press.

Covey, S. R. (1989). *The 7 habits of highly effective people: Powerful lessons in personal change.* New York: Free Press.

Crowell, S. (1989). A new way of thinking: The challenge of the future. Educational *Leadership, 7*(1), 60–63.

Damasio, A. R. (1994). *Descartes' error: Emotion, reason, and the human brain.* New York: G. P. Putnam's Sons.

DeSoto, H. (2000). *The mystery of capital.* New York: Basic Books.

Edvinsson, L., & Malone, M. S. (1997). *Intellectual capital: Realizing your company's true value by finding its hidden brainpower.* New York: HarperCollins.

Egan, K. (1986). *Teaching as story telling.* Chicago: University of Chicago Press.

Egan, K. (1989). Memory, imagination, and learning: Connected by the story. *Phi Delta Kappan, 70*(6), 455–459.

Fassler, D. G., & Dumas, L. S. (1997). *Help me, I'm sad.* New York: Penguin.

Feuerstein, R., Rand, Y., Hoffman, M., & Miller, R. (1980). *Instrumental enrichment: An intervention program for cognitive modifiability.* Baltimore: University Park Press.

Freire, P. (2000). *Pedagogy of the oppressed: 30th anniversary edition.* New York: Continuum International Publishing Group.

Gladwell, M. (2000). *The tipping point: How little things make a big difference.* New York: Little, Brown.

Glickman, C. D. (1990). *Supervision of instruction: A developmental approach* (2nd ed.). Boston: Allyn & Bacon.

Goleman, D. (1995). *Emotional intelligence: Why it can matter more than IQ.* New York: Bantam Books.

Good, T. L., & Brophy, J. E. (1991). *Looking in classrooms* (5th ed.). New York: HarperCollins.

Greene, V. E., & Enfield, M. L. (2004). *Framing your thoughts: Written expression* (Rev. ed.). Bloomington, MN: Language Circle Enterprises.

Greenspan, S. I., & Benderly, B. L. (1997). *The growth of the mind and the endangered origins of intelligence.* Reading, MA: Perseus Books.

Harrison, L. E., & Huntington, S. P. (Eds.). (2000). *Culture matters: How values shape human progress.* New York: Basic Books.

Hart, B., & Risley, T. R. (1995). *Meaningful differences in the everyday experience of young American children.* Baltimore: Paul H. Brookes.

Hock, D. (1999). *Birth of the chaordic age.* San Francisco: Berrett-Koehler.

Howard, P. J. (2000). *The owner's manual for the brain* (2nd ed.). Austin, TX: Bard Press.

Hunter, M. (1982). *Mastery teaching.* El Segundo, CA: TIP Publications.

Idol, L., & Jones, B. F. (Eds.). (1991). *Educational values and cognitive instruction: Implications for reform.* Mahwah, NJ: Erlbaum.

Jensen, E. (1994). *The learning brain.* Del Mar, CA: Turning Point.

Jones, B. F., Pierce, J., & Hunter, B. (1988). Teaching students to construct graphic representations. *Educational Leadership, 46*(4), 20–25.

Jordan, H., Mendro, R., & Weerasinghe, D. (1997, July). *Teacher effects on longitudinal student achievement: A report on research in progress.* Retrieved June 16, 2009, from http://www.dallasisd.org/inside_disd/depts/evalacct/research/articles/Jordan-Teacher-Effects-on-Longitudinal-Student-Achievement-1997.pdf

Joyce, B., & Showers, B. (1988). *Student achievement through staff development.* New York: Longman.

Joyce, B., & Weil, M. (1986). *Models of teaching* (3rd ed.). Boston: Allyn & Bacon.

Marzano, R. J., & Arredondo, D. (1986). *Tactics for thinking.* Aurora, CO: Mid-Continent Regional Educational Laboratory.

McCarthy, B. (1996). *About learning.* Barrington, IL: Excel.

McTighe, J., & Lyman, F. T., Jr. (1988). Cueing thinking in the classroom: The promise of theory-embedded tools. *Educational Leadership, 45*(7), 18–24.

O'Dell, C., & Grayson, J. C., Jr., with Essaides, N. (1998). *If only we knew what we know.* New York: Free Press.

Oshry, B. (1995). Seeing systems: *Unlocking the mysteries of organizational life.* San Francisco: Berrett-Koehler.

Palincsar, A. S., & Brown, A. L. (1984). The reciprocal teaching of comprehension-fostering and comprehension-monitoring activities. *Cognition and Instruction, 1*(2), 117–175.

Porter, A. C., & Brophy, J. (1988). Synthesis of research on good teaching: Insights from the work of the Institute for Research on Teaching. *Educational Leadership, 45*(8), 74–85.

Resnick, L. B., & Klopfer, L. (Eds.). (1989). *Toward the thinking curriculum: Current cognitive research.* Alexandria, VA: Association for Supervision and Curriculum Development.

Ridley, M. (2000). *Genome: The autobiography of a species in 23 chapters.* New York: HarperCollins.

Rieber, R. W. (Ed.). (1997). *The collected works of L. S. Vygotsky: Vol. 4. The history of the development of higher mental functions.* New York: Plenum Press.

Rosenholtz, S. J. (1989). *Teachers' workplace: The social organization of schools.* New York: Longman.

Sanders, W. L., & Rivers, J. C. (1996). Cumulative and residual effects of teachers on future student academic achievement. Retrieved May 21, 2009, from http://www.mccsc. edu/~curriculum/cumulative%20and%20residual%20effects%20of%20teachers.pdf

Sapolsky, R. M. (1998). *Why zebras don't get ulcers.* New York: W. H. Freeman.

Senge, P., McCabe, N. H. C., Lucas, T., Kleiner, A., Dutton, J., & Smith, B. (2000). *Schools that learn: A fifth discipline fieldbook for educators, parents, and everyone who cares about education.* New York: Broadway Business.

Senge, P., Ross, R., Smith, B., Roberts, C., & Kleiner, A. (1994). *The fifth discipline fieldbook: Strategies and tools for building a learning organization.* New York: Doubleday-Currency.

Sharron, H., & Coulter, M. (2004). *Changing children's minds: Feuerstein's revolution in the teaching of intelligence.* Highlands, TX: aha! Process.

Shulman, L. S. (1987). Assessment for teaching: An initiative for the profession. *Phi Delta Kappan, 69*(1), 38–44.

Shulman, L. S. (1988). A union of insufficiencies: Strategies for teacher assessment in a period of educational reform. *Educational Leadership, 46*(3), 36–41.

Stewart, T. A. (1997). *Intellectual capital: The new wealth of organizations.* New York: Doubleday-Currency.

Sveiby, K. E. (1997). *The new organizational wealth: Managing and measuring knowledge-based assets.* San Francisco: Berrett-Koehler.

Walberg, H. J. (1990). Productive teaching and instruction: Assessing the knowledge base. *Phi Delta Kappan, 71*(6), 470–478.

Watson, B., & Konicek, R. (1990). Teaching for conceptual change: Confronting children's experience. *Phi Delta Kappan, 71*(9), 680–685.

Wiggins, G., & McTighe, J. (1998). *Understanding by design.* Alexandria, VA: Association for Supervision and Curriculum Development.

Wilson, E. O. (1998). *Consilience: The unity of knowledge.* New York: Alfred A. Knopf.

Wise, A. (1995). *The high performance mind: Mastering brainwaves for insight, healing, and creativity.* New York: Tarcher/Putnam.

Wong, H. K., & Wong, R. T. (1998). *The first day of school: How to be an effective teacher* (Rev. ed.). Mountainview, CA: Author.

Appendix C

Research on the Brains of Children in Poverty Using EEG Scans

University of California, Berkeley, did research using EEG scans to compare the brains of poor children ages 9 and 10 with middle-class children (*Journal of Cognitive Neuroscience,* 2009). Mark Kishiyama, lead researcher, indicated that the brain patterns in children from poverty were quite similar to adults who have had strokes and therefore have lesions in their prefrontal cortex. The study asked the children to push a button when a tilted triangle appeared. Most low-income children had difficulty identifying the tilted triangle and blocking out the distractions, which is a key function of the prefrontal cortex. The study found that these effects are reversible but need highly intensive interventions.

What additional studies have found is that most low-income children have these disparities in neurocognitive development: language, memory ability, working memory, and executive function (Farah et al., 2006). However, visual and spatial cognitive ability did not differ significantly from middle-class children.

What does the prefrontal part of the brain do? It is the site of the executive function and working memory. Farah et al. (2006) define the prefrontal executive system as doing three things: (1) working memory ("hold information 'online' and maintain it over an interval and manipulate it"), (2) cognitive control ("resist the routine or most easily available response in favor of a more task-appropriate response"), and (3) reward processing ("regulating our responses in the face of rewarding stimuli … resisting the immediate pull of an attractive stimulus to maximize more long-term gains"). What the executive system does is impact behavioral self-regulation, adult intelligence, and problem-solving ability (Davis et al., 2002; Duncan et al., 1995; Engle et al., 1999; Gray et al., 2003).

Furthermore, research at Cornell University researched 339 poor children in upstate rural New York from 1997 to 2006. Ninety-seven percent of these children were Caucasian. "The findings suggest that poverty, over the course of childhood and early adolescence increases allostatic load, and this dysregulation, in turn, explains some of the subsequent deficits in working memory four years later" (Schamberg, 2008). The allostatic load, as noted previously, is the adjustments of the human body's neuroendocrine, nervous, cardiovascular, metabolic, and immune systems to the demands of the environment. The more stressful the environment, the greater the dysregulation of the system. Because poverty environments are so stressful and unstable, the constant adjustments impact working memory by increasing the allostatic load. The greater the allostatic load, the less the working memory system functions—particularly for non-survival tasks.

Examples of working memory/executive function in the classroom would include the following:

- Giving multiple directions at once and the student being unable to follow them
- Planning
- Task completion
- Behavioral self-regulation
- Ability to identify options

In short, it is most of the input strategies as identified by Feuerstein.

What Does This Mean in Practice?

1. We have to teach students to plan (executive function).
2. Visual images can be used to translate to new ideas using mental models. Visual imaging capability is not impacted by poverty.
3. Direct-teach the input strategies through games and classroom activities.
4. Vocabulary acquisition can be taught by using sketching, a visual activity.
5. Procedural processes using step sheets can be taught to develop executive function.
6. Mediate all learning by teaching the what (vocabulary), the why (meaning and relevance), and the how (the process: executive function).
7. Have students make a plan for their behavior, then give them rewards based upon their ability to meet their own plan. Each plan includes an academic goal and a behavioral goal.
8. Details (executive function) are assisted through visuals and step sheets.
9. Well-organized, non-chaotic schools and classrooms reduce allostatic load. Classroom management is a must because it allows working memory to function better.
10. Use visuals to translate from the sensory to the abstract representational world of paper, ideas, number, letter, drawings, etc.
11. Question making is a key function in problem solving (executive function). Teach students to develop their own multiple-choice questions.

Appendix D

What Does the Research Say About Intergenerational Transfer of Knowledge?

Intergenerational transfer of knowledge has been documented in the research. A study done in Australia followed more than 8,500 children for 14 years—from the first clinic visit for pregnancy to age 14 (Najman et al., 2004). The study found that the occupational status of the child's maternal grandfather independently predicted the child's verbal comprehension levels at age 5 and the nonverbal reasoning scores at age 14.

Why would the maternal grandfather's occupation be so predictive? The occupation would tell you the level of stability in the household and be a predictor of the level of education in the family. Because the mother is so instrumental in the early nurturing of the child and the vocabulary that the child hears, it would follow that the mother's access to knowledge and vocabulary would be based on her own childhood experiences; thus the maternal grandfather's occupation would be instrumental in predicting achievement. A U.S. study by Hart and Risley (1995) found that children ages 1–4 in professional households are exposed to far more words than children ages 1–4 in poverty households.

It would be very easy for educators to now dismiss any attempt to educate children by saying, in effect, "Well, it depends on what their grandfather did." But someone taught the grandfather, and someone taught the mother. Therefore, current educators can impact two generations through the students they have in their classrooms and through parent training.

The key issues here are language acquisition and the development of the prefrontal/executive functions of the brain.

What Does This Mean in Practice?

1. You cannot teach what you do not know. Parent training for parents in poverty should be about human capacity development of the adult—i.e., giving adults language to talk about their own experience, having adults develop their own future story, teaching adults to plan and ask questions, teaching them how to analyze and leverage their own resources, and teaching them to build their own literacy base by recording their personal stories (see *Getting Ahead in a Just-Gettin'-By World*: www.ahaprocess.com).

2. To decrease allostatic load in adults, it is important to give them the tools—planning, resource analysis, problem solving, etc.—that will make their lives less stressful. These are all tools that are part of prefrontal/executive function. If the adult came from generational poverty, chances are these brain functions are not well developed for him/her as well.

Appendix E

Levels of Processing

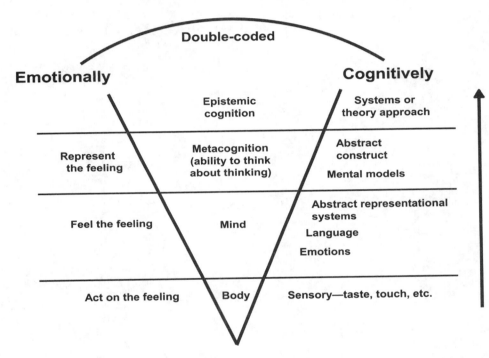

This diagram shows what separates the body, the mind, the ability to think, and the ability to analyze. What separates the body from the mind are emotions; what separates the mind from metacognition (ability to think) are mental models or abstract representations; what separates metacognition (ability to think) from epistemic cognition is the ability to analyze the framework or the theoretical structure of one's thinking.

Payne (2005) elaborates using the example of a welder. At the body level, he or she welds. This level involves the senses—vision and touch, in this example—and the person acts on his or her senses/feelings. At the next level, the mind, the welder can talk about welding and feel the feeling that comes with a job well done. At the mind level, the welder uses language to express feelings and thoughts, and at metacognition he or she welds against a blueprint. At the level of epistemic cognition, the welder can assess blueprints for structural strength. A systems approach or theory approach is involved.

In the research on "situated learning" (Lave and Wenger, 1991), the authors reveal "how different schooling is from the activities and culture that give meaning and purpose to what students learn elsewhere." Lave and Wenger focus on the behavior of JPFs (just plain folks) and record that the ways they learn are quite distinct from what students are asked to do (Brown, Collins, and Duguid, 1989).

	Just plain folks	Student	Practicing individual or apprentice
Reason with	Casual stories	Laws	Casual models
Act on	Situations	Symbols	Conceptual situations
Resolve	Emergent problems and dilemmas	Well-defined problems	Ill-defined problems
Produce	Negotiable meaning and socially constructed understanding	Fixed meaning and immutable concepts	Negotiable meaning and socially constructed understanding

Source: "Situated Cognition and the Culture of Learning" by John Seely Brown, Allan Collins, and Paul Duguid. *Educational Researcher.* Vol. 18, No. 1. January-February 1989. pp. 32–42.

Situated-learning research further indicates that the learning occurs in a context within a set of relationships and cultural norms. Lave and Wenger state that for newcomers to the group "the purpose is not to learn *from* talk as a substitute for legitimate peripheral participation; it is to learn *to* talk as a key to legitimate peripheral participation" (1991, pages 108–109). Wenger (1999, pages 73–84) adds that this participation creates a *shared repertoire* of communal resources, which he defines as routines, behaviors, vocabulary, etc.

In other words, hidden rules come out of the environment and are situated in context, culture, and relationships. Furthermore, in the situated-learning approach, learning is always contextualized and relationship-based. School learning, on the other hand, is decontextualized and abstract (on paper, devoid of immediate relationships, using generalized representations).

Rubric for Analysis of Point of View
(highlight the indicators that apply to the story)

SELECTED STORY	USE OF DIALOGUE	USE OF STORY STRUCTURE	USE OF WORD CHOICE	USE OF CHARACTER DEVELOPMENT	PLOT OR CHARACTER OMISSIONS	TELLER
Story A	Dialogue used to develop plot Dialogue used to develop character (i.e., indicate intelligence) Dialogue used to convey feelings	Story starts in middle and uses flashbacks Story uses chronological order (in time) Story is story within story Story is stream of consciousness Episodic story structure (series of situations involving one character)	Words often used to convey feelings Words used to convey action Words used to describe Word choice is angry, happy, bitter, ___ Use of pronouns (I, we, she)	Main character developed through interactions with other characters Main character developed through dialogue about main character Main character developed through situations Main character developed through conflicts Main character developed through absence	What is *not* in dialogue about main character Key scenes that are only referenced or omitted Accuracy of character comments about self or others Story told by only one person	Told in third person Told in first person Told through dreams Told as retelling Told in present tense Told in past tense
Story B	Dialogue used to develop plot Dialogue used to develop character (i.e., indicate intelligence) Dialogue used to convey feelings	Story starts in middle and uses flashbacks Story uses chronological order (in time) Story is story within story Story is stream of consciousness Episodic story structure (series of situations involving one character)	Words often used to convey feelings Words used to convey action Words used to describe Word choice is angry, happy, bitter, ___ Use of pronouns (I, we, she)	Main character developed through interactions with other characters Main character developed through dialogue about main character Main character developed through situations Main character developed through conflicts Main character developed through absence	What is *not* in dialogue about main character Key scenes that are only referenced or omitted Accuracy of character comments about self or others Story told by only one person	Told in third person Told in first person Told through dreams Told as retelling Told in present tense Told in past tense

Bibliography

Abernathy, C. (2003). Training materials for Understanding Learning workshop.

Ackerman, B. P., & Brown, E. D. (2010). Physical and psychosocial turmoil in the home and cognitive development. In G. W. Evans & T. D. Wachs (Eds.), *Chaos and children's development: Levels of analysis and mechanisms,* 35–48. Washington, DC: American Psychological Association.

Adelabu, D. H. (2006). Future outlook among African American students. *Academic Exchange Quarterly, 10*(2), 44–50.

Adelabu, D. H. (2008). Future time perspective, hope, and ethnic identity among African American adolescents. *Urban Education, 43*(3), 347–360.

Adger, C. (1994). *Enhancing the delivery of services to black special education American Psychiatric Association students from non-standard English backgrounds.* ERIC (Education Resources Information Center) Document Reproduction Service No. ED370377.

Agran, M., Blanchard, C., Wehmeyer, M., & Hughes, C. (2001). Teaching students to self-regulate their behavior: The differential effects of student- vs. teacher-delivered reinforcement. *Research in Developmental Disabilities, 22*(4), 319–332.

Alderfer, C. P. (1972). *Existence, relatedness, and growth.* New York, NY: Free Press.

Allee, V. (1997). *The knowledge evolution: Building organizational intelligence.* Newton, MA: Butterworth-Heinemann.

Allen, J. (2004). *Tools for teaching content literacy.* Portland, ME: Stenhouse.

American Psychiatric Association. (1994). *Diagnostic and statistical manual of mental disorders: DSM-4* (4th ed.). Washington, DC: Author.

American Psychiatric Association. (2013). *Diagnostic and statistical manual of mental disorders: DSM-5* (5th ed.). Washington, DC: Author.

Amyx, D., & Bristow, D. (2004). Future time orientation and student expectations: An empirical investigation. *Delta Pi Epsilon Journal, 46*(1), 1–17.

Anderson, J. R. (1996). *The architecture of cognition.* Mahwah, NJ: Erlbaum.

Andrade, H. G. (1999a). The role of instructional rubrics and self-assessment in learning to write: A smorgasbord of findings. ERIC Document Reproduction Service No. ED431029.

Andrade, H. G. (1999b). Student self-assessment: At the intersection of metacognition and authentic assessment. ERIC Document Reproduction Service No. ED431030.

Andrade, H. L., Du, Y., & Wang, X. (2008). Putting rubrics to the test: The effect of a model, criteria generation, and rubric-referenced self-assessment on elementary school students' writing. *Educational Measurement, 27*(2), 3–13.

Andreas, S., & Faulkner, C. (Eds.). (1994). *NLP: The new technology of achievement*. New York, NY: William Morrow.

Andriessen, I., Lens, W., & Phalet, K. (2004). How future goals enhance motivation and learning in multicultural classrooms. *Educational Psychology Review, 16*(1), 59–89.

Antonakis, J. (2004). On why 'emotional intelligence' will not predict leadership effectiveness beyond IQ or the 'big five': An extension and rejoinder. *Organizational Analysis, 12*(2), 171–182.

Apperly, I. A., Williams, E., & Williams, J. (2004). Three- to four-year-olds' recognition that symbols have a stable meaning: Pictures are understood before written words. *Child Development, 75*(5), 1510–1522.

April, A. (2001). Toward a finer description of the connection between arts education and student achievement. *Arts Education Policy Review, 102*(5), 25–26.

Aronoff, M. (1994). *Morphology by itself: Stems and inflectional classes* (No. 22). Cambridge, MA: MIT Press.

The arts and educational reform: Ideas for schools and communities. (1994). ERIC Document Reproduction Service No. ED365621.

Asbury, C., & Rich, B. (Eds.). (2008). *Learning, arts and the brain: The Dana Consortium report on arts and cognition*. New York, NY: Dana Foundation.

Ashkanasy, N. M., & Dasborough, M. T. (2003). Emotional awareness and emotional intelligence in leadership teaching. *Journal of Education for Business, 79*(1), 18–22.

Assisting students struggling with reading: Response to intervention (RTI) and multi-tier intervention in the primary grades. (2009). Retrieved from https://ies.ed.gov/ncee/wwc/Docs/PracticeGuide/rti_reading_pg_021809.pdf

Association for Career and Technical Education. (2017). Home. Retrieved from https://www.acteonline.org

Ausubel, D. P., Novak, J. D., & Hanesian, H. (1968). *Educational psychology: A cognitive view*. New York, NY: Holt, Rinehart & Winston.

Ausubel, D. P., & Youssef, M. (1963). Role of discriminability in meaningful parallel learning. *Journal of Educational Psychology, 54*, 331–336.

Awbrey, S. M. (2005). General education reform as organizational change: Integrating cultural and structural change. *The Journal of General Education, 54*(1), 1–21.

Baddeley, A., & Hitch, G. J. (2010). Working memory. *Scholarpedia, 5*(2), 3015.

Bagby, J. H., Rudd, L. C., & Woods, M. (2005). The effects of socioeconomic diversity on the language, cognitive and social-emotional development of children from low-income backgrounds. *Early Child Development and Care, 175*(5), 395–405.

Baghban, M. (2007). Scribbles, labels, and stories: The role of drawing in the development of writing. *Young Children, 62*(1), 20–26.

Bailey, M. (1995). *The impact of integrating visuals in an elementary creative writing process*. ERIC Document Reproduction Service No. ED391492.

Bailey, R., Armour, K., Kirk, D., Jess, M., Pickup, I., & Sandford, R. (2009). The educational benefits claimed for physical education and school sport: An academic review. *Research Papers in Education, 24*(1), 1–27.

Bakunas, B., & Holley, W. (2004). Teaching organizational skills. *Clearing House, 77*(3), 92–97.

Bandura, A. (1991). Social theory of self-regulation. *Organizational Behavior and Human Decision Processes, 50,* 248–287.

Bandura, A. (1997). *Self-efficacy: The exercise of control.* New York, NY: Freeman.

Bandura, A., & Cervone, D. (1983). Self-evaluation and self-efficacy mechanisms governing the motivational effects of goal systems. *Journal of Personality and Social Psychology, 45*(5), 1017–1028. Retrieved from https://web.stanford.edu/dept/psychology/bandura/pajares/Bandura1983JPSP.pdf

Bandura, A., & Wood, R. E. (1989). Effect of perceived controllability and performance standards on self-regulation of complex decision-making. *Journal of Personality and Social Psychology, 56,* 805–814.

Barbuto, J. E., & Burbach, M. E. (2006). The emotional intelligence of transformational leaders: A field study of elected officials. *The Journal of Social Psychology, 146*(1), 51–64.

Barley, Z., & Beesley, A. D. (2007). Rural school success: What can we learn? *Journal of Research in Rural Education, 22*(1), 1–16.

Barnett, R. C., Gareis, K. C., James, J. B., & Steele, J. (2001). *Planning ahead: College seniors' concerns about work-family conflict.* ERIC Document Reproduction Service No. ED457506.

Barrouillet, P., Bernardin, S., & Camos, V. (2004). Time constraints and resource sharing in adults' working memory spans. *Journal of Experimental Psychology 133,* 83–100.

Barter, B. (2007). Communities in schools: A Newfoundland school and community outreach in need of stability. *Alberta Journal of Educational Research, 53*(4), 359–372.

Basics of nonviolent communication (NVC). (2009). PuddleDancer Press. Retrieved from http://www.nonviolentcommunication.com/aboutnvc/aboutnvc.htm

Bassuk, E. L., Buckner, J. C., Weinreb, L. F., Browne, A., Bassuk, S., Dawson, R., & Perloff, J. N. (1997). Homelessness in female-headed families: Childhood and adult risk and protective factors. *American Journal of Public Health, 87*(2), 241–248.

Baumeister, R. F., Hutton, D. G., & Cairns, K. J. (1990). Negative effects of praise on skilled performance. *Basic and Applied Social Psychology, 11*(2), 131–149.

Baydar, N., Brooks-Gunn, J., & Furstenberg Jr., F. F. (1993). Early warning signs of functional illiteracy: Predictors in childhood and adolescence. *Child Development 64*(3), 815–829.

Beatham, M. D. (2009). Tools of inquiry: Separating tool and task to promote true learning. *Journal of Educational Technology Systems, 37*(1), 61–70.

Beck, I. L., McKeown, M. G., & Kucan, L. (2002). *Bringing words to life: Robust vocabulary instruction.* New York, NY: Guilford Press.

Becker, K. A., Krodel, K. M., & Tucker, B. H. (2009). *Understanding and engaging under-resourced college students: A fresh look at economic class and its influence on teaching and learning in higher education.* Highlands, TX: aha! Process.

Beers, K. (2003). *When kids can't read: What teachers can do.* Portsmouth, NH: Heinemann.

Beeson, E., & Strange, M. (2003). Why rural matters: The continuing need for every state to take action on rural education. *Journal of Research in Rural Education, 18*(1), 3–16.

Begley, S. (2007). *Train your mind, change your brain: How a new science reveals our extraordinary potential to transform ourselves.* New York, NY: Ballantine Books.

Behrmann, M., & Jerome, M. K. (2002). Assistive technology for students with mild disabilities: Update 2002. ERIC Document Reproduction Service No. ED463595.

Berliner, D. C. (1988, October). Implications of studies of expertise in pedagogy for teacher education and evaluation. Paper presented at Educational Testing Service Invitational Conference on New Directions for Teacher Assessment, New York, NY.

Berne, E. (1996). *Games people play: The basic handbook of transactional analysis.* New York, NY: Ballantine Books.

Berzonsky, M. D., Branje, S. J. T., & Meeus, W. (2007). Identity-processing style, psychosocial resources, and adolescents' perceptions of parent-adolescent relations. *Journal of Early Adolescence, 27*(3), 324–345.

Bianchi, A. J., & Lancianese, D. A. (2005). No child left behind? Role/identity development of the 'good student.' *International Journal of Educational Policy, Research, and Practice, 6*(1), 3–29.

Biemiller, A. (2000). Vocabulary: The missing link between phonics and comprehension. *Perspectives, 26*(4), 26–30.

Biemiller, A. (2006). Vocabulary development and instruction: A prerequisite for school learning. In D. K. Dickinson & S. B. Neuman (Eds.), *Handbook of early literacy research, volume 2,* 41–51. New York, NY: Guilford Press.

Biemiller, A., & Boote, C. (2006). An effective method for building meaning vocabulary in primary grades. *Journal of Educational Psychology, 98*(1), 44–62.

Billig, S. H. (2002). Support for K–12 service-learning practice: A brief review of the research. *Educational Horizons, 80*(4), 184–189.

Black, P., & Wiliam, D. (1998). *Inside the black box: Raising standards through classroom assessment.* London, England: Granada Learning.

Blair C. (2010). Stress and the development of self-regulation in context. *Child Development Perspectives, 4,* 181–88. doi:10.1111/j.1750-8606.2010.00145.x

Blair, C., & Raver, C. C. (2012). Child development in the context of adversity. *American Psychologist, 67,* 309–18. doi:10.1037/a0027493

Bloom, B. (1976). *Human characteristics and school learning.* New York, NY: McGraw-Hill.

Boulware-Gooden, R., Carreker, S., Thornhill, A., & Joshi, R. M. (2007). Instruction of metacognitive strategies enhances reading comprehension and vocabulary achievement of third-grade students. *Reading Teacher, 61*(1), 70–77.

Bowles, T. (2008). The relationship of time orientation with perceived academic performance and preparation for assessment in adolescents. *Educational Psychology, 28*(5), 551–565.

Bowman, H. (2011). Is there a future in architectural modeling of mind? Paper presented at Philip Barnard retirement symposium, MRC Applied Psychology Unit, Cambridge, UK.

Bradley, R. H., & Corwyn, R. F. (2002). Socioeconomic status and child development. *Annual Review of Psychology, 53,* 371–399. doi:10.1146/annurev.psych.53.100901.135233

Bradley, R. H., Corwyn, R. F., McAdoo, H. P., & Garcia-Coll, C. (2001). The home environments of children in the United States, part I: Variations by age, ethnicity, and poverty status. *Child Development, 72,* 1844–1867. doi:10.1111/1467-8624.t01-1-00382

Brandt, R. (1988). On assessment of teaching: A conversation with Lee Shulman. *Educational Leadership, 46*(3), 42–46.

Bransford, J. D., Brown, A. L., & Cocking, R. R. (Eds.). (1999). *How people learn: Brain, mind, experience and school.* Washington, DC: National Academy Press.

Brink, J., Capps, E., & Sutko, A. (2004). Student exam creation as a learning tool. *College Student Journal, 38*(2), 262–272.

Britsch, B., & Wakefield, W. D. (1998). *The influence of ethnic identity status and gender-role identity on social anxiety and avoidance in Latina adolescents.* ERIC Document Reproduction Service No. ED442895.

Brody, G. H., & Flor, D. L. (1997). Maternal psychological functioning, family processes, and child adjustment in rural, single-parent, African American families. *Developmental Psychology, 33,* 1000–1011. doi:10.1037/0012-1649.33.6.1000

Brody, G. H., Stoneman, Z., & Flor, D. L. (1996). Parental religiosity, family processes, and youth competence in rural, two-parent African American families. *Developmental Psychology, 32,* 696–706. doi:10.1037/0012-1649.32.4.696

Brookover, W. B., Beady, C., Flood, P., Schweitzer, J., & Wisenbaker, J. (1979). *School social systems and student achievement: Schools can make a difference.* New York, NY: Bergin.

Brooks, R. (1991). *The self-esteem teacher.* Loveland, OH: Treehaus Communications.

Brooks-Gunn, J., Guo, G., & Furstenberg Jr., F. F. (1993). Who drops out of and who continues beyond high school? A 20-year study of black youth. *Journal of Research in Adolescence 37*(3), 271–294.

Brophy, J. E. (1981). Teacher praise: A functional analysis. *Review of Educational Research, 51*(1), 5–32.

Brown, A., (2012, October 30). With poverty comes depression, more than other illnesses. Gallup. Retrieved from http://www.gallup.com/poll/158417/poverty-comes-depression-illness.aspx

Brown, J. S., Collins, A., & Duguid, P. (1989). Situated cognition and the culture of learning. *Educational Researcher, 18*(1), 32–42.

Bruce, C., Snodgrass, D., & Salzman, J. A. (1999). A tale of two methods: Melding Project Read and guided reading to improve at-risk students' literacy skills. ERIC Document Reproduction Service No. ED436762.

Brumbach, B. H., & Figueredo, J. F. (2009). Effects of harsh and unpredictable environments in adolescence on development of life history strategies: A longitudinal test of an evolutionary model. Retrieved from http://www.u.arizona.edu/~ajf/pdf/Brumbach,%20Figueredo,%20&%20Ellis%202009.pdf

Bruner, J. (1996). *The culture of education.* Cambridge, MA: Harvard University Press.

Buckner, M., Reese, E., & Reese, R. (1987). Eye movement as an indicator of sensory components in thought. *Journal of Counseling Psychology, 34*(3), 283–287.

Burke, P. J., Owens, T. J., Serpe, R., & Thoits, P. A. (Eds.). (2003). *Advances in identity theory and research.* New York, NY: Springer.

Burton, L. J., & VanHeest, J. L. (2007). The importance of physical activity in closing the achievement gap. *Quest, 59*(2), 212–218.

Burts, D. C., Schmidt, H. M., Durham, R. S., Charlesworth, R., & Hart, C. H. (2007). Impact of the developmental appropriateness of teacher guidance strategies on kindergarten children's interpersonal relations. *Journal of Research in Childhood Education, 21*(3), 290–301.

Butera, L. M., Giacone, M. V., & Wagner, K. A. (2008). Decreasing off-task behavior through a dot/point reward system and portfolio reflection with second, fifth, and sixth graders. ERIC Document Reproduction Service No. ED500845.

Caine Learning Center. (2014). Home page. Retrieved from http://cainelearning.com

Caine, R. N., & Caine, G. (1991). *Making connections: Teaching and the human brain.* Alexandria, VA: Association for Supervision and Curriculum Development.

Caine, R. N., & Caine, G. (1997). *Education on the edge of possibility.* Alexandria, VA: Association for Supervision and Curriculum Development.

Callicott, K. J., & Park, H. (2003). Effects of self-talk on academic engagement and academic responding. *Behavioral Disorders, 29*(1), 48–64.

Campbell, F., & Ramey, C. (1994). Effects of early intervention on intellectual and academic achievement: A follow-up of children from low income families. *Child Development, 65,* 684–698. doi:10.1111/j.1467-8624.1994.tb00777

Campbell, T. (2006). The distant exploration of wolves: Using technology to explore student questions about wolves. *Journal of College Science Teaching, 35*(7), 16–21.

Capezio, P. (2000). *Powerful planning skills.* Wayne, NJ: Career Press.

Carlson, J. I., Luiselli, J. K., Slyman, A., & Markowski, A. (2008). Choice-making as intervention for public disrobing in children with developmental disabilities. *Journal of Positive Behavior Interventions, 10,* 86–90.

Carr, E. G., & Carlson, J. I. (1993). Reduction of severe behavior problems in the community using a multicomponent treatment approach. *Journal of Applied Behavior Analysis, 26*(2), 157–172.

Carrell, P. L. (1987). Content and formal schemata in ESL reading. *TESOL Quarterly, 21*(3), 461–481.

Chagnon, F. (2007). Coping mechanisms, stressful events and suicidal behavior among youth admitted to juvenile justice and child welfare services. *Suicide and Life-Threatening Behavior, 37*(4), 439–452.

Chalk, J. C., Hagan-Burke, S., & Burke, M. D. (2005). The effects of self-regulated strategy development on the writing process for high school students with learning disabilities. *Learning Disability Quarterly, 28*(1), 75–87.

Chalmers, D., & Lawrence, J. A. (1993). Investigating the effects of planning aids on adults' and adolescents' organization of a complex task. *International Journal of Behavioral Development, 16*(2), 191–214.

Champaign, J., Colvin, K. F., Liu, A., Fredericks, C., Seaton, D., & Pritchard, D. E. (2014). Correlating skill and improvement in two MOOCs with a student's time on tasks. In *Proceedings of the first ACM conference on learning @ scale conference,* 11–20. New York, NY: ACM Press. doi:10.1145/2556325.2566250

Cheung, A., & Slavin, R. E. (2005). Effective reading programs for English language learners and other language-minority students. *Bilingual Research Journal, 29*(2), 241–267.

Children's Defense Fund Minnesota. (2017). Home page. Retrieved from http://www.cdf-mn.org

Chin, C., & Kayalvizhi, G. (2002). Posing problems for open investigations: What questions do pupils ask? *Research in Science and Technological Education, 20*(2), 269–287.

Chin, C., & Osborne, J. (2008). Students' questions: A potential resource for teaching and learning science. *Studies in Science Education, 44*(1), 1–39.

Chödrön, P. (2012). *Living beautifully with uncertainty and change.* Boulder, CO: Shambhala.

Chomitz, V. R., Slining, M. M., McGowan, R. J., Mitchell, S. E., Dawson, G. F., & Hacker, K. A. (2009). Is there a relationship between physical fitness and academic achievement? Positive results from public school children in the Northeastern United States. *Journal of School Health, 79*(1), 30–37.

Chomsky, C. (1972). Stages in language development and reading exposure. *Harvard Educational Review, 42*(1), 1–33.

Chomsky, N. (2002). *Syntactic structures.* Berlin, Germany: De Gruyter.

Cinamon, R. G., & Rich, Y. (2002). Profiles of attribution of importance to life roles and their implications for work-family conflict. *Journal of Counseling Psychology, 49,* 212–220.

Clark, R. C. (2008). *Building expertise: Cognitive methods for training and performance improvement.* San Francisco, CA: Pfeiffer.

Clark, R., Nguyen, F., & Sweller, J. (2005). *Efficiency in learning: Evidence-based guidelines to manage cognitive load.* Hoboken, NJ: Wiley.

Classwide peer tutoring: What Works Clearinghouse intervention report. (2007). ERIC Document Reproduction Service No. ED499239.

Cleary, T. J., Gubi, A., & Prescott, M. V. (2010). Motivation and self-regulation assessments in urban and suburban schools: Professional practices and needs of school psychologists. *Psychology in the Schools, 47*(10), 985–1002. doi:10.1002/pits.20519

Cole, C., & Majd, M. (2003). Tucker Signing Strategies for Reading national study. Bloomington: Indiana University. Retrieved from http://www.ahaprocess.com/files/Tuckernationalstudy1.pdf

Coles, R. (1989). *The call of stories: Teaching and the moral imagination.* Boston, MA: Houghton Mifflin.

Collier, P. J., & Morgan, D. L. (2008). Is that paper really due today? Differences in first-generation and traditional college students' understandings of faculty expectations. *Higher Education, 55*(4), 425–446.

Collins, E., & Clark, H. (2013). *Supporting young people to make change happen: A review of theories of change.* Sydney, Australia: Act Knowledge and Oxfam.

Comer, J. (1995). Lecture given at Education Service Center, Region IV, Houston, TX.

Committee on the Support for Thinking Spatially: The Incorporation of Geographic Information Science Across the K–12 Curriculum, Committee on Geography, National Research Council. (2006). *Learning to think spatially: GIS as a support system in the K–12 curriculum.* Washington, DC: National Academies Press.

Communities in Schools. (2009). Home page. Retrieved from https://www.communitiesinschools.org

Conger, R. D., & Donnellan, M. B. (2007). An interactionist perspective on the socioeconomic context of human development. *Annual Review of Psychology, 58,* 175–199. doi:10.1146/annurev.psych.58.110405.085551

Conger, R. D., Conger, K. J., & Elder Jr., G. H. (1997). *Family economic hardship and adolescent adjustment: Mediating and moderating processes.* In J. Brooks-Gunn & G. Duncan (Eds.), *Consequences of growing up poor,* 288–310. New York, NY: Russell Sage.

Conlon, T. (2009). Towards sustainable text concept mapping. *Literacy, 43*(1), 20–28.

Connell, J. P., & Kubisch, A. C. (1998). Applying a theory of change approach to the evaluation of comprehensive community initiatives: Progress, prospects and problems. *New Approaches to Evaluating Community Initiatives, 2*(15–44), 1–16.

Conway, H. W. (2006). *Collaboration for kids: Early-intervention tools for schools and communities.* Highlands, TX: aha! Process.

Corcoran, M., & Adams, T. (1997). Race, sex and intergenerational poverty. In G. Duncan & J. Brooks-Gunn (Eds.), *Consequences of growing up poor.* New York, NY: Russell Sage.

Coryn, C. L., Noakes, L. A., Westine, C. D., & Schröter, D. C. (2011). A systematic review of theory-driven evaluation practice from 1990 to 2009. *American Journal of Evaluation, 32*(2), 199–226.

Costa, A., & Garmston, R. (1986). *The art of cognitive coaching: Supervision for intelligent teaching.* Sacramento, CA: California State University Press.

Covey, S. R. (1989). *The 7 habits of highly effective people: Powerful lessons in personal change.* New York, NY: Free Press.

Cox, H. A., & Stephens, L. J. (2006). The effect of music participation on mathematical achievement and overall academic achievement of high school students. *International Journal of Mathematical Education in Science and Technology, 37*(7), 757–763.

Coyle, C., & Cole, P. (2004). A videotaped self-modeling and self-monitoring treatment program to decrease off-task behavior in children with autism. *Journal of Intellectual and Developmental Disability, 29*(1), 3–16.

Crescentini, C., Seyed-Allaei, S., Vallesi, A., & Shallice, T. (2012). Two networks involved in producing and realizing plans. *Neuropsychologia, 50,* 1521–1535. doi:10.1016/j. neuropsychologia.2012.03.005

Crook, S. R., & Evans, G. W. (2013). The role of planning skills in the income-achievement gap. *Child Development 85*(2), 405–411. doi:10.1111/cdev.12129

Crowell, S. (1989). A new way of thinking: The challenge of the future. *Educational Leadership, 7*(1), 60–63.

Curie, P., deBrueys, M., Exnicios, J., & Prejean, M. (1987). *125 ways to be a better student.* East Moline, IL: Lingui Systems.

Daly, M., & Valletta, R. (2004). Inequality and poverty in the United States: The effects of rising male wage dispersion and changing family behavior. Retrieved from http://www. frbsf.org/econrsrch/workingp/2000/wp00-06.pdf

Damasio, A. R. (1994). *Descartes' error: Emotion, reason, and the human brain.* New York, NY: G. P. Putnam's Sons.

Daniels, M. (1994). The effects of sign language on hearing children's language development. *Communication Education, 43,* 291–298.

Daniels, M. (1996). Seeing language: The effect over time of sign language on vocabulary development in early childhood education. *Child Study Journal, 26,* 193–208.

Daniels, M. (2001). *Dancing with words: Signing for hearing children's literacy.* Westport, CT: Bergin & Garvey.

Davelaar, E. J., Goshen-Gottstein, Y., Haarmann, H. J., & Usher, M. (2005). The demise of short-term memory revisited: Empirical and computational investigations of recency effects. *Psychology Review Journal, 112*(1), 3–42.

Delfitto, D. (2006). *The Blackwell companion to syntax* (vols. 1–5). Hoboken, NJ: Wiley.

Dembo, M. H., & Eaton, M. J. (2000). Self-regulation of academic learning in middle-level schools. *The Elementary School Journal, 100,* 473–490. doi:10.1086/499651

Dermody, M. M., & Speaker Jr., R. B. (1999). Reciprocal strategy training in prediction, clarification, question generating and summarization to improve reading comprehension. *Reading Improvement, 36*(1), 16–23.

DeSoto, H. (2000). *The mystery of capital.* New York, NY: Basic Books.

DeVol, P. E. (2006). *Getting ahead in a just-gettin'-by world: Building your resources for a better life.* (2nd ed.). Highlands, TX: aha! Process.

DeVol, P. E. (2013). *Getting ahead in a just-gettin'-by world: Building your resources for a better life.* (3rd ed.). Highlands, TX: aha! Process.

DeVol, P. E., & Krodel, K. M. (2010). *Investigations into economic class in America.* Highlands, TX: aha! Process.

DeVol, P. E., Payne, R. K., & Dreussi Smith, T. (2017). *Bridges out of poverty: Strategies for professionals and communities training supplement* (Rev. ed.). Highlands, TX: aha! Process.

Dewey, E. (1938). Behavior development in infants. *Occupational Therapy and Rehabilitation, 17*(1), 61.

DeWitz, S. J., Woolsey, M. L., & Walsh, W. B. (2009). College student retention: An exploration of the relationship between self-efficacy beliefs and purpose in life among college students. *Journal of College Student Development, 50*(1), 19–34.

Diaconis, P., & Mosteller, F. (1989). Methods of studying coincidences. *Journal of the American Statistical Association, 84*(408), 853–861.

Diemer, M. A. (2002). Constructions of provider role identity among African American men: An exploratory study. *Cultural Diversity and Ethnic Minority Psychology, 8*(1), 30–40.

Domagala-Zysk, E. (2006). The significance of adolescents' relationships with significant others and school failure. *School Psychology International, 27*(2), 232–247.

Donovan, M. S., & Bransford, J. D. (2005). *How students learn: History, mathematics, and science in the classroom.* Washington, DC: National Academies Press.

Dreher, M. J., & Singer, H. (1980). Story grammar instruction unnecessary for intermediate grade students. *The Reading Teacher, 34*(3), 261–268.

Dulewicz, V., & Higgs, M. (2000). Emotional intelligence: A review and evaluation study. *Journal of Managerial Psychology, 15*(4), 341–372.

Duncan, G. J. (2012). Give us our daily breadth. *Child Development, 83,* 6–15. doi:10.1111/j.1467-8624.2011.01679.x

Duncan, G. J., & Brooks-Gunn, J. (Eds.). (1997). *Consequences of growing up poor.* New York, NY: Russell Sage.

Duncan, G. J., & Brooks-Gunn, J. (1997). Income effects across the life span: Integration and interpretation. In G. J. Duncan & J. Brooks-Gunn (Eds.), *Consequences of growing up poor,* 596–610. New York, NY: Russell Sage.

Dweck, C. S. (1986). Motivational processes affecting learning. *American Psychologist, 41,* 1040–1048.

Dweck, C. S. (2006). *Mindset: The new psychology of success.* New York, NY: Ballantine Books.

Dweck, C. S. (2008). Can personality be changed? The role of beliefs in personality and change. *Current Directions in Psychological Science, 17*(6), 391–394.

Dweck, C. S., & Leggett, E. L. (1988). A social-cognitive approach to motivation and personality. *Psychological Review, 95,* 256–273.

Dyer, K., Dunlap, G., & Winterling, V. (1990). Effects of choice making on the serious problem behaviors of students with severe handicaps. *Journal of Applied Behavioral Analysis, 23*(4), 515–524.

Earl, S., Carden, F., & Smutylo, T. (2001). Outcome mapping. *Building learning and reflection into development programs.* Ottawa, Ontario, Canada: International Development Research Center.

Educational Epiphany (2012). Home. Retrieved from http://educationalepiphany.com

Edvinsson, L., & Malone, M. S. (1997). *Intellectual capital: Realizing your company's true value by finding its hidden brainpower.* New York, NY: HarperCollins.

Egan, K. (1986). *Teaching as story telling.* Chicago, IL: University of Chicago Press.

Egan, K. (1989). Memory, imagination, and learning: Connected by the story. *Phi Delta Kappan, 70*(6), 455–59.

Elliott, M., Gray, B., & Lewicki, R. (2003). Lessons learned about the framing of intractable environmental conflicts. In R. Lewicki, B. Gray, & M. Elliott (Eds.), *Making sense of intractable environmental conflicts: Concepts and cases,* 409–436. Washington, DC: Island Press.

Elliott, M., Kaufman, S., Gardner, R., & Burgess, G. (2002). Teaching conflict assessment and frame analysis through interactive web-based simulations. *The International Journal of Conflict Management, 13*(4), 320–340.

Ellis, B. J., Figueredo, A. J., Brumbach, B. H., & Schlomer, G. L. (2009). Fundamental dimensions of environmental risk: The impact of harsh versus unpredictable environments on the evolution and development of life history strategies. *Human Nature, 20,* 204–268. doi:10.1007/s12110-009-9063-7

Ellis, K. D. (2004). *Putting the pieces together.* Highlands, TX: aha! Process.

Emmons, R. A., & McCullough, M. E. (2003). Counting blessings versus burdens: An experimental investigation of gratitude and subjective well-being in daily life. *Journal of Personality and Social Psychology, 84*(2), 377–389.

Engle, R. W., & Kane, M. J. (2004). Executive attention, working memory capacity and two-factor theory of cognitive control. In B. Ross (Ed.), *The Psychology of Learning and Motivation,* 145–199. New York, NY: Elsevier.

Epstein, M. L., Lazarus, A. D., Calvano, T. B., Matthews, K. A., Hendel, R. A., Epstein, B. B., & Brosvic, G. M. (2002). Immediate feedback assessment technique promotes learning and corrects inaccurate first responses. *The Psychological Record, 52,* 187–201.

Ericsson, I. (2008). Motor skills, attention and academic achievements: An intervention study in school years 1–3. *British Educational Research Journal, 34*(3), 301–313.

Erikson, E. (1988). Youth: Fidelity and diversity. *Daedalus, 117*(3), 1–24.

Evans, G. W. (2004). The environment of childhood poverty. *American Psychologist, 59,* 77–92. doi:10.1037/0003-066X.59.2.77

Evans, G. W., Eckenrode, J., & Marcynyszyn, L. A. (2010). Poverty and chaos. In G. W. Evans & T. D. Wachs (Eds.), *Chaos and its influence on children's development: An ecological perspective,* 225–238. Washington, DC: American Psychological Association.

Evans, G. W., & Kim, P. (2012). Childhood poverty, chronic stress, self-regulation and coping. *Child Development Perspectives, 7*(1), 43–48. doi:10.1111/cdep.12013

Evans, G. W., & Rosenbaum, J. (2008). Self-regulation and the income-achievement gap. *Early Childhood Research Quarterly, 23,* 504–514. doi:10.1016/j.ecresq.2008.07.002

Evans, P. (1992). *The verbally abusive relationship: How to recognize it and how to respond.* Cincinnati, OH: Adams Media.

Evertson, C. M., & Weinstein, C. S. (Eds.). (2006). *Handbook of classroom management: Research, practice, and contemporary issues.* Mahwah, NJ: Erlbaum.

Fain, T., Turner, S., & Ridgeway, G. (2008, October). *Los Angeles County Juvenile Justice Crime Prevention Act: RAND quarterly report.* Santa Monica, CA: RAND Corporation.

Faircloth, B. S., & Hamm, J. V. (2005). Sense of belonging among high school students representing four ethnic groups. *Journal of Youth and Adolescence, 34*(4), 293–309.

Farah, M. J., Noble, K. G., & Hurt, H. (2006). Poverty, privilege, and brain development: Empirical findings and ethical implications. Retrieved from https://pdfs.semanticscholar.org/721e/0fd8bf020f62cf8791dc5c7d10d69c41ece7.pdf

Farah, M. J., Shera, D. M., Savage, J. H., Betancourt, L., Giannetta, J. M., Brodsky, N. L., ... Hurt, H. (2006). Childhood poverty: Specific associations with neurocognitive development. *Brain Research, 1110*(1), 166–174. doi:10.1016/j.brainres.2006.06.072

Farbman, D., & Kaplan, C. (2005). *Time for a change: The promise of extended time schools for promoting student achievement.* Boston, MA: Massachusetts 2020.

Farmer, T. W., Dadisman, K., Latendresse, S. J., Thompson, J., Irvin, M. J., & Zhang, L. (2006). Educating out and giving back: Adults' conceptions of successful outcomes of African American high school students from impoverished rural communities. Retrieved from http://jrre.vmhost.psu.edu/wp-content/uploads/2014/02/21-10.pdf

Farmer-Hinton, R. L. (2002). When time matters: Examining the impact and distribution of extra instructional time. ERIC Document Reproduction Service No. ED479926.

Farrell, A. D., Erwin, E. H., Allison, K. W., Meyer, A., Sullivan, T., Camou, S., ... Esposito, L. (2007). Problematic situations in the lives of urban African American middle school students: A qualitative study. *Journal of Research on Adolescence, 17*(2), 413–454.

Farson, R. (1996). *Management of the absurd.* New York, NY: Touchstone.

Fassler, D. G., & Dumas, L. S. (1997). *Help me, I'm sad.* New York, NY: Penguin.

Fedor, D. B. (1991). Recipient responses to performance feedback: A proposed model and its implications. *Research in Personnel and Human Resources Management, 9,* 73–120.

Feeney, T. J., & Ylvisaker, M. (2008). Context-sensitive cognitive-behavioral supports for young children with TBI: A second replication study. *Journal of Positive Behavior Interventions, 10*(2), 115–128.

Ferguson, R. (2008). *Toward excellence with equity: An emerging vision for closing the achievement gap.* Cambridge, MA: Harvard Education Press.

Fernyhough, C., & Fradley, E. (2005). Private speech on an executive task: Relations with task difficulty and task performance. *Cognitive Development, 20*(1), 103–120.

Feuerstein, R. (1980). *Instrumental enrichment: An intervention program for cognitive modifiability.* Baltimore, MD: University Park Press.

Feuerstein, R. (1990). The theory of structural modifiability. In B. Presseisen (Ed.), *Learning and thinking styles: Classroom interaction.* Washington, DC: National Education Association.

Feuerstein, R. (1998a). *Glossary of MLE, LPAD and IE terms and concepts.* Jerusalem, Israel: International Center for the Enhancement of Learning Potential.

Feuerstein, R. (1998b). *The theory of mediated learning experience: About human as a modifiable being* [Hebrew]. Jerusalem, Israel: Ministry of Defense Publications.

Feuerstein, R. et al. (2003). *Feuerstein's theory and applied systems: A reader.* Jerusalem, Israel: ICELP Press.

Feuerstein, R., Falik, L., Rand, Y., & Feuerstein, R. S. (2006). *Creating and enhancing cognitive modifiability: The Feuerstein instrumental enrichment program.* Jerusalem, Israel: ICELP Press.

Feuerstein, R., Feuerstein, R. S., & Feuerstein, A. (2003). *Learning potential assessment device—basic: Manual.* Jerusalem, Israel: ICELP Press.

Feuerstein, R., Klein, P., & Tannenbaum, A. (Eds.). (1991). *Mediated learning experience: Theoretical, psychosocial, and learning implications.* Tel Aviv, Israel, and London, England: Freund.

Feuerstein, R., Mintzker, Y., Feuerstein, R. S., Ben Shachar, N., Cohen, M., & Rathner, A. (2001). *Mediated learning experience: Guidelines for parents.* Jerusalem, Israel: ICELP Press.

Feuerstein, R., & Rand, Y., with Engels, N., & Feuerstein, R. S. (2006). *Don't accept me as I am* (Rev. English ed.). Jerusalem, Israel: ICELP Press.

Feuerstein, R., Rand, Y., Hoffman, M., & Miller, R. (1980). *Instrumental enrichment: An intervention program for cognitive modifiability.* Baltimore, MD: University Park Press.

Fields, C. (2003). Training materials for Understanding Learning workshop.

Fisher, D., Brozo, W., Frey, N., & Ivey, G. (2006). *50 content area strategies for adolescent literacy.* Upper Saddle River, NJ: Prentice Hall.

Fisher, D., & Frey, N. (2008). *Wordwise and content rich: Five essential steps to teaching academic vocabulary.* Portsmouth, NH: Heinemann.

Fisher, R., & Ury, W. (1983). *Getting to YES: Negotiating agreement without giving in.* New York, NY: Penguin.

Fox, J. E. (1999). 'It's time to go home!' Reframing dismissal routines. *Dimensions of Early Childhood, 27*(3), 11–15.

Fraser, M. W., Galinsky, M. J., Smokowski, P. R., Day, S. H., Terzian, M. A., Rose, R. A., & Guo, S. (2005). Social information-processing skills training to promote social competence and prevent aggressive behavior in the third grades. *Journal of Consulting and Clinical Psychology, 73*(6), 1045–1055.

Freed, M., Hess, R., & Ryan, J. (Eds.). (2002). *The educator's desk reference: A sourcebook of educational information and research.* Westport, CT: Praeger.

Freedman, J., & Combs, G. (1996). *Narrative therapy: The social construction of preferred realities.* New York, NY: Norton.

Freire, P. (2000). *Pedagogy of the oppressed: 30th anniversary edition.* New York, NY: Continuum International.

Friedman, S. L., & Haywood, S. C. (1994). *Child care and child development: The NICHD Study of Early Child Care.* New York, NY: Academic Press.

Fuchs, L. S., Fuchs, D., Prentice, K., Hamlett, C. L., Finelli, R., & Courey, S. J. (2004). Enhancing mathematical problem solving among third-grade students with schema-based instruction. *Journal of Educational Psychology, 96*(4), 635–647.

Funnell, S. C., & Rogers, P. J. (2011). *Purposeful program theory: Effective use of theories of change and logic models* (Vol. 31). Hoboken, NJ: Wiley.

Gaddy, S. A., Bakken, J. P., & Fulk, B. M. (2008). The effects of teaching text-structure strategies to postsecondary students with learning disabilities to improve their reading comprehension on expository science text passages. *Journal of Postsecondary Education and Disability, 20*(2), 100–119.

Gajria, M., Jitendra, A. K., Sood, S., & Sacks, G. (2007). Improving comprehension of expository text in students with LD: A research synthesis. *Journal of Learning Disabilities, 40*(3), 210–225.

Gallagher, E. (2013). The effects of teacher-student relationships: Social and academic outcomes of low-income middle and high school students. Retrieved from http://steinhardt.nyu.edu/appsych/opus/issues/2013/fall/gallagher

Galton, M., Hargreaves, L., & Pell, T. (2009). Group work and whole-class teaching with 11- to 14-year-olds compared. *Cambridge Journal of Education, 39*(1), 119–140.

Gambill, J. M., Moss, L. A., & Vescogni, C. D. (2008). The impact of study skills and organizational methods on student achievement. ERIC Document Reproduction Service No. ED501312.

Garcia-Ros, R., Perez-Gonzalez, F., & Hinojosa, E. (2004). Assessing time management skills as an important aspect of student learning: The construction and evaluation of a time management scale with Spanish high school students. *School Psychology International, 25*(2), 167–183.

Gianakos, I. (1995). The relation of sex role identity to career decision-making self-efficacy. *Journal of Vocational Behavior, 46*(2), 131–143.

Gillies, R. M. (2004). The effects of cooperative learning on junior high school students during small group learning. *Learning and Instruction, 14*(2), 197–213.

Gillies, R. M. (2008). The effects of cooperative learning on junior high school students' behaviors, discourse and learning during a science-based learning activity. *School Psychology International, 29*(3), 328–347.

Giota, J. (2006). Why am I in school? Relationships between adolescents' goal orientation, academic achievement and self-evaluation. *Scandinavian Journal of Educational Research, 50*(4), 441–461.

Gladwell, M. (2000). *The tipping point: How little things make a big difference.* New York, NY: Little, Brown.

Gladwell, M. (2008). *Outliers: The story of success.* New York, NY: Little, Brown.

Glickman, C. D. (1990). *Supervision of instruction: A developmental approach* (2nd ed.). Boston, MA: Allyn & Bacon.

Goddard, Y. L., & Sendi, C. (2008). Effects of self-monitoring on the narrative and expository writing of four fourth-grade students with learning disabilities. *Reading and Writing Quarterly, 24*(4), 408–433.

Godley, A. J., & Minnici, A. (2008). Critical language pedagogy in an urban high school English class. *Urban Education, 43*(3), 319–346.

Goldratt, E. M. (1990). *Theory of constraints.* Great Barrington, MA: Great River Press.

Goleman, D. (1995). *Emotional intelligence: Why it can matter more than IQ.* New York, NY: Bantam Books.

Goleman, D. (2006). *Social intelligence: The new science of human relationships.* New York, NY: Bantam Books.

Good, M., & Adams, G. R. (2008). Linking academic social environments, ego-identity formation, ego virtues, and academic success. *Adolescence, 43*(170), 221–236.

Good, T. L., & Brophy, J. E. (1991). *Looking in classrooms* (5th ed.). New York, NY: HarperCollins.

Goodman, J., Wood, R. E., & Hendrickx, M. (2004). Feedback specificity, exploration, and learning. *Journal of Applied Psychology 89*(2), 248–262.

Gordon, C. J., & Braun, C. (1983). Using story schema as an aid to reading and writing. *The Reading Teacher, 37*(2), 116–121.

Gouzouasis, P., Guhn, M., & Kishor, N. (2007). The predictive relationship between achievement and participation in music and achievement in core grade 12 academic subjects. *Music Education Research, 9*(1), 81–92.

Grant, A. M., & Gino, F. (2010). A little thanks goes a long way: Explaining why gratitude expressions motivate prosocial behavior. *Journal of Personality and Social Psychology, 98*(6), 946–955.

Grant, K. E., Compas, B. E., Stuhlmacher, A. F., Thurm, A. E., McMahon, S. D., & Halpert, J. A. (2003). Stressors and child and adolescent psychopathology: Moving from markers to mechanisms of risk. *Psychological Bulletin, 129,* 447–466. doi:10.1037/0033-2909.129.3.447

Gredler, M. E. (2004). Games and simulations and their relationships to learning. In D. H. Jonassen (Ed.), *Handbook of research on educational communications and technology,* 571–582. Mahwah, NJ: Erlbaum.

Green, G., Rhodes, J., Hirsch, A. H., Suarez-Orozco, C., & Camic, P. M. (2008). Supportive adult relationships and the academic engagement of Latin American immigrant youth. *Journal of School Psychology, 46*(4), 393–412.

Greene, B. A., & DeBacker, T. K. (2004). Gender and orientations toward the future: Links to motivation. *Educational Psychology Review, 16*(2), 91–120.

Greene, B. A., Miller, R. B., Crowson, H. M., Duke, B. L., & Akey, K. L. (2004). Predicting high school students' cognitive engagement and achievement: Contributions of classroom perceptions and motivation. *Contemporary Educational Psychology, 29*(4), 462–482.

Greene, J. A., Moos, D. C., Azevedo, R., & Winters, F. I. (2008). Exploring differences between gifted and grade-level students' use of self-regulatory learning processes with hypermedia. *Computers and Education, 50*(3), 1069–1083.

Greene, V. E., & Enfield, M. L. (2004). *Framing your thoughts: Written expression* (Rev. ed.). Bloomington, MN: Language Circle Enterprises.

Greenspan, S. I., & Benderly, B. L. (1997). *The growth of the mind and the endangered origins of intelligence.* Reading, MA: Perseus Books.

Griffin, J. A., & Friedman, S. L. (2007). *NICHD study of early childcare and youth development.* Bethesda, MD: National Institutes of Health.

Grigsby, B. L. (2005). *African American male students' perceptions of social, emotional, physical, and academic variables in their transition from elementary school to middle school.* Unpublished doctoral dissertation, Texas A&M University, College Station, TX.

Groesser, S. N. (2012). Mental model of dynamic systems. In N. M. Seel (Ed.). *The encyclopedia of the sciences of learning* (Vol. 5), 2195–2200. New York, NY: Springer.

Guastello, E. F., Beasley, T. M., & Sinatra, R. C. (2000). Concept mapping effects on science content comprehension of low achieving inner-city seventh graders. *Remedial and Special Education, 21*(6), 356–364.

Guay, F., Marsh, H. W., Senecal, C., & Dowson, M. (2008). Representations of relatedness with parents and friends and autonomous academic motivation during the late adolescence-early adulthood period: Reciprocal or unidirectional effects? *British Journal of Educational Psychology, 78*(4), 621–637.

Guidelines for the first days of school. (n.d.). Research Development Center for Teacher Education, Research on Classrooms, University of Texas, Austin. Comparable document retrievable from https://www.stcloudstate.edu/ignite/_files/documents/classroom-management/procedures-elementary.pdf

Gunzelmann, G. (2008). Strategy generalization across orientation tasks: Testing a computational cognitive model. *Cognitive Science, 32*(5), 835–861.

Gürses, A., Cetinkaya, S., Dogar, C., & Sahin, E. (2015). Determination of levels of use of basic process skills of high school students. *Procedia Social and Behavioral Sciences, 191*, 644–650.

Gyselinck, V., Meneghetti, C., De Beni, R., & Pazzaglia, F. (2009). The role of working memory in spatial text processing: What benefit of imagery strategy and visuospatial abilities? *Learning and Individual Differences, 19*(1), 12–20.

Haager, D., Klingner, J., & Vaughn, S. (Eds.). (2007). *Evidence-based reading practices for response to intervention.* Baltimore, MD: Paul H. Brookes.

Hafner, J. C., & Hafner, P. M. (2003). Quantitative analysis of the rubric as an assessment tool: An empirical study of student peer-group rating. *International Journal of Science Education, 25*(12), 1509–1528.

Hagaman, J. L., & Reid, R. (2008). The effects of the paraphrasing strategy on the reading comprehension of middle school students at risk for failure in reading. *Remedial and Special Education, 29*(4), 222–234.

Hall, K. M., Sabey, B. L., & McClellan, M. (2005). Expository text comprehension: Helping primary-grade teachers use expository texts to full advantage. *Reading Psychology, 26*(3), 211–234.

Halvorson, H. G. (2010). *Succeed: How we can reach our goals—2010.* New York, NY: Hudson Street Press.

Hamilton, J. L. (2007). The use of self-management skills with kindergarten through third grade students with emotional and behavior disorders: Investigation of findings. ERIC Document Reproduction Service No. ED497000.

Hammond, C., Linton, D., Smink, J., & Drew, S. (2007). *Dropout risk factors and exemplary programs: A technical report.* Clemson, SC: National Dropout Prevention Center/Network.

Hammond, D. (2011, September 10). Summer vacation hurts poor children—but is year-round school the answer? *Huffington Post.* Retrieved from http://www.huffingtonpost.com/darell-hammond/year-round-school-summer-vacation_b_894707.html

Harris, K. R., Graham, S., Friedlander, B., & Laud, L. (2013). Bring powerful writing strategies into your classroom! Why and how. *Reading Teacher, 66*(7), 538–542. Retrieved from http://www.thinksrsd.com/wp-content/uploads/2014/07/HGFL-Reading-Teacher-21.pdf

Harris, M. (2008). The effects of music instruction on learning in the Montessori classroom. *Montessori Life, 20*(3), 24–31.

Harrison, L. E., & Huntington, S. P. (Eds.). (2000). *Culture matters: How values shape human progress.* New York, NY: Basic Books.

Hart, B., & Risley, T. R. (1995). *Meaningful differences in the everyday experience of young American children.* Baltimore, MD: Paul H. Brookes.

Hartman, H. (2002). *Human learning and instruction.* New York, NY: City College of City University of New York.

Harvard Mental Health Letter. (2011, November). In praise of gratitude. Retrieved from http://www.health.harvard.edu/newsletter_article/in-praise-of-gratitude

Haskitz, A. (1996). A community service program that can be validated. *Phi Delta Kappan, 78*(2), 163–164.

Hattie, J. (2008). *Visible learning: A synthesis of over 800 meta-analyses relating to achievement.* London, England: Routledge.

Hattie, J. (2012). *Visible learning for teachers: Maximizing impact on learning.* London, England: Routledge.

Hattie, J. (2015). The applicability of visible learning to higher education. *Scholarship of Teaching and Learning in Psychology, 1,* 79–91.

Hattie, J., & Yates, G. (2014). *Visible learning and the science of how we learn.* London, England: Routledge.

Head, M. H., & Readence, J. E. (1986). Anticipation guides: Meaning through prediction. In E. K. Dishner, T. W. Bean, J. E. Readence, & D. W. Moore (Eds.), *Reading in the content areas: Improving classroom instruction* (2nd ed.), 229–234. Dubuque, IA: Kendall/Hunt.

Heath, S. B. (2001). Three's not a crowd: Plans, roles, and focus in the arts. *Educational Researcher, 30*(7), 10–17.

Heckman, J. J. (2006). Skill formation and the economics of investing in disadvantaged children. *Science, 30,* 1900–1902. doi:10.1126/science.1128898

Herman, T., Colton, S., & Franzen, M. (2008). Rethinking outreach: Teaching the process of science through modeling. *PLOS Biology, 6*(4), e86. doi:10.1371/journal.pbio.0060086

Hill, H. C., Blunk, M. L., Charalambous, Y., Lewis, J. M., Phelps, G. C., Sleep, L., & Ball, D. L. (2008). Mathematical knowledge for teaching and the mathematical quality of instruction: An exploratory study. *Cognition and Instruction, 26*(4), 430–511.

Hock, D. (1999). *Birth of the chaordic age.* San Francisco, CA: Berrett-Koehler.

Hock, M., & Mellard, D. (2005). Reading comprehension strategies for adult literacy outcomes. *Journal of Adolescent and Adult Literacy, 49*(3), 192–200.

Hock, M. F., Schumaker, J. B., & Deshler, D. D. (2003). *Possible selves: Nurturing student motivation.* Lawrence, KS: Edge Enterprises.

Hoff, E. (2003). The specificity of environmental influence: Socioeconomic status affects early vocabulary via maternal speech. *Child Development, 74,* 1368–1378. doi:10.1111/1467-8624.00612

Hoff, E. (2006). How social contexts support and shape language development. *Developmental Review, 26,* 55–88. doi:10.1016/j.dr.2005.11.002

Hoffman, A. (2003). Teaching decision making to students with learning disabilities by promoting self-determination. ERIC Document Reproduction Service No. ED481859.

Hollingsworth, J., & Ybarra, S. (2000). *Analyzing classroom instruction: Curriculum calibration.* Retrieved from http://www.dataworks-ed.com

Hollins, E. R. (Ed.). (2015). *Rethinking field experiences in preservice teacher preparation: Meeting new challenges for accountability.* London, England: Routledge.

Horstmanshof, L., & Zimitat, C. (2007). Future time orientation predicts academic engagement among first-year university students. *British Journal of Educational Psychology, 77*(3), 703–718.

Howie, D. R. (2003). *Thinking about the teaching of thinking.* Wellington, New Zealand: Council for Educational Research.

Howard, P. J. (2000). *The owner's manual for the brain* (2nd ed.). Austin, TX: Bard Press.

Howatt, A. P. R., & Widdowson, H. G. (2004). *A history of ELT.* Oxford, England: Oxford University Press.

Hsu, J. (2008, August). The secrets of storytelling: Why we love a good yarn. Retrieved from http://www.scientificamerican.com/article.cfm?id=the-secrets-of-storytelling

Huan, V. S. (2006). The role of social and personal identities among at-risk and non-at-risk Singapore youths during peer mediation. *Education Journal, 34*(2), 97–113.

Huang, J., Maassen van den Brink, H., & Groot, W. (2009). A meta-analysis of the effect of education on social capital. *Economics of Education Review, 28*(4), 454–464.

Hughes, C., Ensor, R., Wilson, A., & Graham, A. (2010). Tracking executive function across the transition to school: A latent variable approach. *Developmental Neuropsychology, 35,* 20–36. doi:10.1080/87565640903325691

Hunter, M. (1982). *Mastery teaching.* El Segundo, CA: TIP Publications.

Hurst, N. (2011, June 13). Federal welfare programs can have negative effects on children's cognitive scores. University of Missouri News Bureau. Retrieved from http://munews.missouri.edu/news-releases/2011/0607-federal-welfare-programs-can-have-negative-effects-on-children%E2%80%99s-cognitive-scores-mu-researchers-find/

Idol, L., & Jones, B. F. (Eds.). (1991). *Educational values and cognitive instruction: Implications for reform.* Mahwah, NJ: Erlbaum.

Irwin, J., LaGory, M., Ritchey, F., & Fitzpatrick, K. (2008). Social assets and mental distress among the homeless: Exploring the roles of social support and other forms of social capital on depression. *Social Science and Medicine, 67*(12), 1935–1943.

Irvin, J., & Rose, E. (1995). *Starting early with study skills: A week-by-week guide for elementary students.* Needham Heights, MA: Allyn & Bacon.

Jackson, E. T. (2013). Interrogating the theory of change: Evaluating impact investing where it matters most. *Journal of Sustainable Finance & Investment, 3*(2), 95–110.

Jaser, S. S., Fear, J. M., Reeslund, K. L., Champion, J. E., Reising, M. M., & Compas, B. E. (2008). Maternal sadness and adolescents' responses to stress in offspring of mothers with and without a history of depression. *Journal of Clinical Child and Adolescent Psychology, 37*(4), 736–746.

Jensen, E. (1994). *The learning brain.* Del Mar, CA: Turning Point.

Jensen, K. (2015). Chart. Retrieved from http://www.ahaprocess.com

Jiménez, L., Dekovic, M., & Hidalgo, V. (2009). Adjustment of school-aged children and adolescents growing up in at-risk families: Relationships between family variables and individual, relational and school adjustment. *Children and Youth Services Review, 31,* 654–661.

Johnson, D. W., & Johnson, R. T. (1996). Conflict resolution and peer mediation programs in elementary and secondary schools: A review of the research. *Review of Educational Research, 66*(4), 459–506.

Johnson, L. S. (2008). Relationship of instructional methods to student engagement in two public high schools. *American Secondary Education, 36*(2), 69–87.

Jones, B. F., Pierce, J., & Hunter, B. (1988). Teaching students to construct graphic representations. *Educational Leadership, 46*(4), 20–25.

Jones, S. M., Bailey, R., & Partee, A. (2016, September 12). How to target intergenerational poverty with a basic life skill. Retrieved from https://www.aspeninstitute.org/aspen-journal-of-ideas/target-intergenerational-poverty-basic-life-skill/

Joos, M. (1967). The styles of the five clocks. In R. D. Abraham & R. C. Troike (Eds.), *Language and cultural diversity in American education,* 145–149. Englewood Cliffs, NJ: Prentice Hall.

Jordan, H., Mendro, R., & Weerasinghe, D. (1997, July). Teacher effects on longitudinal student achievement: A report on research in progress. Retrieved from http://www.dallasisd.org/cms/lib/TX01001475/Centricity/Shared/evalacct/research/articles/Jordan-Teacher-Effects-on-Longitudinal-Student-Achievement-1997.pdf

Joshi, R. M. (2005). Vocabulary: A critical component of comprehension. *Reading and Writing Quarterly, 21*(3), 209–219.

Joyce, B., & Showers, B. (1988). *Student achievement through staff development.* New York, NY: Longman.

Joyce, B., & Weil, M. (1986). *Models of teaching* (3rd ed.). Boston, MA: Allyn & Bacon.

Kamps, D. M., Greenwood, C., Arreaga-Mayer, C., Veerkamp, M. B., Utley, C., Tapia, Y., … Bannister, H. (2008). The efficacy of ClassWide Peer Tutoring in middle schools. *Education and Treatment of Children, 31*(2), 119–152.

Karpman, S. (1968). Fairy tales and script drama analysis. *Transactional Analysis Bulletin, 7*(26), 39–43.

Karpman, S. B. (1974). Overlapping egograms. *Transactional Analysis Journal, 4*(4), 16–19.

Kashima, Y., Foddy, M., & Platow, M. (Eds.). (2002). *Self and identity: Personal, social and symbolic.* Mahwah, NJ: Erlbaum.

Kaylor, M., & Flores, M. M. (2007). Increasing academic motivation in culturally and linguistically diverse students from low socioeconomic backgrounds. *Journal of Advanced Academics, 19*(1), 66–89.

Kerpelman, J. L., Eryigit, S., & Stephens, C. J. (2008). African American adolescents' future education orientation: Associations with self-efficacy, ethnic identity, and perceived parental support. *Journal of Youth and Adolescence, 37*(8), 997–1008.

Killingsworth, M., & Gilbert, D. (2010). A wandering mind is an unhappy mind. *Science, 330*(6006), 932.

Kilpatrick, J., Swafford, J., & Findell, B. (Eds.). (2001). *Adding it up: Helping children learn mathematics.* Washington, DC: Mathematics Learning Study Committee, National Research Council.

King-Sears, M. E. (2008). Using teacher and researcher data to evaluate the effects of self-management in an inclusive classroom. *Preventing School Failure, 52*(4), 25–36.

Kinney, D. W. (2008). Selected demographic variables, school music participation, and achievement test scores of urban middle school students. *Journal of Research in Music Education, 56*(2), 145–161.

Kirby, N. F., & Downs, C. T. (2007). Assessment and the disadvantaged student: Potential for encouraging self-regulated learning? *Assessment and Evaluation in Higher Education, 32*(4), 475–494.

Kirkpatrick, L. C., & Klein, P. D. (2009). Planning text structure as a way to improve students' writing from sources in the compare-contrast genre. *Learning and Instruction, 19*(4), 309–321.

Kishiyama, M. M., Boyce, W. T., Jiménez, A. M., Perry, L. M., & Knight, R. T. (2009). Socioeconomic disparities affect prefrontal function in children. *Journal of Cognitive Neuroscience, 21*(6), 1106–1115.

Koch, L. M., Gross, A. M., & Kolts, R. (2001). Attitudes toward black English and code switching. *Journal of Black Psychology, 27*(1), 29–42.

Koegel, P., Melamid, E., & Burnam, M. A. (1995). Childhood risk factors of homelessness among homeless adults. *American Journal of Public Health, 85*(12), 1642–1649.

Koppenaal, L., & Glanzer, M. (1990). An examination of the continuous distractor task and the 'long-term recency effect.' *Memory & Cognition 18*(2), 183–195.

Kourea, L., Cartledge, G., & Musti-Rao, S. (2007). Improving the reading skills of urban elementary students through total class peer tutoring. *Remedial and Special Education, 28*(2), 95–107.

Kozulin, A. (2001). *Psychological tools: A sociocultural approach to education.* Cambridge, MA: Harvard University Press.

Krauss, S., Brunner, M., Kunter, M., Baumert, J., Blum, W., Neubrand, M., & Jordan, A. (2008). Pedagogical content knowledge and content knowledge of secondary mathematics teachers. *Journal of Educational Psychology, 100*(3), 716–725.

Krueger, K. A., & Dayan, P. (2009). Flexible shaping: How learning in small steps helps. *Cognition, 110*(3), 380–394.

Kulhavy, R. W. (1977). Feedback in written instruction. *Review of Educational Research, 47,* 211–232.

Kulik, J. A., & Kulik, C. C. (1988). Timing of feedback and verbal learning. *Review of Educational Research, 58*(1), 79–97.

Kunsch, C. A., Jitendra, A. K., & Sood, S. (2007). The effects of peer-mediated instruction in mathematics for students with learning problems: A research synthesis. *Learning Disabilities Research and Practice, 22*(1), 1–12.

Laird, J., Cataldi, E. F., Ramani, S., & Chapman, C. (2008). Dropout and completion rates in the United States: 2006. National Center for Education Statistics. Retrieved from https://nces.ed.gov/pubs2008/2008053.pdf

Lambert, N. M., & Fincham, F. D. (2011). Expressing gratitude to a partner leads to more relationship maintenance behavior. *Emotion, 11*(1), 52–60.

Langford, P. A., Rizzo, S. K., & Roth, J. M. (2003). *Improving student comprehension in content areas through the use of reading strategies.* Unpublished master's thesis, Saint Xavier University, Chicago, IL.

Lave, J. (1988). *Cognition in practice: Mind, mathematics and culture in everyday life.* Cambridge, England: Cambridge University Press.

Lave, J., & Wenger, E. (1991). *Situated learning: Legitimate peripheral participation.* Cambridge, England: Cambridge University Press.

Lazareve, O. F. (2012). Relational learning in a context of transposition: A review. *Journal of the Experimental Analysis of Behavior, 97*(2), 231–248.

Lee, S. Y., & Olszewski-Kubilius, P. (2006). The emotional intelligence, moral judgment, and leadership of academically gifted adolescents. *Journal for the Education of the Gifted, 30*(1), 29–67.

Leech, G. N. (2008). *Language in literature: Style and foregrounding*. Harlow, England: Pearson Longman.

Leemkuil, H., Jong, T. D., & Ootes, S. (2000). Review of educational use of games and simulations. University of Twente. Retrieved from http://doc.utwente.nl/28235/1/review_of_educational.pdf

Leinhardt, G., & Greeno, J. G. (1991). The cognitive skill of teaching. In P. Goodyear (Ed.), *Teaching knowledge and intelligent tutoring*, 233–268. Norwood, NJ: Ablex.

Lennon, C., & Burdick, H. (2004). The lexile framework as an approach for reading measurement and success. Retrieved from https://lexile.com/research/1/

Leondari, A. (2007). Future time perspective, possible selves, and academic achievement. *New Directions for Adult and Continuing Education, 114*, 17–26.

Liaw, F., & Brooks-Gunn, J. (1994). Cumulative familial risks and low-birthweight children's cognitive and behavioral development. *Journal of Clinical Child Psychology, 23*(4), 360–372.

Lin, H., & Chen, T. (2006). Decreasing cognitive load for novice EFL learners: Effects of question and descriptive advance organizers in facilitating EFL learners' comprehension of an animation-based content lesson. *System, 34*(3), 416–431.

Littlewood, J. E. (1986). *Littlewood's miscellany*. Cambridge, England: Cambridge University Press.

Lloyd, J. E. V., & Hertzman, C. (2009). From kindergarten readiness to fourth-grade assessment: Longitudinal analysis with linked population data. *Social Science and Medicine, 68*(1), 111–123.

Lodewyk, K. R., Winne, P. H., & Jamieson-Noel, D. L. (2009). Implications of task structure on self-regulated learning and achievement. *Educational Psychology, 29*(1), 1–25.

Louv, R. (2006). *The cradle of prosperity: Raising the new American economy*. Cambridge, MA: National Scientific Council on the Developing Child.

Lucas, J. H., & Stallworth, J. R. (2003). Providing difficult feedback: TIPS for the problem learner. *Family Medicine, 35*(8), 544–546.

Lujan, M. L. (2006). *Critical thinking*. Tyler, TX: Mentoring Minds.

Lyman, F. (1981). The responsive classroom discussion. In A. S. Anderson (Ed.), *Mainstreaming Digest*, 109–113. College Park, MD: University of Maryland College of Education.

Macaulay, R. (2002). Adverbs and social class revisited. *University of Pennsylvania Working Papers in Linguistics, 8*(3), 11.

Mackinnon, A., & Amott, N., with McGarvey, C. (2006). Mapping change: Using a theory of change to guide planning and evaluation. Retrieved from http://www.grantcraft.org/assets/content/resources/theory_change.pdf

Maguire, E. A., Frith, C. D., & Morris, R. G. (1999). The functional neuroanatomy of comprehension and memory: The importance of prior knowledge. *Brain, 122*(10), 1839–1850.

Mahalingam, M., Schaefer, F., & Morlino, E. (2008). Promoting student learning through group problem solving in general chemistry recitations. *Journal of Chemical Education, 85*(11), 1577–1581.

Malewski, E., & Phillion, J. (2009). International field experiences: The impact of class, gender and race on the perceptions and experiences of preservice teachers. *Teaching and Teacher Education, 25*(1), 52–60.

Malka, A., & Covington, M. V. (2005). Perceiving school performance as instrumental to future goal attainment: Effects on graded performance. *Contemporary Educational Psychology, 30*(1), 60–80.

Malmberg, L.-E., Ehrman, J., & Lithen, T. (2005). Adolescents' and parents' future beliefs. *Journal of Adolescence, 28*(6), 709–723.

Malone, T. W. (1981). Toward a theory of intrinsically motivating instruction. *Cognitive Science, 5*(4), 333–370.

Manfra, L., & Winsler, A. (2006). Preschool children's awareness of private speech. *International Journal of Behavioral Development, 30*(6), 537–549.

Marcia, J. E. (1966). Development and validation of ego-identity status. *Journal of Personality and Social Psychology, 3*(5), 551.

Martin, M. M. B., Rosselle, C., & Tarrida, A. (2007). Formulation of 'questions-answers' in teaching-learning process as a way of improving learning of students at university level. Retrieved from http://scholars.fhsu.edu/cgi/viewcontent.cgi?article=1123&context=alj

Marzano, R. J. (2000). *What works in classroom instruction.* Alexandria, VA: Association for Supervision and Curriculum Development.

Marzano, R. J. (2004). *Building background knowledge for academic achievement: Research on what works in schools.* Alexandria, VA: Association for Supervision and Curriculum Development.

Marzano, R. J. (2007). *The art and science of teaching: A comprehensive framework for effective instruction.* Alexandria, VA: Association for Supervision and Curriculum Development.

Marzano, R. J., & Arredondo, D. (1986). *Tactics for thinking.* Aurora, CO: Mid-Continent Regional Educational Laboratory.

Marzano, R. J., Pickering, D. J., & Pollock, J. E. (2001). *Classroom instruction that works: Research-based strategies for increasing student achievement.* Alexandria, VA: Association for Supervision and Curriculum Development.

Mason, B. J., & Bruning, R. (2001). Providing feedback in computer-based instruction: What the research tells us. Retrieved from https://www.researchgate.net/publication/247291218_Providing_Feedback_in_Computer-based_Instruction_What_the_Research_Tells_Us

Mason, L. H., & Shriner, J. G. (2008). Self-regulated strategy development instruction for writing an opinion essay: Effects for six students with emotional/behavior disorders. *Reading and Writing, 21*(1), 71–93.

Mattox, K., Hancock, D., & Queen, J. A. (2005). The effect of block scheduling on middle school students' mathematics achievement. *NASSP Bulletin, 89*(642), 3–13.

Mayer, R. E. (2003). Elements of a science of e-learning. *Journal of Educational Computing Research, 29*(3), 297–313.

Mayer, R. E. (2005). Cognitive theory of multimedia learning. In R. E. Mayer (Ed.), *The Cambridge Handbook of Multimedia Learning.* New York, NY: Cambridge University Press.

McCarthy, B. (1996). *About learning.* Barrington, IL: Excel.

McConaughy, S. H. (1982). Developmental changes in story comprehension and levels of questioning. *Language Arts, 59*(6), 580–600.

McCormack, T., & Atance, C. M. (2011). Planning in young children: A review and synthesis. *Developmental Review, 31,* 1–31. doi:10.1016/j.dr.2011.02.002

McCrudden, M. T., Schraw, G., & Lehman, S. (2009). The use of adjunct displays to facilitate comprehension of causal relationships in expository text. *Instructional Science, 37*(1), 65–86.

McIntosh, K., Campbell, A. L., Carter, D. R., & Dickey, C. R. (2009). Differential effects of a tier two behavior intervention based on function of problem behavior. *Journal of Positive Behavior Interventions, 11*(2), 82–93.

McLoyd, V. C. (1998). Socioeconomic disadvantage and child development. *American Psychologist, 53,* 185–204. doi:10.1037//0003-066X.53.2.185

McManus, D. O., Dunn, R., & Denig, S. J. (2003). Effects of traditional lecture versus teacher-constructed and student-constructed self-teaching instructional resources on short-term science achievement and attitudes. *American Biology Teacher, 65*(2), 93–102.

McTighe, J., & Lyman Jr., F. T. (1988). Cueing thinking in the classroom: The promise of theory-embedded tools. *Educational Leadership, 45*(7), 18–24.

McWhorter, J. (2000). *Losing the race: Self-sabotage in black America.* New York, NY: Harper Perennial.

Mental models for English/language arts: Grades 6–12. (2007). Highlands, TX: aha! Process.

Mental models for math: Grades 6–12. (2006). Highlands, TX: aha! Process.

Merrill, J. (1987). Levels of questioning and forms of feedback: Instructional factors in courseware design. *Journal of Computer-Based Instruction, 14,* 18–22.

MetaMetrics. (2017). Home page. Retrieved from https://www.metametricsinc.com

Meyer, B. J. F., & Poon, L. W. (2001). Effects of structure strategy training and signaling on recall of text. *Journal of Educational Psychology, 93*(1), 141–159.

Miller, S. C. (2007). *Until it's gone: Ending poverty in our nation, in our lifetime.* Highlands, TX: aha! Process.

Milliken, B. (2007). *The last dropout: Stop the epidemic.* Carlsbad, CA: Hay House.

Mills, A. (1999). Pollyanna and the not so glad game. *Children's Literature, 27,* 87–104.

Mistar, J. (2011). A study of the validity and reliability of self-assessment. *TEFLIN Journal, 22*(1), 1–10.

Mithaug, D. K. (2002). 'Yes' means success: Teaching children with multiple disabilities to self-regulate during independent work. *Teaching Exceptional Children, 35*(1), 22–27.

Miyake, A., Friedman, N. P., Emerson, M. J., Witzki, A. H., & Howerter, A. (2000). The unity and diversity of executive functions and their contribution to 'frontal lobe' tasks: A latent variable analysis. *Cognitive Psychology, 41,* 49–100. doi:10.1006/cogp.1999.0734

Mohan, B., & Slater, T. (2006). Examining the theory/practice relation in a high school science register: A functional linguistic perspective. *Journal of English for Academic Purposes, 5*(4), 302–316.

Molfese, D. L., Freeman, R. B., & Palermo, D. S. (1975). The ontogeny of brain lateralization for speech and nonspeech stimuli. *Brain and Language, 2,* 356–368.

Montague, M., & Bos, C. S. (1986). The effect of cognitive strategy training on verbal math problem solving performance of learning disabled adolescents. *Journal of Learning Disabilities, 19,* 1–9. doi:10.1177/002221948601900107

Montaño-Harmon, M. R. (1991). Discourse features of written Mexican Spanish: Current research in contrastive rhetoric and its implications. *Hispania, 74*(2), 417–425.

Montelongo, J., Berber-Jiménez, L., Hernandez, A. C., & Hosking, D. (2006). Teaching expository text structures. *Science Teacher, 73*(2), 28–31.

Moore, D. W., Prebble, S., Robertson, J., Waetford, R., & Anderson, A. (2001). Self-recording with goal setting: A self-management program for the classroom. *Educational Psychology, 21*(3), 255–265.

Moreno, R. (2004). Decreasing cognitive load for novice students: Effects of explanatory versus corrective feedback in discovery-based multimedia. *Instructional Science, 32,* 99–113.

Morris, P., Huston, A., Duncan, G., Crosby, D., & Bos, J. (2001). How welfare and work policies affect children: A synthesis of research. MDRC. Retrieved from https://nyuscholars.nyu.edu/en/publications/how-welfare-and-work-policies-affect-children-a-synthesis-of-rese

Morrison, J. A., & Young, T. A. (2008). Using science trade books to support inquiry in the elementary classroom. *Childhood Education, 84*(4), 204–208.

Mory, E. H. (1994). Adaptive feedback in computer-based instruction: Effects of response certitude on performance, feedback-study time, and efficiency. *Journal of Educational Computing Research, 11*(3), 263–290.

Mueller, C. M., & Dweck, C. S. (1998). Praise for intelligence can undermine children's motivation and performance. *Journal of Personality and Social Psychology, 75*(1), 33–52.

Nagy, W. E., & Anderson, R. C. (1984). How many words are there in printed school English? *Reading Research Quarterly, 19,* 304–330.

Najman, J. M., Aird, R., Bor, W., O'Callaghan, M., Williams, G. M., & Shuttlewood, G. J. (2004). The generational transmission of socioeconomic inequalities in child cognitive development and emotional health. *Social Science and Medicine, 58*(6), 1147–1158.

Najman, J. M., Hayatbakhsh, M. R., Heron, M. A., Bor, W., O'Callaghan, M. J., & Williams, G. M. (2009). The impact of episodic and chronic poverty on child cognitive development. *The Journal of Pediatrics, 154*(2), 284–289.

Nam, Y., & Huang, J. (2009). Equal opportunity for all? Parental economic resources and children's educational attainment. *Children and Youth Services Review, 31*(6), 625–634.

Narciss, S., & Huth, K. (2004). How to design informative tutoring feedback for multimedia learning. In H. M. Niegemann, D. Leutner, & R. Brunken (Eds.), *Instructional design for multimedia learning,* 181–195. Munster, NY: Waxmann.

National Institute of Child Health and Human Development. (2000). *Report of the National Reading Panel. Teaching children to read: An evidence-based assessment of the scientific research literature on reading and its implications for reading instruction* (NIH Publication No. 00–4769). Washington, DC: U.S. Government Printing Office.

National Research Council. (2006). *Learning to think spatially: GIS as a support system in the K–12 curriculum.* Washington, DC: National Academies Press.

Nelson, M. (2000). A case of preservice elementary teachers exploring, retelling, and reframing. *Research in Science Education, 30*(4), 417–433.

Nelson, L. H., White, K. R., & Grewe, J. (2012). Evidence for website claims about the benefits of teaching sign language to infants and toddlers with normal hearing. *Infant and Child Development, 21*(5), 474–502.

Neuman, S. B. (2006). Speak up! *Early Childhood Today, 20*(4), 12–13.

Neuman, S. B., & Celano, D. (2006). The knowledge gap: Implications of leveling the playing field for low-income and middle-income children. *Reading Research Quarterly, 41*(2), 176–201.

Ngu, B. H., Mit, E., Shahbodin, F., & Tuovinen, J. (2009). Chemistry problem solving instruction: A comparison of three computer-based formats for learning from hierarchical network problem representations. *Instructional Science, 37*(1), 21–42.

Nielsen: Income influences TV viewership. (2015, December 10). *Medialife Magazine.* Retrieved from http://medialifemagazine.com/175972-2

Noble, K. G., McCandliss, B. D., & Farah, M. J. (2007). Socioeconomic gradients predict individual differences in neurocognitive abilities. *Developmental Science, 10,* 464–480. doi:10.1111/j.1467-7687.2007.00600.x

Noble, K. G., Norman, N. F., & Farah, M. J. (1998). Neurocognitive correlates of socioeconomic status in kindergarten children. *Developmental Science, 8,* 74–87.

Norcross, J. C., Krebs, P. M., & Prochaska, J. O. (2011). Stages of change. *Journal of Clinical Psychology, 67*(2), 143–154.

O'Dell, C., & Grayson Jr., J. C., with Essaides, N. (1998). *If only we knew what we know.* New York, NY: Free Press.

Ogle, D. (1986, February). K-W-L: A teaching model that develops active reading of expository text. *The Reading Teacher, 39*(6), 564–570. Published by International Reading Association Stable. Retrieved from http://www.jstor.org/stable/20199156

Olmedo, I. M. (2009). Blending borders of language and culture: Schooling in La Villita. *Journal of Latinos and Education, 8*(1), 22–37.

Oshry, B. (1995). *Seeing systems: Unlocking the mysteries of organizational life.* San Francisco, CA: Berrett-Koehler.

Ostad, S. A., & Askeland, M. (2008). Sound-based number facts training in a private speech internalization perspective: Evidence for effectiveness of an intervention in grade 3. *Journal of Research in Childhood Education, 23*(1), 109–124.

Paas, F., Renkl, A., & Sweller, J. (2003). Cognitive load theory and instructional design: Recent developments. *Educational Psychologist, 38,* 1–4.

Palincsar, A. S., & Brown, A. L. (1984). The reciprocal teaching of comprehension-fostering and comprehension-monitoring activities. *Cognition and Instruction, 1*(2), 117–175.

Pape, S. J., & Wang, C. (2001). Middle school children's strategic behavior: Classification and relation to academic achievement and mathematical problem solving. *International Science, 31,* 419–449. doi:10.1023/A:1025710707285

Paquette, K. R., Fello, S. E., & Jalongo, M. R. (2007). The talking drawings strategy: Using primary children's illustrations and oral language to improve comprehension of expository text. *Early Childhood Education Journal, 35*(1), 65–73.

Parker, M., & Hurry, J. (2007). Teachers' use of questioning and modeling comprehension skills in primary classrooms. *Educational Review, 59*(3), 299–314.

Pasley, K., Furtis, T. G., & Skinner, M. L. (2002). Effects of commitment and psychological centrality on fathering. *Journal of Marriage and Family, 64*(1), 130–138.

Payne, R. K. (1996). *A framework for understanding and working with students and adults from poverty.* Baytown, TX: RFT Publishing.

Payne, R. K. (2002). *Understanding learning: The how, the why, the what.* Highlands, TX: aha! Process.

Payne, R. K. (2005). *Learning structures* (4th ed.). Highlands, TX: aha! Process.

Payne, R. K. (2006). *Working with parents: Building relationships for student success.* Highlands, TX: aha! Process.

Payne, R. K. (2013). *A framework for understanding poverty: A cognitive approach* (5th ed.). Highlands, TX: aha! Process.

Payne, R. K. (2017). *Under-resourced learners: 8 strategies to boost student achievement* (2nd ed.). Highlands, TX: aha! Process.

Payne, R. K., DeVol, P. E., & Dreussi Smith, T. (2009). *Bridges out of poverty: Strategies for professionals and communities* (4th ed.). Highlands, TX: aha! Process.

Payne, R. K., & Krabill, D. L. (2002). *Hidden rules of class at work.* Highlands, TX: aha! Process.

Payne, R. K., & Magee, D. S. (2001). *Meeting standards & raising test scores—When you don't have much time or money.* Highlands, TX: aha! Process.

Peer tutoring and response groups: What Works Clearinghouse intervention report. (2007). ERIC Document Reproduction Service No. ED499296.

Penn State University. (2001, November 20). Sign language enriches learning for hearing children. Retrieved from https://www.eurekalert.org/pub_releases/2001-11/ps-sle112001.php

Perkinson, M. (2017, June 6). Personal conversation with coauthor.

Perrino, T., Gonzalez-Soldevilla, A., Pantin, H., & Szapocznik J. (2000). The role of families in adolescent HIV prevention: A review. *Clinical Child and Family Psychology Review, 3*(2), 81–96.

Perry, N. E., & Rahim, A. (2011). Studying self-regulated learning in classrooms. In B. J. Zimmerman & D. H. Schunk (Eds.), *Handbook of self-regulation of learning and performance,* 122–136. Educational Psychology Handbook Series. New York, NY: Routledge.

Petermann, F., & Natzke, H. (2008). Preliminary results of a comprehensive approach to prevent antisocial behaviour in preschool and primary school pupils in Luxembourg. *School Psychology International, 29*(5), 606–626.

Peters, G. (2002). *Perceptions of principals and teachers regarding frames used in decision-making.* Unpublished dissertation, University of Alabama.

Peterson, L. D., Young, K., Richard, S., Charles, L., West, R. P., & Hill, M. (2006). Using self-management procedures to improve classroom social skills in multiple general education settings. *Education and Treatment of Children, 29*(1), 1–21.

Phalet, K., Andriessen, I., & Lens, W. (2004). How future goals enhance motivation and learning in multicultural classrooms. *Educational Psychology Review, 16*(1), 59–89.

Pilavin, J. A., & Callero, P. L. (1991). *Giving blood: The development of an altruistic identity.* Baltimore, MD: Johns Hopkins University Press.

Piro, J. M., & Ortiz, C. (2009). The effect of piano lessons on the vocabulary and verbal sequencing skills of primary grade students. *Psychology of Music, 37*(3), 325–347. doi:10.1177/0305735608097248

Pitner, R. O., & Astor, R. A. (2008). Children's reasoning about poverty, physical deterioration, danger, and retribution in neighborhood contexts. *Journal of Environmental Psychology, 28*(4), 327–338.

Porter, A. C., & Brophy, J. (1988). Synthesis of research on good teaching: Insights from the work of the Institute for Research on Teaching. *Educational Leadership, 45*(8), 74–85.

Positive Psychology Program. (2017, February 28). What is gratitude and what is its role in positive psychology? Retrieved from https://positivepsychologyprogram.com/gratitude-appreciation

Po-ying, C. (2007). How students react to the power and responsibility of being decision makers in their own learning. *Language Teaching Research, 11*(2), 225–241.

The proof is in the classroom. (2017). Project Read. Retrieved from https://www.projectread.com/research/the-proof-is-in-the-classroom

PuddleDancer Press. (2009). Home page. Retrieved from http://www.nonviolentcommunication.com/aboutnvc/aboutnvc.htm

Putnam, R. D. (2000). *Bowling alone: The collapse and revival of American community.* New York, NY: Simon & Schuster.

Quilligan, S. (2007). Communication skills teaching: The challenge of giving effective feedback. *The Clinical Teacher, 4,* 100–105.

Rafferty, Y., & Shinn, M. (1991). The impact of homelessness on children. *American Psychologist, 46*(11), 1170–1179.

Rapee, R. M., Gaston, J. E., & Abbott, M. J. (2009). Testing the efficacy of theoretically derived improvements in the treatment of social phobia. *Journal of Consulting and Clinical Psychology, 77*(2), 317–327.

Ratey, J., & Hageman, E. (2008). *Spark: The revolutionary new science of exercise and the brain.* New York, NY: Little, Brown.

Rauscher, F. H. (1999). Music exposure and the development of spatial intelligence in children. *Bulletin of the Council for Research in Music Education, 142,* 35–47.

Raver, C. C. (2004). Placing emotional self-regulation in sociocultural and socioeconomic contexts. *Child Development, 75,* 346–353. doi:10.1111/j.1467-8624.2004.00676.x

Razumnikova, O. M. (2005). The interaction between gender stereotypes and life values as factors in the choice of profession. *Russian Education and Society, 47*(12), 21–33.

Reddy, L. A., De Thomas, C. A., Newman, E., & Chun, V. (2009). School-based prevention and intervention programs for children with emotional disturbance: A review of treatment components and methodology. *Psychology in the Schools, 46*(2), 132–153.

Reiner, M. (2009). Sensory cues, visualization and physics learning. *International Journal of Science Education, 31*(3), 343–364.

Reis, S. M., Colbert, R. D., & Hebert, T. P. (2005). Understanding resilience in diverse, talented students in an urban high school. *Roeper Review, 27*(2), 110.

Renkl, A. (2005). The worked-out-example principle in multimedia learning. In R. E. Mayer (Ed.), *The Cambridge handbook of multimedia learning.* Cambridge, England: Cambridge University Press.

Renkl, A., Atkinson, R. K., & Grosse, C. S. (2004). How fading worked solution steps works—A cognitive load perspective. *Instructional Science, 32*(1), 59–82.

Resnick, L. B., & Klopfer, L. (Eds.). (1989). *Toward the thinking curriculum: Current cognitive research.* Alexandria, VA: Association for Supervision and Curriculum Development.

Richards, A. G. (2003). Arts and academic achievement in reading: Functions and implications. *Art Education, 56*(6), 19–23.

Richards, J. C., & Anderson, N. A. (2003). How do you know? A strategy to help emergent readers make inferences. *Reading Teacher, 57*(3), 290–293.

Ridley, M. (2000). *Genome: The autobiography of a species in 23 chapters.* New York, NY: HarperCollins.

Rieber, L. P. (2005). Multimedia learning in games, simulations, and microworlds. In R. E. Mayer (Ed.), *The Cambridge handbook of multimedia learning,* 549–567. Cambridge, England: Cambridge University Press.

Rieber, R. W. (Ed.). (1997). *The collected works of L. S. Vygotsky: Vol. 4. The history of the development of higher mental functions.* New York, NY: Plenum Press.

Riley, L. P., LaMontagne, L. L., Hepworth, J. T., & Murphy, B. A. (2007). Parental grief responses and personal growth following the death of a child. *Death Studies, 31*(4), 277–299.

Rimm-Kaufman, S. E., & Chiu, Y.-J. I. (2007). Promoting social and academic competence in the classroom: An intervention study examining the contribution of the 'responsive classroom' approach. *Psychology in the Schools, 44*(4), 397–413.

Robbins, R. N., & Bryan, A. (2004). Relationships between future orientation, impulsive sensation seeking, and risk behavior among adjudicated adolescents. *Journal of Adolescent Research, 19*(4), 428–445.

Rocha, E. (2008). Expanded learning time in action: Initiatives in high-poverty and high-minority schools and districts. Retrieved from http://www.americanprogress.org/issues/2008/07/elt_report1.html

Rogevich, M. E., & Perin, D. (2008). Effects on science summarization of a reading comprehension intervention for adolescents with behavior and attention disorders. *Exceptional Children, 74*(2), 135–154.

Rohrer, T. (2006). Image schemata in the brain. In B. Hampe (Ed.), *From perception to meaning: Image schemas in cognitive linguistics,* 165–198. Berlin, Germany: De Gruyter.

Roscoe, R. D., & Chi, M. T. H. (2008). Tutor learning: The role of explaining and responding to questions. *Instructional Science, 36*(4), 321–350.

Rosenberg, M. B. (2015). *Nonviolent communication: A language of life* (3rd ed.). Encinitas, CA: PuddleDancer Press.

Rosenholtz, S. J. (1989). *Teachers' workplace: The social organization of schools.* New York, NY: Longman.

Ross, D. D., Bondy, E., Gallingane, C., & Hambacher, E. (2008). Promoting academic engagement through insistence: Being a warm demander. *Childhood Education, 84*(3), 142–146.

Ross, J. A., & Starling, M. (2008). Self-assessment in a technology-supported environment: The case of grade 9 geography. *Assessment in Education, 15*(2), 183–199.

Ross, T. (2003). Training materials for Understanding Learning workshop.

Ryan, R., Fauth, R., & Brooks-Gunn, J. (2006). Childhood poverty: Implications for school readiness and early childhood education. In B. Spodek & O. Saracho (Eds.), *Handbook of research on the education of young children,* 323–347. Mahwah, NJ: Erlbaum.

Ryken, A. E. (2006). Goin' somewhere: How career technical education programs support and constrain urban youths' career decision-making. *Career and Technical Education Research, 31*(1), 49–71.

Sadler, D. R. (1989). Formative assessment and the design of instructional systems. *Instructional Science, 18,* 119. doi:10.1007/BF00117714

Sadler, D. R. (2013). 'Opening up feedback: Teaching learners to see.' In S. Merry, M. Price, D. Carless, & M. Taras (Eds.), *Reconceptualizing feedback in higher education: Developing dialogue with students,* 54–63. London, England: Routledge.

Sain, J. (2004). *Daily math skills review, grade 4: Practice for mastery of math standards.* Highlands, TX: aha! Process.

Sanchez, B., Reyes, O., & Singh, J. (2006). Makin' it in college: The value of significant individuals in the lives of Mexican American adolescents. *Journal of Hispanic Higher Education, 5*(1), 48–67.

Sansone, R. A., & Sansone, L. A. (2010). Gratitude and well being: The benefits of appreciation. *Psychiatry, 7*(11), 18–22.

Sapolsky, R. M. (1998). *Why zebras don't get ulcers.* New York, NY: W. H. Freeman.

Sarsour, K., Sheridan, M., Jutte, D., Nuru-Jeter, A., Hinsh, S., & Boyce, W. T. (2011). Family socioeconomic status and child executive functions: The roles of language, home environment, and single parenthood. *Journal of the International Neuropsychological Society, 17,* 120–132. doi:10.1017/S1355617710001335

Scales, P. C., Benson, P. L., Roehlkepartain, E. C., Sesma Jr., A., & van Dulmen, M. (2006). The role of developmental assets in predicting academic achievement: A longitudinal study. *Journal of Adolescence, 29*(5), 691–708.

Schacter, J. (2001). Reading programs that work: An evaluation of kindergarten through third-grade reading instructional programs. *ERS Spectrum, 19*(4), 12–25.

Schamberg, M. (2008). The cost of living in poverty: Long-term effects of allostatic load on working memory. Retrieved from http://ecommons.library.cornell.edu/bitstream/1813/10814/1/Schamberg%20-%20Pov%2c%20Load%2c%20Working%20Mem.pdf

Schellenberg, R. C., Parks-Savage, A., & Rehfuss, M. (2007). Reducing levels of elementary school violence with peer mediation. *Professional School Counseling, 10*(5), 475–481.

Scherff, L., & Singer, N. R. (2008). Framing and re-framing through computer-mediated communication: Providing pre-service teachers with alternate support structures. *Learning Inquiry, 2*(3), 151–167.

Schmidt, H., & Moust, J. (2000). Factors affecting small group tutorial learning: A review of research. In D. Evenson & C. Hmelo (Eds.), *Problem-based learning: A research perspective on learning interactions,* 19–51. Mahwah, NJ: Erlbaum.

Schnotz, W., & Kurschner, C. (2008). External and internal representations in the acquisition and use of knowledge: Visualization effects on mental model construction. *Instructional Science, 36*(3), 175–190.

Scholnick, E. K., & Freidman, S. L. (1993). Planning in context: Developmental and situational considerations. *International Journal of Behavioral Development, 16,* 145–167. doi:10.1177/016502549301600204

Schraw, G., Brooks, D., & Crippen, K. J. (2005). Using an interactive, compensatory model of learning to improve chemistry teaching. *Journal of Chemical Education, 82*(4), 637–640.

Schwartz, F., & White, K. (2000). Making sense of it all: Giving and getting online course feedback. In K. W. White & B. H. Weight (Eds.), *The online teaching guide: A handbook of attitudes, strategies, and techniques for the virtual classroom,* 57–72. Boston, MA: Allyn & Bacon.

Scott, E. (2016, December 29). Reduce stress and improve your life with positive self talk. Retrieved from https://www.verywell.com/how-to-use-positive-self-talk-for-stress-relief-3144816

Seaton, D. T., Reich, J., Nesterko, S. O., Mullaney, T., Waldo, J., Ho, A. D., & Chuang, I. (2014). 14.73x the challenges of global poverty MITx on edX course report—2013 spring. MITx Working Paper #11. doi:10.2139/ssrn.2382296

Seebaum, M. (1999). *A picture is worth a thousand words*. Highlands, TX: aha! Process.

Seginer, R. (2008). Future orientation in times of threat and challenge: How resilient adolescents construct their future. *International Journal of Behavioral Development, 32*(4), 272–282.

Seligman, M. E. P. (2002). *Authentic happiness*. New York, NY: Free Press.

Seligman, M. E. P., Steen, T. A., Park, N., & Peterson, C. (2005). Positive psychology progress: Empirical validation of interventions. *American Psychologist, 60*(5), 410–421.

Senge, P., McCabe, N. H. C., Lucas, T., Kleiner, A., Dutton, J., & Smith, B. (2000). *Schools that learn: A fifth discipline fieldbook for educators, parents, and everyone who cares about education*. New York, NY: Broadway Business.

Senge, P., Ross, R., Smith, B., Roberts, C., & Kleiner, A. (1994). *The fifth discipline fieldbook: Strategies and tools for building a learning organization*. New York, NY: Doubleday-Currency.

Shamir, A., & Lazerovitz, T. (2007). Peer mediation: Intervention for scaffolding self-regulated learning among children with learning disabilities. *European Journal of Special Needs Education, 22*(3), 255–273.

Shamir, A., Tzuriel, D., & Rozen, M. (2006). Peer mediation: The effects of program intervention, maths level, and verbal ability on mediation style and improvement in maths problem solving. *School Psychology International, 27*(2), 209–231.

Sharron, H., & Coulter, M. (2004). *Changing children's minds: Feuerstein's revolution in the teaching of intelligence*. Highlands, TX: aha! Process.

Shenk, D. S. (1962). Personal conversation with coeditor.

Shenk, D. W. (2012). Chess program a success [letter to editor]. Retrieved from http://www.goshennews.com/opinion/letters_to_the_editor/goshen-chess-program-a-success/article_a71a6913-6e70-560e-93f3-fa906985d614.html

Shenk, D. W. (2017). Personal recollection.

Shonkoff, J. P., & Phillips, D. A. (Eds.). (2000). *From neurons to neighborhoods: The science of early childhood development*. Washington, DC: National Academy Press.

Shulman, L. S. (1987). Assessment for teaching: An initiative for the profession. *Phi Delta Kappan, 69*(1), 38–44.

Shulman, L. S. (1988). A union of insufficiencies: Strategies for teacher assessment in a period of educational reform. *Educational Leadership, 46*(3), 36–41.

Sibley, B. A., Ward, R. M., Yazvac, T. S., Zullig, K., & Potteiger, J. A. (2008). Making the grade with diet and exercise. *AASA Journal of Scholarship and Practice, 5*(2), 38–45.

Simonsen, B., Fairbanks, S., Briesch, A., Myers, D., & Sugai, G. (2008). Evidence-based practices in classroom management: Considerations for research to practice. *Education and Treatment of Children, 31*(3), 351–380.

Singh, C. (2008). Assessing student expertise in introductory physics with isomorphic problems. I. Performance on nonintuitive problem pair from introductory physics. doi:10.1103/PhysRevSTPER.4.010104

Sirin, S. R. (2005). Socioeconomic status and academic achievement: A meta-analytic review of research. *Review of Educational Research, 75,* 417–453. doi:10.3102/00346543075003417

Skipper, J. I., Goldin-Meadow, S., Nusbaum, H. C., & Small, S. L. (2007). Speech-associated gestures, Broca's area, and the human mirror system. *Brain and Language, 101*(3), 260–277.

Slaski, M., & Cartwright, S. (2002). Health, performance and emotional intelligence: An exploratory study of retail managers. *Stress and Health, 18*(2), 63–68.

Smith, C., Wiser, M., Anderson, C., & Krajcik, J. (2006). Implications of research on children's learning for standards and assessment: A proposed learning progression for matter and atomic-molecular theory. *Measurement, 14*(1&2), 1–98.

Smith, G. G., & Kurthen, H. (2007). Front-stage and back-stage in hybrid e-learning face-to-face courses. *International Journal on E-Learning, 6*(3), 455.

Smith, J. R., Brooks-Gunn, J., & Klebanov, P. (1997). The consequences of living in poverty for young children's cognitive and verbal ability and early school achievement. In G. J. Duncan & J. Brooks-Gunn (Eds.), *Consequences of growing up poor.* New York, NY: Russell Sage.

Smith, R. E., Bayen, U. J., & Martin, C. (2010). The cognitive processes underlying event-based prospective memory in school-age children and young adults: A formal model based study. *Developmental Psychology, 46,* 230–244. doi:10.1037/a0017100

Souther, E. (2008a). *Facilitator guide for the R rules: A guide for teens to identify and build resources.* Highlands, TX: aha! Process.

Souther, E. (2008b). *The R rules: A guide for teens to identify and build resources.* Highlands, TX: aha! Process.

Southgate, D. E., & Roscigno, V. J. (2009). The impact of music on childhood and adolescent achievement. *Social Science Quarterly, 90*(1), 4–21.

Spears D. (2011). Economic decision making in poverty depletes behavioral control. *The B.E. Journal of Economic Analysis and Policy, 72,* 1–42. doi:10.2202/1935-1682.2973

Stamou, E., Theodorakis, Y., Kokaridas, D., Perkos, S., & Kessanopoulou, M. (2007). The effect of self-talk on the penalty execution in goalball. *British Journal of Visual Impairment, 25*(3), 233–247.

Star, J. R., & Rittle-Johnson, B. (2008). Flexibility in problem solving: The case of equation solving. *Learning and Instruction, 18*(6), 565–579.

Steiner, C. (1994). *Scripts people live: Transactional analysis of life scripts.* New York, NY: Grove Press.

Stenner, A. J., Fisher Jr., W. P., Stone, M. H., & Burdick, D. S. (2013). Causal Rasch models. *Frontiers in Psychology, 4,* 536.

Stenner, A. J., & Smith III, M. (1989). *The Lexile frame for reading.* Durham, NC: MetaMetrics.

Sternberg, R., & Grigorenko, E. (2002): *Dynamic testing.* Cambridge, England: Cambridge University Press.

Stewart, R. M., Benner, G. J., Martella, R. C., & Marchand-Martella, N. E. (2007). Three-tier models of reading and behavior: A research review. *Journal of Positive Behavior Interventions, 9*(4), 239–253.

Stewart, T. A. (1997). *Intellectual capital: The new wealth of organizations.* New York, NY: Doubleday-Currency.

Stichter, J. P., Lewis, T. J., Whittaker, T. A., Richter, M., Johnson, N. W., & Trussell, R. P. (2009). Assessing teacher use of opportunities to respond and effective classroom management strategies: Comparisons among high- and low-risk elementary schools. *Journal of Positive Behavior Interventions, 11*(2), 68–81.

Stoeger, H., & Ziegler, A. (2008). Evaluation of a classroom based training to improve self-regulation in time management tasks during homework activities with fourth graders. *Metacognition and Learning, 3*(3), 207–230.

Stone, R. H., Boon, R. T., Fore III, C., Bender, W. N., & Spencer, V. G. (2008). Use of text maps to improve the reading comprehension skills among students in high school with emotional and behavioral disorders. *Behavioral Disorders, 33*(2), 87–98.

Straus, M. A. (2000). *Beating the devil out of them: Corporal punishment in American families and its effects on children* (2nd ed.). New Brunswick, NJ: Transaction.

Strayhorn, T. L. (2011). Bridging the pipeline: Increasing underrepresented students' preparation for college through a summer bridge program. *American Behavioral Scientist, 55*(2), 142–159. doi:10.1177/0002764210381871

Sullivan, F. R. (2008). Robotics and science literacy: Thinking skills, science process skills and systems understanding. *Journal of Research in Science Teaching, 45*(3), 373–394.

Sveiby, K. E. (1997). *The new organizational wealth: Managing and measuring knowledge-based assets.* San Francisco, CA: Berrett-Koehler.

Swan, K., van't Hooft, M., Kratcoski, A., & Unger, D. (2005). Uses and effects of mobile computing devices in K–8 classrooms. *Journal of Research on Technology in Education, 38*(1), 99–112.

Tabachnick, S. E., Miller, R. B., & Relyea, G. E. (2008). The relationships among students' future-oriented goals and subgoals, perceived task instrumentality, and task-oriented self-regulation strategies in an academic environment. *Journal of Educational Psychology, 100*(3), 629–642.

Tanenhaus, M. K., Spivey-Knowlton, M. J., Eberhard, K. M., & Sedivy, J. C. (1995). Integration of visual and linguistic information in spoken language comprehension. *Science, 268*(5217), 1632–1634.

Taplin, D. H., Clark, H., Collins, E., & Colby, D. C. (2013). Theory of change. *Act Knowledge: Technical Papers,* 1–22.

Templeton, S., Invernizzi, M., Johnston, F., & Bear, D. (2008). *Word sorts for syllables and affixes spellers.* Englewood Cliffs, NJ: Prentice Hall.

Teräs, M. (2007). *Intercultural learning and hybridity in the culture laboratory.* Helsinki, Finland: Helsinki University Press.

Texas administrative code, title 19, part II, chapter 112. Texas essential knowledge and skills for science. (n.d.). Retrieved from http://ritter.tea.state.tx.us/rules/tac/chapter112/index.html

Texas Assessment of Knowledge and Skills. (2003). Pearson Education in collaboration with Texas Education Agency.

Therrien, W. J. (2004). Fluency and comprehension gains as a result of repeated reading. *Remedial and Special Education, 25*(4), 252.

Thompson, D. D., & McDonald, D. M. (2007). Examining the influence of teacher-constructed and student-constructed assignments on the achievement patterns of gifted and advanced sixth-grade students. *Journal for the Education of the Gifted, 31*(2), 198–226.

Thompson, R. L., Vinson, D. P., & Vigliocco, G. (2009). The link between form and meaning in American Sign Language: Lexical processing effects. *Journal of Experimental Psychology, 35*(2), 550–557.

Thornton, S. (2008). *Seven days in the art world.* New York, NY: Norton.

Tomporowski, P. D., Davis, C. L., Miller, P. H., & Naglieri, J. A. (2008). Exercise and children's intelligence, cognition, and academic achievement. *Educational Psychology Review, 20*(2), 111–131.

Traore, R. (2008). Cultural connections: An alternative to conflict resolution. *Multicultural Education, 15*(4), 10–14.

Tremarche, P. V., Robinson, E. M., & Graham, L. B. (2007). Physical education and its effect on elementary testing results. *Physical Educator, 64*(2), 58–64.

Tucker, B. H. (2005). *The journey of Al and Gebra to the land of algebra.* Highlands, TX: aha! Process.

Tucker, B. H. (2007). *Reading by age 5.* Highlands, TX: aha! Process.

Tucker, B. H. (2012). *Tucker signing strategies for reading* (Rev. ed.) [manual and DVD]. Highlands, TX: aha! Process.

Tzuriel, D., & Shamir, A. (2007). The effects of peer mediation with young children (PMYC) on children's cognitive modifiability. *British Journal of Educational Psychology, 77*(1), 143–165.

Ury, W., Fisher, R., & Patton, B. (1991). *Getting to yes: Negotiating an agreement without giving in* (2nd ed.). Boston, MA: Houghton Mifflin Harcourt.

van den Bos, K. P., Nakken, H., Nicolay, P. G., & van Houten, E. J. (2007). Adults with mild intellectual disabilities: Can their reading comprehension ability be improved? *Journal of Intellectual Disability Research, 51*(11), 835–849.

Vanderbilt University. (2017). What is service learning or community engagement? Retrieved from https://cft.vanderbilt.edu/guides-sub-pages/teaching-through-community-engagement

van der Schoot, M., Vasbinder, A. L., Horsley, T. M., & van Lieshout, E. C. D. M. (2008). The role of two reading strategies in text comprehension: An eye fixation study in primary school children. *Journal of Research in Reading, 31*(2), 203–223.

Van Meter, P., Aleksic, M., Schwartz, A., & Garner, J. (2006). Learner-generated drawing as a strategy for learning from content area text. *Contemporary Educational Psychology, 31*(2), 142–166.

VanLehn, K., Lynch, C., Schulze, K., Shapiro, J. A., Shelby, R., Taylor, L., … Wintersgill, M. (2005). The Andes physics tutoring system: Lessons learned. *International Journal of Artificial Intelligence in Education, 15*(3), 147–204.

Veerkamp, M. B., Kamps, D. M., & Cooper, L. (2007). The effects of ClassWide Peer Tutoring on the reading achievement of urban middle school students. *Education and Treatment of Children, 30*(2), 21–51.

Vestal, A., & Jones, N. A. (2004). Peace building and conflict resolution in preschool children. *Journal of Research in Childhood Education, 19*(2), 131.

Vickerstaff, S., Heriot, S., Wong, M., Lopes, A., & Dossetor, D. (2007). Intellectual ability, self-perceived social competence, and depressive symptomatology in children with high-functioning autistic spectrum disorders. *Journal of Autism and Developmental Disorders, 37*(9), 1647–1664.

Wagner, T. (2008). *The global achievement gap.* New York, NY: Basic Books.

Walberg, H. J. (1984). Improving educational productivity. *Educational Leadership, 41*(8), 19–27.

Walberg, H. J. (1990). Productive teaching and instruction: Assessing the knowledge base. *Phi Delta Kappan, 71*(6), 470–478.

Waring, T. M. (2010). New evolutionary foundations: Theoretical requirements for a science of sustainability. *Ecological Economics, 69,* 718–730.

Watson, B., & Konicek, R. (1990). Teaching for conceptual change: Confronting children's experience. *Phi Delta Kappan, 71*(9), 680–685.

Watson, S., & Miller, T. (2009). Classification and the dichotomous key: Tools for teaching identification. *Science Teacher, 76*(3), 50–54.

Weekes, H. (2005). Drawing students out: Using sketching exercises to hone observation skills. *Science Teacher, 72*(1), 34–37.

Weitzman, B. C., Silver, D., & Dillman, K. N. (2002). Integrating a comparison group design into a theory of change evaluation: The case of the Urban Health Initiative. *American Journal of Evaluation, 23*(4), 371–385.

Wenger, E. (1999). *Communities of practice: Learning, meaning, and identity.* Cambridge, England: Cambridge University Press.

Wenzlaff, R. M., & Wegner, D. M. (2000). Thought suppression. *Annual Review of Psychology, 51*(1), 59–91.

Whalon, K., & Hanline, M. F. (2008). Effects of a reciprocal questioning intervention on the question generation and responding of children with autism spectrum disorder. *Education and Training in Developmental Disabilities, 43*(3), 367–387.

Wheeler, R. S. (2008). Becoming adept at code-switching. *Educational Leadership, 65*(7), 54–58.

Wiggins, G., & McTighe, J. (1998). *Understanding by design.* Alexandria, VA: Association for Supervision and Curriculum Development.

Willcox, G. (1982). The feeling wheel: A tool for expanding awareness of emotions and increasing spontaneity and intimacy. *Transactional Analysis Journal, 12*(4), 274–276. doi:10.1177/036215378201200411

Williams, A., Rouse, K., Seals, C., & Gilbert, J. (2009). Enhancing reading literacy in elementary children using programming for scientific simulations. *International Journal on E-Learning, 8*(1), 57–69.

Williams, J. P. (2005). Instruction in reading comprehension for primary-grade students: 'A focus on text structure.' *Journal of Special Education, 39*(1), 6–18.

Williams, J. P., Hall, K. M., & Lauer, K. D. (2004). Teaching expository text structure to young at-risk learners: Building the basics of comprehension instruction. *Exceptionality, 12*(3), 129–144.

Williams, J. P., Hall, K. M., Lauer, K. D., Stafford, K. B., DeSisto, L. A., & deCani, J. S. (2005). Expository text comprehension in the primary grade classroom. *Journal of Educational Psychology, 97*(4), 538–550.

Williams, J. P., Stafford, K. B., Lauer, K. D., Hall, K. M., & Pollini, S. (2009). Embedding reading comprehension training in content-area instruction. *Journal of Educational Psychology, 101*(1), 1–20.

Wilson, E. O. (1998). *Consilience: The unity of knowledge.* New York, NY: Alfred A. Knopf.

Wise, A. (1995). *The high performance mind: Mastering brainwaves for insight, healing, and creativity.* New York, NY: Tarcher/Putnam.

Wolff, J. (2002). Proven practices: 'More time on task' benefits students at risk. In evidence: Policy reports from the CFE trial, vol. 5. ERIC Document Reproduction Service No. ED472576.

Wong, H. K., & Wong, R. T. (1998). *The first day of school: How to be an effective teacher* (Rev. ed.). Mountainview, CA: Author.

Woodward-Kron, R. (2008). More than just jargon: The nature and role of specialist language in learning disciplinary knowledge. *Journal of English for Academic Purposes, 7*(4), 234–249.

Wright, J. C., & Huston, A. C. (1995). *Effects of educational TV viewing of lower income preschoolers on academic skills, school readiness, and school adjustment one to three years later: A report to Children's Television Workshop.* Lawrence, KS: University of Kansas.

Yeung, W.-J. J., & Pfeiffer, K. M. (2009). The black-white test score gap and early home environment. *Social Science Research, 38*(2), 412–437.

You do the math: Explaining basic concepts behind math problems improves children's learning. (2009). *ScienceDaily.* Retrieved from http://www.sciencedaily.com/releases/2009/04/090410143809.htm

Yumusak, N., Sungur, S., & Cakiroglu, J. (2007). Turkish high school students' biology achievement in relation to academic self-regulation. *Educational Research and Evaluation, 13*(1), 53–69.

Zakin, A. (2007). Metacognition and the use of inner speech in children's thinking: A tool teachers can use. *Journal of Education and Human Development 1*(2), 1–14.

Ziesemer, C., Marcoux, L., & Marwell, B. E. (1994). Homeless children: Are they different from other low-income children? *Social Work, 39*(6), 658–668.

Zima, B. T., Wells, K. B., & Freeman, H. (1994). Emotional and behavioral problems and severe academic delays among sheltered homeless children in Los Angeles County. *American Journal of Public Health, 84*(2), 260–264.

Zimmerman, B. J. (2011). Motivational sources and outcomes of self-regulated learning and performance. In B. J. Zimmerman & D. H. Schunk (Eds.), *Handbook of self-regulation of learning and performance,* 49–64. New York, NY: Routledge.

Zimmerman, B. J., & Cleary, T. J. (2004). Self-regulation empowerment program: A school-based program to enhance self-regulated and self-motivated cycles of student learning. *Psychology in the Schools, 41*(5), 537–550. doi:10.1002/pits.10177

Zuckerman, E. L. (2005). *Clinician's thesaurus: The guide to conducting interviews and writing psychological reports* (6th ed.). New York, NY: Guilford.

Zull, J. E. (2002). *The art of changing the brain: Enriching the practice of teaching by exploring the biology of learning.* Sterling, VA: Stylus.

About the Authors

Ruby K. Payne, Ph.D., is founder of aha! Process and an author, speaker, publisher, and career educator. She is a leading expert on the mindsets of economic class and on crossing socioeconomic lines in education and work. Recognized internationally for her foundational book, *A Framework for Understanding Poverty,* now in its 5th revised edition (1996, 2013), which has sold more than 1,500,000 copies, Dr. Payne has helped students and adults of all economic backgrounds achieve academic, professional, and personal success.

Dr. Payne's expertise stems from more than 30 years of experience in public schools. Dr. Payne has traveled extensively and has presented her work throughout North America, and in Europe, Australia, China, and India.

Dr. Payne has written or coauthored more than a dozen books. Another publication is *Bridges Out of Poverty* (1999, revised 2009), coauthored with Philip E. DeVol and Terie Dreussi Smith, which offers strategies for building sustainable communities. Her career-long goal for raising student achievement and overcoming economic class barriers has become a cornerstone for efforts toward school improvement by educational districts across the United States. In 2013 "Achievement for All: Keys to Educating Middle Grades Students in Poverty" was published by AMLE (Association for Middle Level Education).

Sequels to her original *Framework* book include *School Improvement: 9 Systemic Processes to Raise Achievement* (2010), coauthored with Dr. Donna Magee; *Research-Based Strategies: Narrowing the Achievement Gap for Under-Resourced Students* (2009); *Under-Resourced Learners: 8 Strategies to Boost Student Achievement* (2008); *Crossing the Tracks for Love: What to Do When You and Your Partner Grew Up in Different Worlds* (2005); *Hidden Rules of Class at Work* (2002), coauthored with Don Krabill; *Living on a Tightrope: a Survival Handbook for Principals* (2001), coauthored with Dr. William Sommers; and *What Every Church Member Should Know About Poverty* (1999), coauthored with Bill Ehlig.

In 2011 two of her publications were recognized with awards: *Removing the Mask: How to Identify and Develop Giftedness in Students from Poverty* received a Gold Medal from Independent Publishers for Education, and *Boys in Poverty: Understanding DropOut* (Solution Tree Press) received the Distinguished Achievement Award from Association of Educational Publishers for Professional Development. Both were coauthored with the late Dr. Paul Slocumb.

Payne received a bachelor's degree from Goshen College, Goshen, IN; master's degree in English Literature from Western Michigan University, Kalamazoo, MI; and her doctorate in Educational Leadership and Policy from Loyola University, Chicago, IL.

Bethanie H. Tucker, Ed.D., is coauthor of *Research-Based Strategies;* she has had an extensive career in education. Researching and field-testing instructional strategies have been major foci of her work.

Following her initial classroom teaching position in the 1970s, she studied and implemented research-based strategies for teaching reading through the use of art to Title I students in Pittsylvania County, VA. Later she worked as a member of a team to identify approaches for meeting the needs of academically gifted students in neighboring Halifax County.

While teaching in the Education Department at Averett University in Danville, VA, Dr. Tucker's research in the fields of American Sign Language and reading led to the development of *Tucker Signing Strategies for Reading* (both a 2001 book and a program), a strategy for teaching letter/sound associations through hand signs. Continued success with this pilot program led to grant-funded projects and, finally, to working with Dr. Ruby K. Payne and aha! Process, Inc., based in Highlands, TX.

Since 2000 Dr. Tucker has conducted hundreds of workshops for aha! Process worldwide, including Research-Based Strategies, A Framework for Understanding Poverty, Bridges Out of Poverty, Tucker Signing Strategies for Reading, and Understanding and Engaging Under-Resourced College Students. She is frequently invited to give keynote presentations for various organizations.

Dr. Tucker holds three academic degrees, all in education: B.S. from Averett University and M.S. and Ed.D. from the University of Virginia, Charlottesville.

In addition to *Tucker Signing Strategies,* she is author of *Mr. Base Ten Invents Mathematics* (2002) and *The Journey of Al and Gebra to the Land of Algebra* (2005); she is coauthor of *Understanding and Engaging Under-Resourced College Students* (2009). All were published by aha! Process. She also wrote a children's book, *The Story of Mrs. Santa Claus* (2007), published by Waterway Publishers.

She and her husband, William, were married in 1978. They reside in the countryside near Alton, VA.

WE'D LIKE TO HEAR FROM YOU!

Join us on Facebook
www.facebook.com/rubypayne
www.facebook.com/ahaprocess

Twitter
www.twitter.com/ahaprocess
#PovertyChat
#BridgesOutofPoverty

Pinterest
www.pinterest.com/ahaprocess

Subscribe to our YouTube channel
www.youtube.com/ahaprocess

Respond to our blog
www.ahaprocess.com/blog

Download free resources
www.ahaprocess.com

Visit our online store for related titles by Dr. Payne and Dr. Tucker

- *Under-Resourced Learners: 8 Strategies to Improve Student Achievement* (Payne)
- *How Much of Yourself Do You Own? A Process for Building Your Emotional Resources* (Payne & O'Neill-Baker)
- *Working with Students: Discipline Strategies for the Classroom* (Payne)
- *Removing the Mask: How to Identify and Develop Giftedness in Students from Poverty* (Payne & Slocumb)
- *Tucker Signing Strategies for Reading* (Tucker)
- *Understanding and Engaging Under-Resourced College Students* (Becker, Krodel, & Tucker)

Go to www.ahaprocess.com/events for online offerings, including Trainer Certification for Framework and more